LIFE AMONG THE ANTHROS AND OTHER ESSAYS

CLIFFORD GEERTZ

Life among the Anthros AND OTHER ESSAYS

Edited by FRED INGLIS

PRINCETON UNIVERSITY PRESS
Princeton and Oxford

Library of Congress Cataloging-in-Publication Data

Geertz, Clifford.
   Life among the anthros and other essays / by Clifford Geertz, edited by Fred Inglis.
      p. cm.
   Includes bibliographical references and index.
   ISBN 978-0-691-14358-3 (alk. paper)
      1. Anthropology—Philosophy.   2. Anthropology—Research.   3. Anthropology—
Fieldwork.   I. Inglis, Fred.   II. Title.
GN33.G44 2010
301.01—dc22

                                                                                            009043977

British Library Cataloging-in-Publication Data is available

This book has been composed in Adobe Garamond
Printed on acid-free paper. ∞
press.princeton.edu
Printed in the United States of America
10 9 8 7 6 5 4 3 2 1

CONTENTS

LIFE AMONG THE ANTHROS AND OTHER ESSAYS

The Comic Vision of Clifford Geertz

I

Once upon a time, in October 1988, just weeks before the cold war swallowed itself in a tumble of falling masonry in Berlin, overloaded Trabants pouring past the raised barriers at Hungarian checkpoints, a sea of vengeful fists and faces booing their hateful overlord off his balcony in Bucharest, a full-page advertisement in affirmative defense of being a liberal appeared in the *New York Times*.

An unorganized group of prominent academics and intellectuals had united briefly to pay up in order to rebut their president, the amiable, lethal, hotly ideological, charmingly anti-intellectual Ronald Reagan, who had turned "liberal" into a term of open and contemptuous abuse.

It has pretty well stayed that way, the forty-third president notwithstanding, for the succeeding twenty-odd years. The signatories said:

> Extremists of the right and of the left have long attacked liberalism as their greatest enemy. In our own time liberal democracies have been crushed by such extremists. Against any encouragement of this tendency in our own country . . . we feel obliged to speak out.[1]

Clifford Geertz was one of the signatories. He had never been a fellow traveler of a *marxisant* persuasion, still less the kind of fundamental federalist the U.S. government hired to do its dirtiest work in Indochina and in Chile. He was a "quiet American," all right, but he spoke in the purest accents and very rapidly the active, historical, self-critical, and unmartyred liberalism which John Dewey took from John Stuart Mill and Thomas Hill Green, and turned it into the plain prose of the best that Americans thought and said in the twentieth century.

In one of his finest essays, in which he sought to identify both the moral point and the common ground of all inquiry into the human sciences,[2] Geertz fell to puzzling out "some of the most thoroughly entrenched tropes of the liberal imagination." The latter phrase is of course the title of Lionel Trilling's famous collection of essays, and Geertz's essay was given as a Trilling Memorial Lecture at Columbia. Those tropes included—in one of Geertz's characteristic, inclusive, and disorienting lists—the integrity of other cultures; the sanctity of all human life (cruelty toward which is, for liberals, the one worst thing, so Richard Rorty says); the principle of equality as between men and women, supremely, but also as between classes, races, and generations; and the always mixed but largely brutal and desolate legacy of colonialism.

Typically, Geertz interpolates a parenthesis before his list, saying of the liberal imagination—the making and remaking of which he takes as his subject and his life's work—that it is "an imagination, I'd best confess, I more or less share," that "more or less" being the weightiest part of his confession, an aside which propels him to that edge of the stage from which the moral and intellectual commentator on human goings-on can best speak: near the exit but still an actor, perfectly audible but sotto voce; judging the action but not inflecting it; speaking always with as much intelligence, precision, and beauty as he knows how.

Not that this minor lord-at-court is detached from the actions—or only as detached as he can manage and keep his balance. Indeed, Geertz is programmatically off-balance, always seeking out those moments where momentum veers and those moral truths about ourselves and others which, our having supposed them to be fairly dependable, suddenly elude us in ways typical of any imaginative construction capable, first, of gripping us, and then of changing, however slightly, the direction of our lives (*King Lear*, *Cosi Fan Tutte*, the end of cold war, the natures of Islam, the making of a president).

So the lesson of that essay and of Geertz's life is this: that we apprehend other lives not by trying to get *behind* the elaborate behaviors and ideas with which they dramatize their being, but by seeing through (the pun holds up) the spectacles which constitute their meanings and their minds.

This business of "seeing through" the lenses you happen to have picked up and got used to goes very deep. When you remove your spectacles, it's hard to see anything. Good ones are custom-made; they will hardly suit anybody else. So it is with the glasses ground by liberalism. Geertz put his name and his reputation to the advertisement in the *New York Times* because he and his associates rightly felt that, catchall term that it is, their common property marked out as liberalism was being wantonly defiled by the abuse of mere power. And in the name of what? In the names—no doubt, the mixed and motley names—of neoconservatism, or the doctrine of small government and big money; of old nationalism, or the certainty of American righteousness; of a Godhead confidently enlisted on the side of both big money and Old Glory.

The fragments of liberalism were to be shored against these rough and ruinous beasts, and in the more than twenty years since the advertisement appeared, there has been a hidden, unfinished, and titanic struggle going on for the soul of America as it flickered elusively behind and between the stipulations and amendments of the Constitution.

Geertz remained an undaunted and tireless officer in the liberal vanguard, never more so than in the pages of the *New York Review of Books*. It is, however, the very nature of his intellectual achievement—as you might say, the magnification and varifocalism of the lenses he has ground—to put freedom or variety of seeing, the sheer multifariousness of the ways there are of being human, the certainty that differing people will live and die for these extreme peculiarities, bang in the center of his and our vision.

Once one can see the strangeness of other people as familiar, then the familiarity of one's own streets becomes estranged. This is a liberalism with a strong tinge of realism. As Geertz himself wrote,

> We can at least say something (not of course that we always do) with some concreteness to it. I have never been able to understand why such comments as "your conclusions, such as they are, only cover two million people [Bali], or fifteen million [Morocco], or sixty-five million [Java], and only over some years or centuries," are supposed to be criticisms. Of course, one can be wrong, and probably, as often as not, one is. But "just" or "merely" trying to figure out Japan, China, Zaire, or the Central Eskimo (or better, some aspect of their life along some chunk of their world line) is not chopped liver, even if it looks less impressive than explanations, theories, or whatnot which have as their object "History," "Society," "Man," "Woman," or some other grand and elusive upper-case entity.[3]

One cannot doubt that such a thing can be called liberalism; the concept of freedom is intrinsic to it, but that freedom is itself a constitutive value. It is not merely the desirable, nonmoral circumstance of action—"freedom to . . ." and "freedom from . . ." as Isaiah Berlin had it. It is the *content* of action, freely chosen, self-willed (or culture-willed), the product of an Emersonian self-reliance, dreamed up by America, for sure, but open to everybody to take up and live for themselves. That there are then better and worse ways to live in such freedom only needs pointing out to those cartoonists who pretend that liberalism has no way of distinguishing between good and bad, intelligent or stupid.

Brief lives and the history of nations may go reasonably well, or they may go crazily. The human scientists, each in their particular, overlapping idioms, tell their tales of human endeavor, each understanding them as best they can, and step back. The happiest result is not then "universal" as opposed to "local" (though if he had to, Geertz would always vote "local"); it is a distinct answer to a particular historical question.

II

It is therefore wholly consistent with such a way of doing things that Geertz's enormous oeuvre should be dominated by the essay form. A few years ago he remarked that the world as it is—diffuse, changeable, particles hurtling upon and away from each other, "globalized" only in the sense that its populations are forever on the move to somewhere else, refugees, immigrants, tourists, salesmen, mercenaries—is amenable only to "mosaic or *pointilliste*" ways of seeing.

If the form is enforced by the facts, it is also the one in which Geertz has made himself most at home. He started out, as rookie anthropologists had to in those days, by taking as subject a medley of large topics, some as specific as individual towns (Modjokuto, eponym for Indonesia, and Sefrou, standing in for Morocco), others configuring whole fields of meaning (his doctoral dissertation was called, in the plural and with no definite article, "Religions of Java"; his publishers inserted "the" and the singular), modes of production (*Agricultural Involution*), social bonding (*Kinship in Bali*). But as he moved away from the heavy engineering and social structuration of the classics of old anthropology, he found the lightness of the world's being as anchored to the earth by its history, for sure, but that history as compounded not so much by solid systems (class, nation, firm belief, fixed relations) as by time, chance, accident, and patterned desperation (maybe quiet, often noisy).

He found this out in the best American way: by going to see what he could see, unarmed except with his own genius, his good manners, his gift of tongues, an excellent egalitarianism, and a style of speech-in-writing which not only turned his prose into an exquisite instrument of pure science, but placed him in that great tradition of American thinkers—William James, Oliver Wendell Holmes, John Dewey, Edmund Wilson, Yvor Winters—whose discursive writing is one of the glories of literature in English. Now that Geertz's own discovery of the uncertainty principle brought to all the sciences of humankind by the quiddity of the individual observer's eye and words is a truism of postmodernity, the force of Nietzsche's strictly personal admonition for the arts of thought is all the more piercing.

> One thing is needful, to "give style" to one's character—a great and rare art. It is practiced by those who survey all the strengths and weaknesses of their nature and then fit them into an artistic plan until every one of them appears as art and reason and even weaknesses delight the eye. In the end, when the work is finished, it becomes evident how the constraint of a single taste governed and formed everything large and small. Whether this taste was good or bad is less important than one might suppose, if only it was a single taste![4]

This kind of thing is no good to those busy module-managers trying to devise courses in social-scientific methodology for doctoral students. It is, however, precisely Geertz's concern to refuse and, if possible, paralyze the assumptions which direct such courses and which pour concrete over the brains of those who have to take them. The ideology of methodology is always a function of the bureaucratic authority which orders and ratifies the qualifications.[5] The closer these courses in method come to the making of policy (and as the lectures in this collection indicate, Geertz was well aware of the way his ideas might be bent, for good and ill, to policy purposes), the more their function is to suppress disagreement and wave away conflict in order to ensure the complicity of the oppressed in the preferences of the management.

The inimitability of Geertz's style makes it intractable to discourses upon method. The style is the man, all right, and in being distinctively so cannot be turned into a technique. That same style in his hands is radically opposed to a view of human inquiry (so much influenced at present by the abominable machinations of managerialism) as the deployment of *skills* and the technology of subordination. The discipline of interpretation leads, when it is well pursued, to exact *expression*, and as an antipositivist philosopher much admired by Geertz, R. G. Collingwood, wrote, "Expression is an activity of which there can be no technique."[6]

Art, supremely, is the exact expression of thought and feeling; technique is by definition instrumental, its aim reproducibility. One studies Geertz's thought not as an exercise in (as the unspeakable language has it) "higher-order study skills," but (as Collingwood also puts it, of reading a great poet) in order

> not merely [to] understand the poet's expression of his, the poet's emotions, [but that] he is also expressing emotions of his own in the poet's words, which have thus become his own words. As Coleridge put it, we know a man for a poet by the fact that he makes us poets.[7]

That is what it is to find oneself under the influence of a great writer, and I do not doubt that Geertz is one such. In his hands, the essay has the imaginative force, compression, clear light, and sharp memorability of the short poem. The greatest short poems in the language, Yvor Winters observed, derive their force and complexity from the demands of the form and its accrued conventions as realized by the writer. They can allude to an action without having to recount a whole narrative. They permit, even encourage, aphorism and judicious generalization. They demand the matching of due passion to relevant experience, of motive to emotion. Reason and rhetoric must be at poise (or the poem will collapse into rant). Necessarily the poem issues in moral judgment (which is not to say, in sentencing).

Clifford Geertz's essays do these things and pass these tests. That is what makes them works of art and human science in action, rather than applications of method. To read them is not to be drilled but to think, the thinking being done informed by the best feelings of which one is capable in the carrying out of the task of interpretation to hand. Geertz is both friend and master; inasmuch as we, his readers, look for instruction, we are his students.

III

Most of the reviews and articles which follow appeared first in the *New York Review of Books*, and if what is plain upon the page is the directness, humor, luminosity, and easy American conversability of the man, then it is worth adding that the pages of the *New York Review* have been notable for almost half a century as the continental, even international, agora of just this manner of intellectual exchange. There is nothing to match it worldwide for its scrupulous, brave, and even-tempered application not just of liberal but of inclusively humanist ideals and principles.

Even there, however, Geertz stands out for wisdom and for a quite colossal breadth of reference—this was a man who spoke and read Arabic, two or three of the countless Indonesian dialects, German, French, Spanish, a phrase or two of Japanese, and his native tongue, a classic American prose straight in the line of Twain and Faulkner, Henry and William James, and James Thurber, his favorite writers.

Given his gifts, the *New York Review* was the ideal place for him to speak, with modest authority, upon nearly forty years' worth of the great world issues; from his first appearance reviewing, with muffled hilarity, his disciplinary ancestor, Malinowski, to his last, "Among the Infidels," a few months before his unexpected death and just after he was knocked down by an uninsured and incompetent driver as he traversed the road on a marked crosswalk.

"Great world issues," however, would never have been how he put it. Everywhere throughout his concise, conversational contributions, he refuses by way of trademark both Grand Theory and Issues in Capital Letters. Facing the facts of risk and the end of the world in his review of Richard Posner's and Jared Diamond's ill-assorted visions of doom, Geertz puts the delirious duo under warning with an epigraph from Cole Porter, and in his conclusion returns us to the necessity of monographic study, piecemeal solutions, face-to-face argufying, Fabianizing (as they say in Britain) amelioration. They may not seem much; they're the best we can do.

A collection of Geertz's reviews, spanning as this one does just about forty years, is therefore far more than a piece of bookmaking. It configures the man and his self-making; it dramatizes his extended encounters with the world's intellectuals, with the world's tempestuous quarrels with itself, with the best, most intelligent and morally most defensible methods (to use the blessed word) one may devise for understanding it.

Printing the full range of reviews from the 1967 essay on Malinowski to his last appearance in the *New York Review*, "Among the Infidels," only a few months before his heart operation went fatally wrong in the late summer of 2006, would take 150,000 words and go beyond the purposes of this collection. For my purpose here is to indicate, in this readable, accessible form, a representative selection from a momentous oeuvre: the work of a traveling American typical in his easy openness to the world in all its peculiarity yet exceptional in the acuteness of his vision, as well as the readiness and accuracy with which he knew what to think, how to connect perception to judgment, and how to settle both—informally as it were—in a vision of the human comedy.

Vision isn't quite the right word, however. Vision comes along with a capital letter on it; let's say instead, Geertz's way of being-in-the-world, a serious man on serious earth, is inseparable from his shaping sense of comedy. In lower case and lowish tones of voice—as his friend and admirer, Robert Darnton complained in a memoir, "he talked too fast and mumbled into his beard"[8]—he embodied in his writing and enacted in his thought a vision (dammit) of the modern comedy and its historical formation.

In this he followed Kenneth Burke, one of the mentors from whom he borrowed (with embellishments from Wittgenstein) his signature concept, "dramatism." Burke distinguished between tragedy, understood as impelled by human evil and the supernatural malevolence of history, and comedy, effortfully contrived by human stupidity and corrigible error, perhaps to be put right by human self-knowledge.[9]

In Geertz's sort-of-literary-critical volume of essays on the founding fathers and mothers of anthropology, he ends his preface by paying the book's formal tribute to Burke, "who has no direct connection to it or me, but whose work has served as its governing inspiration at almost every point."[10]

Burke had discovered in I. A. Richards the definition of a symbolic act as "the dancing of an attitude" (Geertz pounced on that). He had launched upon his search and research for "a grammar of motives" framed as *comedy*, for "a comic frame of motives would not only avoid the sentimental denial of materialistic factors in human acts. It would also avoid the cynical brutality that comes when such sensitivity is outraged." Burke then, with confident quirkiness, roundly defines comedy as "the maximum of forensic complexity."

Geertz was much seized by the comedy of things; indeed, there is no thinker of our time who is funnier. He has a blunt way with the widespread insistence of contemporary political and sociological writers, borrowed no doubt from journalism, always to be looking for the truth *behind* the facts and their appearance, poking about for meanings and motives that, as they suppose, everybody is at pains to conceal, but that are, in the key adverb, "really" what is going on. Geertz's truth, comically plain, is that "the real is as imagined as the imaginary," that public action, symbolic of ourselves, is all there is to go on.[11]

Comedies as written by Geertz are therefore peopled by peoples and without sanctimonious inflection: whether as individual thinkers, as nations trekking towards and away from progress, as churches and their congregations struggling for meaning and furious to strike down the meaningless, or as empires, past or present, doing their best for misery or emancipation.

IV

I have grouped the reviews under two headings before adding what Kierkegaard once described as his "final concluding postscript," composed of the last lectures. The first section, "Sages and Anthropologists" takes in a queer enough *galère*; Geertz once remarked to me that "the *NYR* sends me books about the down-and-outs, the trouserless and the crazies," and it was so. I have, for example, had to exclude Geertz's review of *Ishi's Brain*, the book about the last and most wretched Yahi Indian found mute and cowering in the Californian Sierra in 1911.

But this was exactly how Geertz reordered anthropology for the improvement of Western modernity. He showed the West Atlantic academic world more or less by himself (although Marshall Sahlins and Robert Bellah helped a lot) not only how to understand those millions living on the other side of our imaginative territory but also how we and they might cross the frontiers and live, think, and feel quite differently from the way we do here and now.

This is what he made anthropology do, taking the great opportunity thrown open by the Harvard Department of Human Relations in 1950 (still one of the most thrilling innovations by a university trying to make the world a better place), and carrying his subject to the neighboring disciplines for their edification. This first section is constituted by his meditations on this mighty topic, the help and hindrance of the sages, and the absorption of its lessons into the way we think now. His essay for *Encounter* on Levi-Strauss, at once lethal and handsome, which appeared in a later version in *The Interpretation of Cultures* caused Levi-Strauss to say, wincing, when they met, that "it was a bit hard").

The second section is roundly entitled "Islams and the Fluidity of Nations," and, in the new world crisis since that religion's most hysterical commandoes crashed into the most complacent certainties of world wealth, the title needs no more justification. But in a dictum concluding the essay *Toutes Directions* here (what he called his "house-painting guide") Geertz's admonition long before the World Trade Towers atrocity is that "the Islamic City . . . is losing definition and gaining energy." The minatory moral of that is to locate the multiple sources of the energy and its manifold dramatizations—hence the two-part essay, its title taken, as you'd expect, from a *New Yorker* cartoon, "Which way to Mecca."

Geertz, in spite of himself, also essayed a larger conspectus, and this section includes those reviews in which, majestically and modestly, he tackles the conditions of whole societies and their shifting places in the world. In two cases (in 1990 and 2005), he envisions the state of the world itself, followed by that half unsanctified by maleness. Naturally, his emphasis falls largely on those two areas, one vastly populous, the other still vastly empty but filling up, which provided the dual subject matter of his career: Indonesia and North Africa. But it was the predominant emphasis of his method to teach his reader how to look through the lenses of one society at the peculiarities of another. Always refusing to accept Hegel's category of "world-historical nations," his salutary lesson for his own society was to show it how to look at other principalities making modernity their own un-American way and to draw the moral that their protean shapelessness was the way the world is likely to go. For him, understanding was more a matter of bifocalism than comparativism *tout court*. (He kept uneasily in mind Santayana's remark that people compare when they can't get to the root of the matter.)

This collection is certainly intended to be illustrative—"Look, here's the range; this is what the work was like." It is also celebratory and valedictory. In part 3, "The Idea of Order" (Geertz was an admirer of Wallace Stevens's poetry), the five lectures may as well be read as his farewell to the world. The second is a successor fragment of autobiography and self-evaluation providing a footnote to *After the Fact* in 1995 and to the first chapter of *Available Light* in 2000. But in each of these lectures, Geertz at once lifts his eyes cautiously up to a universal human horizon, while standing as firmly as it allows on the broken and irregular ground beneath his feet.

The autobiographical essay is also a long perspective thrown over American intellectual life and its soldiering in the cold war and postmodernity. The one before it is a paper so far given and published only at the Institute for Advanced Study and uncovering, in his characteristic way, "The Near East in the Far" as well as the future in the present. The third takes up some of the questions posed in an earlier three-part essay in *Available Light*, "The World in Pieces," and once more rehearses the necessity to refuse grand theoretical accounts of globalization, still more the drum-beating anticipation of a clash of civilizations, and to take each oddity on its own terms, whether responded to by the United States or the United Nations. The fourth—the James Frazer lecture—is, as its title announces, a reiteration of his antiuniversalist liberal-imaginative strictures in the name, nonetheless, of that excellent cliché, "common humanity."

Finally, at the height of his powers but barely nine months before his death, he ends with his characteristically unsettling lecture given in memorial of Irving Howe and published in the journal *Dissent*, in which he dismantles some of the most reassuring political commonplaces of the day in order to suggest, without rancor, just how shaky are the nation-based narratives with which the powerful interpret the political world, meanwhile proposing others, preferable because local, because domestic, because less deadly, and holding open the future to its unlikelihood.

For many years Geertz had been talking politics as much as anthropology or history. Indeed, he invented out of the babel of the intellectual tongues of his time the outlines of what R. G. Collingwood asked for of his fellow scholar-citizens, "a science of human affairs."[12] Geertz fashioned such a thing from the medley of what he called the "blurred genres" of contemporary thought,[13] the using and controlling of which his first and last requirement was that human scientists refuse the unspeakable but alas widely spoken and lockjawed jargon of management and the policy sciences, and recover instead, in W. H. Auden's fine phrase, a "sane, affirmative speech."

It is timely to speculate, by way of conclusion, that the development of Geertz's genius, his "style" in Nietzsche's strong sense, owed much to the wisdom and good fortune which placed him, from 1970 until 2006, in the School of Social Science at the Institute for Advanced Study in Princeton. The extreme happiness of this, as he once noted himself, was that in those wonderful surroundings,

> The niche-specialization that occurs with increasing rapidity in the great conglomerate universities is entirely missing, and nobody is ever really delegated to do anything. Economists have to deal with anthropologists, anthropologists with political scientists, political scientists with economists, and so on around the circle, and they all have to make sure the books balance, the appointments get made, and the Nosy Parkers from the government—NEH and all that—get kept properly at bay. It's the social science business we all have to know, not just our own special region of it, and there is surely no alienation from the means of production here.
>
> This leads of course to an intensely personal sort of relationship between the proprietors as full human beings, there being no Deans, Department Heads, Standing Committees or whatever to hide behind, or

for that matter to dump upon, and the line between home and office gets rather blurred. You hold policy meetings in hallways and streets, seminars in homes, discuss problems evenings, Sundays and whatever. And the result of *that* is you either get along as, to use the vernacular term, friends, not just, to use the professional one, colleagues, or the thing doesn't work.[14]

As he went on to say, such arrangements resemble those in a small business, never far away from danger or disaster, its partners united in anxiety and in hope, only doing a few things but obliged to do them extremely well, "for otherwise who needs it?" The result, he said, is "a sort of dialectic of temperaments rather than a division of labor," a powerful alloy of deep friendship between very unalike characters—"the sort of thing that is reputed to have existed in Greece but is rather hard to find in contemporary academia"—compounded of trust, regard, affection, and an argumentatively shared picture of the world.

These homely and amenable morals transpire spontaneously from the reviews and essays which follow. Geertz—himself cordial, generous, warmhearted to a fault, unmanageably funny, irascible when it counted, not a little frightening to us who listened to his quick, funny, murmured, intricate, sometimes inaudible delivery and couldn't always follow—taught in his prose and in his thought the truism that the proper study of humankind is humanity and that you can only do it properly by becoming as fully human as you have it in yourself to be.

PART I

Sages and Anthropologists

On Malinowski

Ten years ago several eminent anthropologists, linguists, and sociologists who had, in one way or another, been students of Bronislaw Malinowski decided that he had been unjustly neglected since his death in 1942 and put together a collection of essays, each of which was devoted to a particular aspect of his work.[1] But, as the writers were frank and competent, the result did rather more to justify the neglect than to end it. Meyer Fortes of Cambridge decided that although Malinowski wrote about Kinship incessantly, he really didn't understand it. S. F. Nadel indicted his religious studies as a simplistic "theology of optimism." J. R. Firth, though sympathetic to his aims, regarded his technical linguistic contribution as consisting of "sporadic comments immersed and perhaps lost in what is properly called his ethnographic analysis." Edmund Leach thought his theoretical writings "not merely dated [but] dead"; Talcott Parsons that he misinterpreted both Durkheim and Freud and had hardly heard of anyone else; Raymond Firth that he failed to grasp economic reasoning; Isaac Schapera that he was unwilling or unable to distinguish law from custom. Only on one point was there unanimous and quite unqualified praise: Malinowski was an incomparable fieldworker. Possessed, in Audrey Richard's words, of "unusual linguistic gifts, lively powers of personal contact and terrific energy," he "achieved a great measure of personal identification with the people he lived with." Pretentious, platitudinous, unsystematic, simpleminded, long-winded, intellectually provincial, and perhaps even somewhat dishonest, he had, somehow, a way with the natives.

Well now we have more direct evidence of just what sort of man this consummate fieldworker was. It takes the form of a very curious document, which its editors have decided to call *A Diary in the Strict Sense of the Term*, apparently

Originally published as "Under the Mosquito Net," *New York Review of Books* 9, no. 4 (14 September 1967). Books under discussion therein are as follows: Bronislaw Malinowski, *A Diary in the Strict Sense of the Term* and Bronislaw Malinowski, *Coral Gardens and Their Magic: I: Soil Tilling and Agricultural Rites in the Trobriand Islands II: The Language of Magic and Gardening.*

in an effort to communicate that it is a diary in a queer sense of the term. Written, in Polish, during 1914–1915, when he was in New Guinea for his first expedition, and in 1917–1918, when he was finishing up his famous Trobriand research, the diary consists, for the most part, neither of a description of his daily activities nor a record of the personal impact those activities had upon him. Rather it depicts a sort of mental tableau whose stereotyped figures—his mother, a boyhood friend with whom he has quarreled, a woman he has loved and wishes to discard, another he is now in love with and wishes to marry— are all thousands of miles away, frozen in timeless attitudes which, in anxious self-contempt, he obsessively contemplates. For this man of "lively powers of personal contact," everything local and immediate in the South Seas seems to have been emotionally offstage, a profitable object of observation or a petty source of irritation. For more than three years, this "diary" suggests, Malinowski worked, with enormous industry, in one world, and lived, with intense passion, in another.

The significance of this fact for anthropology's image of itself is shattering, especially since that image has been so self-congratulatory. Indeed, for a discipline which regards itself as nothing if not broad-minded, it is most unpleasant to discover that its archetypal fieldworker, rather than being a man of catholic sympathies and deep generosity, a man who his Oceanist contemporary R. R. Marett thought could find his way into the heart of the shiest savage, was instead a crabbed, self-preoccupied, hypochrondriacal narcissist, whose fellow-feeling for the people he lived with was limited in the extreme. (He refers to them continually in this diary as—lapsing into English—the bloody, insolent, or disgusting niggers, and virtually never mentions them except to express his contempt for them: "At bottom I am living outside of Kiriwina [the main district of the Trobriands, in which, physically, he was living] although strongly hating the niggers.") For the truth is that Malinowski *was* a great ethnographer, and, when one considers his place in time, one of the most accomplished that has yet appeared. That he was also apparently a disagreeable man thus poses something of a problem.

An iconoclast all his life, Malinowski has, in this gross, tiresome, posthumous work, destroyed one final idol, and one he himself did much to create: that of the fieldworker with extraordinary empathy for the natives. While intensive field research of the sort Malinowski perfected has grown, so has the notion that the success of such research depends upon the establishment of a peculiar bond of sympathy between the anthropologist and the informant, a bond usually referred to as "rapport." Unlike the missionary, the colonial official, the trader (all of whom Malinowski seems to have regarded as fools or worse) or, nowadays, the embassy aide, Coca-Cola representative, journalist, and junketing economist, the anthropologist "understands the people," and, appreciating this, the people in turn reveal to him their innermost thoughts and feelings.

This unsophisticated conception of rapport is, of course, self-serving and sentimental, thus false. Nevertheless, some bond of sympathy is at the heart of effective field research; and the ability to encourage an informant, who has no particular reason for doing so, to talk with some honesty and in some detail about what the anthropologist wants him to talk about is what separates the gifted from the miscast in ethnography. The value of Malinowski's embarrassing example is that, if one takes it seriously, it makes it difficult to defend the sentimental view of rapport as depending on the enfolding of anthropologist and informant into a single moral, emotional, and intellectual universe. In whatever way Malinowski obtained the material for the more than 2500 pages of the major descriptive monographs which he produced on the Trobriands, he didn't do it by becoming one with the natives:

> At 10 I went to Teyava, where I took pictures of a house, a group of girls, and the [food exchanges] and studied the construction of a new house. On this occasion I made one or two coarse jokes, and one bloody nigger made a disapproving remark, whereupon I cursed them and was highly irritated. I managed to control myself on the spot, but was terribly irritated that the nigger had dared to speak to me in such a manner.

In fact, the relationship between an anthropologist and the people he studies is inevitably asymmetrical, and radically so. The two parties come to the encounter with different backgrounds, different expectations, and different purposes. They are not members of a single community, a fact which no amount of murmuring about human brotherhood or the society of all mankind can really obscure. Their interests, their resources, their needs, to say nothing of their positions in life, are all sharply contrasting. They do not see things in the same way nor feel about them in the same way, and so the relationship between them is characterized by moral tension, a fixed ethical ambiguity. Most anthropologists are not so ill-natured as Malinowski, and indeed he seems (though this may merely be a result of his having also been franker than most) something of a deviant, if not an extreme case. But the fact that most good ethnographers are decent and reasonably pleasant men who like and admire the people they work with doesn't really change the situation. The noblest of anthropologists face the problem Malinowski faced: how to penetrate a form of life not merely different from but incompatible with their own.

What saved Malinowski, what kept him from sinking entirely into the emotional swamp the diary describes, was not an enlarged capacity for empathy. There is very little evidence in any of his work that he ever found his way into any savage's heart, even the least shy. The psychology is all generalized, the ideas and emotions all standardized. "The Trobriander" (or, often enough, "The Savage") does this or that, feels this or that, thinks this or that. Individuals appear only momentarily as often suspiciously apt illustrations of some general feature of Trobriand mentality. What saved him was an almost unbelievable capacity for work. For a man who complains in his diary almost every day of lethargy, boredom, illness, despair, or just a general inability to get anything done, he collected a staggering quantity of data. Not universal compassion but an almost Calvinist belief in the cleansing power of work brought Malinowski out of his own dark world of oedipal obsessions and practiced self-pity into Trobriand daily life:

> As for ethnology: I see the life of the natives as utterly devoid of interest or importance, something as remote from me as the life of a dog. During the walk, I made it a point of honor to think about what I am here to do. About the need to collect many documents. I have a general idea about their life and some acquaintance with their language, and if I can only somehow "document" all this, I'll have valuable material.—Must concentrate on my ambitions and work to some purpose. Must organize the linguistic material and collect documents, find better ways of studying the life of women [domestic implements], and system of "social representations." Strong spiritual impulse.

The diary is laced with moral self-exhortation to leave off onanism, pawing native girls, and reading trashy novels and buckle down to doing what he was there to do. When this is combined with the constant theme of self condemnation, the book takes on something of the tone of a Puritan tract:

> Got up at 7. Yesterday, under the mosquito net, dirty thoughts: Mrs. [H.P.]; Mrs. C. and even Mrs. W. . . . I even thought of seducing M. Shook all this off . . . Today got up at 7—sluggish; I lay under the mosquito net and wanted to read a book instead of working. I got up and made the rounds of the village. [Studied barter trade.] I resolved absolutely to avoid all lecherous thoughts, and in my work to finish off the census, if possible, today. At about 9 I went to Kaytabu where I took the census with a bearded old man. Monotonous, stupid work, but indispensable.
>
> Woke up late; under the netting a tendency to let myself go, as usual, which I mastered. Planned details of excursion to Kitava and thought about documenting [native trade]. Wrote down conversations . . . Conversations with [the island chief].
>
> Moral tenets: I must never let myself become aware of the fact that other women [than his fiancée] have bodies, that they copulate. I also

resolve to shun the line of least resistance in the matter of novels. I am very content not to have fallen again into the habit of smoking. Now I must accomplish the same thing in respect to reading. I may read poems and serious things, but I must absolutely avoid trashy novels. And I should read ethnographic works.

The total lack of "moral personality" is disastrous. For instance, my behavior at George's, my pawing of Jab., dancing with her, etc. is caused mainly by a desire to impress other fellows . . . I must have a system of specific formal prohibitions: I must not smoke. I must not touch a woman with suberotic intentions. I must not betray E.R.M. [his fiancée] mentally, i.e., recall my previous relations with women, or think about future ones . . . Preserve the essential inner personality through all difficulties and vicissitudes: I must never sacrifice moral principles or essential work to "posing," to convivial *Stimmung*, etc. My main task now must be: work. *Ergo*: work!

On almost every page one finds something like this. He has erotic fantasies of one sort or another, remembers his mother or his fiancée, is overwhelmed with guilt, and resolves, in spite of severe lassitude, to get down to business, which he does with a vengeance. He then feels, especially if the work goes well, exhausted but euphoric, and discourses, often with real eloquence, on the beauties of the landscape "toward which I have a voluptuous feeling."

The ethnography this expiatory approach to work produced was, as one might expect, detailed, concrete, comprehensive to the point of indiscriminateness, and—the word is inadequate—voluminous. "Working at my present pace," he remarks in one of his more optimistic moods, "I should come back laden with materials as a camel." He did, and each of his major works is an enormous encyclopedia of data on every topic related to its general theme, and even on some topics that are not related at all. *Coral Gardens and Their Magic*, first published in 1935 and just now reissued (and the work Malinowski personally regarded as his best) is a prime example. In its 800 pages, divided into two not very closely integrated volumes, one gets everything from diagrams of house types, layouts of garden plots, and lists of yam exchanges to extensive discussions of Trobriand clan organization, agricultural rituals, gift exchanges, and gardening practices, plus (inserted between a chapter on "The Cultivation of Taro, Palms and Bananas" and one on "Land Tenure") a disquisition on field methods, and (in the second volume) ninety-eight magical texts in the Trobriand language complete with literal and free translations and commentaries. There are sections called "An Ethnographic Theory of the Magical Word," "What Industrial Specialization Looks Like in Melanesia," "A Walk

Through the Gardens," "*Kayaku*—The chief and Magician in Council," "Hunger, Love and Vanity as Driving Forces in the Trobriand Harvest Gift," and "Fruits of the Wood and of the Wild," after which there is a lengthy appendix lamenting the amount of facts he failed to gather (for example, how often the natives calculate the number of seed yams per garden plot).

Malinowski's ex-students were right: it is this great corpus of material, in *Coral Gardens*, in *The Argonauts*, in *Crime and Custom*, in *Sex and Repression in Savage Society*, in *The Sexual Life of Savages*, that remains as his monument. The rest—the biologistic theory of functionalism, the contextual theory of language, the confidence theory of magic, the non-economic interpretation of primitive trade, the extension of family ties approach to social organization now seem at best feeble first steps toward an adequate conceptualization of culture, at worst dogmatic oversimplifications that have done more harm than good. His achievement was to compile a faithful, lifelike, and indeed moving record of a primitive way of life, against psychological odds that would have crushed almost anyone else. For if the Trobrianders are "bloody niggers" in his private diary, in his ethnographic works they are, through a mysterious transformation wrought by science, among the most intelligent, dignified, and conscientious natives in the whole of anthropological literature: men, Malinowski is forever insisting, even as you and I.

Or as he. The insight into Trobriand life Malinowski apparently was unable to gain by human contact he gained by industry. Closed off, by the peculiarities of his own personality, from reaching directly what, in *The Argonauts*, he called the final goal of ethnography, "to grasp the native's point of view, his relation to life, to realize *his* vision of *his* world," he reached it indirectly. Isolated, even estranged, from his subjects emotionally, he struggled to understand them by patiently observing them, talking to them, reflecting about them. Such an approach can carry one only so far. But it carried Malinowski farther than most because, in spite of his personal torments or because of them, he carried on the struggle so relentlessly. "Truly," he says in the concluding sentence of the diary, "I lack real character." Perhaps; but it rather depends on what is meant by character.

On Gandhi

"Whence, however," the *Mahabharata* asks, "does Hope arise?" For twenty years, since his *Childhood and Society* announced the Freudian vocation to be the empowerment of the ego, Erik Erikson has been asking the same question. His whole career has proceeded from a settled determination to turn psychoanalysis away from fascination with weakness toward detection of strength, to dissolve its hospital odor and connect it up with the public aspirations of men. In modern India, where despair is more than an emotion—a quality of the landscape, a dimension of the weather—hope arose most eloquently with Gandhi. In addressing himself to the question of whence, in the convolutions of the Mahatma's life, that hope came, what it consisted in, and why, at least for a while, it caught most of India in its grasp, Erikson has found a most appropriate subject. But he has found as well a most refractory case.

A man who claims to be a saint, as Gandhi did, if not in so many words, certainly in almost every action he took after his return from South Africa in 1915 (he arrived at the banquet, with which Bombay high society greeted him, in peasant dress and announced that he would rather have been received by indentured servants), demands, above all, a moral response. Rather like the little girl who did not know whether she wished to see the dinosaur in the museum until she found out whether it was good or bad, we have to decide how to feel about him before we really understand him, and coming to understand him does not actually help very much in deciding how to feel about him.

Indeed, when it is a dinosaur like Gandhi one is going to see, coming to understand him only makes the problem worse. The deeper the labyrinth of his personality is penetrated the higher rises the tension between admiration and outrage, awe and disgust, trust and suspicion, until the encounter with him becomes as painful and disaccommodating as he wished to make it. It is the triumph of Erikson's book that in uncovering the inner sources of Gandhi's

Originally published as "Gandhi: Non-Violence as Therapy," *New York Review of Books* 13, no. 9 (20 November 1969). The book under discussion therein is as follows: Erik H. Erikson, *Gandhi's Truth, or the Origins of Militant Nonviolence*.

power it does not dissolve but deepens his inherent moral ambiguity, and in so doing extends the intent of his career: to make of himself an exemplary prophet, a man who recommends his character to the world as a saving revelation.

The more prominent features of Gandhi's character are only too well known. His sexual and dietary asceticism, his hatred of filth, his shyness, his restlessness, his penchant for self-inflicted suffering, his moralism, his romanticism, his vanity, have all been described over and over again in what is by now a fairly sizable hagiographic and anti-hagiographic literature both inside India and out. Erikson inspects these familiar traits and traces their roots in Gandhi's childhood and adolescence. But it is to a less noticed aspect of Gandhi's character that he turns as the psychological axis of his religious genius—his ironic, mocking, grating humor.

Erikson's Gandhi is an obsessive tease, a man with an extraordinary capacity to make others feel furious and foolish at the same time. At Benares, the arch symbol of Hindu humility, he dresses up as a pauper and offers a penny to the Well of Knowledge and is duly rewarded by having a custodian of orthodoxy (and, apparently, of the Well) inform him that he will land in hell for his stinginess. In South Africa, he organizes a boycott against the Black Act and then escorts Indians who wish to break it through the picket lines of his own followers. At a meeting with the Viceroy arranged to end his disobedience campaign against the salt tax he draws a packet of salt from his shawl and pours it ceremoniously into his tea. He praises anarchy to lawyers, patience to students, manual labor to civil servants, poverty to economists, simplicity to maharajas, Hindi to college professors, and violence to Annie Besant.

He is always taunting, testing limits, playing, up to some finely calculated point, with others' emotions. The essence of his spiritual gift is an edged gaiety, an Indic variety of kidding on the level, which keeps everyone—intimates, followers, rivals, officials, wisdom seekers from the West—psychologically off balance, unable to find their moral feet with him. Forged into a political instrument this becomes the famous *Satyagraha*, which literally means "truth force" or "perseverance in truth," is usually translated as "passive resistance" or (somewhat better) "militant non-violence," but which could perhaps be most informatively rendered as "mass taunting" or "collective needling." What in the end Gandhi did to colonial India was drive it to distraction.

Erikson centers his investigation of this intricate art around an incident— he calls it "The Event"—which, occurring at the very beginning of Gandhi's Indian career (though, as he was nearly fifty, well along in his life), demonstrates its workings in a parochial, highly personal, micro-context—a small, intense circle of intimates. Working into this "Event," the Ahmedabad textile strike of 1918, from Gandhi's youth and young manhood (Gujerat, London, South Africa), on the far side, and outward from it to the days of his Mahatmaship, when "all India would hold its breath while [he] fasted," on the near, he uses it, like a true clinician, to uncover the psychological materials out of which *Satyagraha* was made.

What made the Ahmedabad strike such a natural for Gandhi was the in-grown character of it all. The workers, many of whom were women, were led by the feminist sister of the main mill owner, one of the earliest of Gandhi's long string of devoted female disciples. Management was led by her less vi-sionary brother, whose wife was also a Gandhi partisan, and who, for all his defensive bluffness, had himself been Gandhi's first important financial backer in India. Together with a few other early adherents—an energetic Bombay social worker, a mousy male secretary, one of Gandhi's squad of attendant nephews—this little group formed a mock family, thick with oblique affec-tions and equivocal motives, which the intrusion of the strike threw into pre-cisely the kind of psychological disarray in which an inspired tease with a passion for toying with others' emotions could effectively maneuver. "I am handling a most dangerous situation here," he wrote exultantly to one of his sons as irresistible sister and immovable brother set out on a collision course, "and preparing to go on to a still more dangerous."

After such promising beginnings, however, the affair turned out, on the surface at least, to be a bit of a fizzle. Seated beneath a bulbul tree Gandhi lectured to thousands of people each afternoon on the principles of *Satya-graha*. He extracted, almost without quite realizing it, a sacred pledge from the workers neither to resume work nor to cause any disturbance until their de-mands had been met. And, when their resolution began to fail, he launched the first of his seventeen famous "fasts to the death." In the end, despairing of the moral fiber of the workers ("After twenty years' experience I have come to the conclusion that I am qualified to take a pledge," he told them with headmaster rudeness. "I see you are not yet so qualified.") he negotiated a settlement between the sibling antagonists which saved the workers' pride, the owners' pocketbook, and his own reputation.

It seemed to Gandhi a rather sordid end to what was to have been a moral revolution. ("My co-workers and I," he wrote later in his *Autobiography*, "had built many castles in the air, but they all vanished for the time being.") But for Erikson it is the point at which Gandhi set definitively off down the road to sainthood, the point at which the philosophy of militant non-violence freed itself from his personal biography to become part of the collective conscious-ness of modern India:

> . . . Casting Ahmedabadis against one another [The Event] was largely a
> local show, like a rehearsal before a provincial audience. This [becomes] es-
> pecially clear when we look back on Ahmedabad from the first nation-wide

Satyagraha exactly one year later. . . . Then hundreds of thousands of Indians of all regions and religions would be on the move; the British Empire itself would be the principal counter-player, and world opinion the awed onlooker. But at least Ahmedabad [was] a real, a craftsmanlike rehearsal, in spite of a few devastating shortcomings such as earnest rehearsals bring to life.

At Ahmedabad, teasing was finally raised to a philosophical plane, taunting exalted into a religious act. To an extent this had already occurred in the agitations in South Africa. But there it had all been rather pragmatic, ad hoc, a day-to-day experimentation with styles and devices, immediate reactions to immediate injustices. At Ahmedabad, where the personal, social, ethical, and practical flowed into one another in such a way as virtually to dissolve the line between private emotions and public acts, such ideological innocence could no longer be maintained. The inner connection between *Satyagraha* as individual experience—what Gandhi taxed the workers with not having—and as collective action—what he taxed himself for not controlling—was openly exposed, and with it the fact that shaming men into virtue was a complex and treacherous business, both less selfish and less pacific than it looked.

The violence that non-violence contains, has, of course, often been noted; since Nietzsche, it has been a commonplace. But what Gandhi came, after Ahmedabad, to believe—and in so doing plunged himself into a forest of puzzles—was that this contained violence was precisely what gave nonviolence its moral grandeur. As a weapon of the weak, *Satyagraha* is reduced to cowardice, it is what the defenseless must do to survive; as a weapon of the strong, it is the highest form of courage, the willingness to suffer evil rather than commit it. From someone powerless to strike back, turning the other cheek is a token of submission, a victim mollifying his tormentor by dissembling his rage. From someone competent to strike back, and even to kill, it is a provocation, an assertion of moral superiority which an aggressor, whether with renewed brutality or crushed repentance, must necessarily acknowledge. The road to true non-violence passes then through the attainment of power, that is of the means of violence, a doctrine which, when stated in the context of India fifty years ago, breathes the same chill of desperate logic as it does in that of the contemporary United States:

> What am I to advise a man to do who wants to kill but is unable owing to his being maimed? Before I can make him feel the virtue of not killing, I must restore to him the arm he has lost. . . . A nation that is unfit to fight cannot from experience prove the virtue of not fighting. I do not infer from this that India must fight. But I do say that India must know how to fight.

I have come to see, what I did not so clearly before, that there is non-violence in violence. This is the big change which has come about. I had not fully realized the duty of restraining a drunkard from doing evil, of killing a dog in agony or one infected with rabies. In all these instances violence is in fact non-violence.

Today I find that everybody is desirous of killing, but most are afraid of doing so or powerless to do so. Whatever is to be the result I feel certain that the power must be restored to India. The result may be carnage. Then India must go through it.

Whether one hears Malcolm X or Dean Rusk in these quotations—and it is part of the now-you-see-it-now-you-don't quality of *Gandhi's Truth* that one can hear something of both—this is clearly dangerous doctrine; the carnage after all did come, martyring Gandhi with it, and, as I write, Ahmedabad, of all places, is the scene of the bloodiest communal riots since Partition. The moral doubletalk to which it can lead is apparent, not only in Gandhi (". . . Our offspring must be strong in physique," he said, urging Indians into the British Army. "If they cannot completely renounce the urge to violence, we may permit them to commit violence, to use their strength to fight and thus make them non-violent"), but, on occasion, in Erikson as well:

In view of the values which the Jews of the diaspora have come to stand for, the belated proof that Jews could fight a national war, may impress many as an historical anachronism. And, indeed, the triumph of Israeli soldiery is markedly subdued, balanced by a certain sadness over the necessity to reenter historical actuality by way of military methods not invented by Jews, and yet superbly used by them. I would go further: is it not possible that such historical proof of a military potential will make peace-loving Jews better potential Satyagrahis?

Yet, however one may prefer the bleak candor of *Realpolitik* to images of a saddened soldiery fighting to advance the cause of pacifism (as Burkhardt said, there is enough hypocrisy in the world already), the argument that a sacred pledge to abstain from the use of force can have moral reality only with respect to people who have a genuine possibility of effectively using force is surely correct. And, as Gandhi himself recognized (". . . This new aspect of non-violence which has revealed itself to me has enmeshed me in no end of problems. . . . I have not found one master-key for all the riddles. . . . My powers of thinking fail me . . .") the acceptance of this hard truth introduces a paradox into the very heart of Gandhian doctrine. As ideological slogans, "Peace Through Strength" and "Strength Through Peace" do not sit altogether comfortably together.

Not, at least, in thought. In action, Erikson argues, this contradiction was transcended by the sheer force of Gandhi's commitment, his readiness when faced with the immediate possibility, a possibility he had had usually himself specifically created, to get hurt rather than to hurt. Like Luther and like St. Francis, two other men with a subversive sense of humor, Gandhi was "a religious actualist," a man for whom truth resides neither in tradition nor in doctrine, but in "that which feels effectively true in action." In the carefully staged politico-moral dramas which he called his "experiments with truth"— Ahmedabad, the salt campaign, Hydari Mansion—Gandhi made his argument that the active decision not to do harm was the basic law of life come alive both to himself and to large masses of Indians. Stymied by the paradox that non-violence is the reciprocal of strength, power the prerequisite of self-command, his "philosophy" dissolved into a collection of colliding homilies and Indic eccentricities. Fired by the same paradox, his "method" focussed into a rising series of studied provocations designed to expose at once the pretensions of colonial society and the impotence of political brutality.

In attempting to clarify the anatomy of this exercise in collective truthfinding, Erikson follows a famous remark of Nehru's to the effect that what Gandhi accomplished for India was "a psychological change, almost as if some expert in psychoanalytic methods had probed deep into the patient's past, found out the origins of his complexes, exposed them to view, and thus rid him of that burden." Erikson constructs an extended parallel between the technique developed by Freud for renewing growth in neurotic individuals and that developed by Gandhi to restore hope to a crippled people. Both relied on engagement at close range between the agent and the subject of change; both attempted to give the subject courage to change by confronting him as a full and equal human being with a latent capacity to trust and love, rather than as a lunatic, an inferior and enemy, or a savage; both eschewed any form of coercion, even moral coercion; both regarded as critical the agent's openness to change as well as the subject's, and saw the process of "cure" as involving a deepening of insight and consequent self-transformation, on both sides. And so on. *Satyagraha* is Analysis writ large; Analysis *Satyagraha* writ small. Politics and therapy coincide.

Perhaps one should not expect an analyst, even an heterodox one, to come to any other conclusions. ("When I began this book, I did not expect to rediscover psychoanalysis in terms of truth, self-suffering and non-violence," he concludes somewhat ingenuously. "But now that I have done so I see better what I hope the reader has come to see with me, namely, that I felt attracted to the Ahmedabad Event. . . because I sensed an affinity between Gandhi's truth and the insights of modern psychology.") But there is in this analogy a rather serious defect: in a clinical encounter ultimate interests merge, in the political one they do not. It is the deliberate exclusion of extrinsic concerns from the therapeutic situation, the stripping away of everything but a common concentration on emotional exploration that gives it, when this in fact occurs, its enormous force. With politics it is just the reverse: the wider the range of divergent concerns with which it can manage to cope the deeper it cuts. As models for each other, the consulting room and the textile strike seem peculiarly likely to mislead.

Yet, even if the therapeutic image of political process, like the therapeutic images of art, law, or education, fails at a general level to do justice to its object, and even distorts it, with respect to Gandhi that image was, as Erikson clearly demonstrates, centrally relevant. And this in turn reveals why, even when brought down to the solid outlines of a polished method, Gandhi's teachings remain, like the man himself, ambiguous and only half-convincing.

Gandhi was, as Erikson is, powerfully attracted by a therapeutic view of politics—one which abstracts from the realities of group solidarity, divergent interest, social hierarchy, and cultural difference (and this in India!) in order to concentrate on exploiting the emotional involvements of individuals in one another's lives. At Ahmedabad, he had a situation in which such exploitation was possible, and though, characteristically, the strike failed, the therapy worked. "I have never come across the like of it," he said in his final speech to the workers. "I had had experience of many such conflicts or heard of them but have not known any in which there was so little ill will or bitterness as in this." And a few days later he wrote to the *Bombay Chronicle* to justify his own role which the paper had questioned as wasting large talents on parochial issues, "I have not known a struggle fought with so little bitterness and such courtesy on either side. This happy result is principally due to the connections with it of Mr. Ambalal Sarabhai [the millowner brother] and Anasuyaben [the labor-leader sister]."

Removed from this intimate context, he would never know it again. And in attempting again and again to re-enact this family drama on the national stage his career revealed both the intrinsic power of attraction that a view of politics as a process of inward change possesses—its ability to move men—and its radical inability, having moved them, to deal with the issues—whether workers' wages or the threat of Partition—thereby raised.

The contrast which appeared already at Ahmedabad between Gandhi's extraordinary ability to shape the personal lives of those immediately around him and his inability to control the direction of the strike as a collective act grew greater and greater as he extended himself across India and into larger and larger mass settings, and became, as violence followed violence to the climax of Partition and his own assassination, the distinguishing feature of his career. Nehru was wrong. Gandhi did not psychoanalyze India, he (though of course not alone) politicized it; and having politicized it, could not—a fact our own "religious actualists," taunting power, toying with social passions, and finding truth "in that which feels effectively true in action" might well ponder—in the end control it.

"Who listens to me today," he wrote just six months before his death,

> . . . I am being told to retire to the Himalayas. Everybody is eager to gar-land my photos and statues. Nobody really wants to follow my advice. . . . Neither the people nor those in power have any use for me.

Today, when his centenary is being celebrated by men for whom he is nei-ther a personal presence nor a moral force but a marketable national treasure, like the Taj Mahal, this is even more true. Erikson's penetrating book, more convincing in describing the dinosaur than in judging him, deepens our un-derstanding not only of the inward sources of personal greatness but those, as well, of its self-defeat.

On Foucault

I

Michel Foucault erupted onto the intellectual scene at the beginning of the Sixties with his *Folie et déraison*, an unconventional but still reasonably recognizable history of the Western experience of madness. He has become, in the years since, a kind of impossible object: a nonhistorical historian, an antihumanistic human scientist, and a counter-structuralist structuralist. If we add to this his tense, impacted prose style, which manages to seem imperious and doubt-ridden at the same time, and a method which supports sweeping summary with eccentric detail, the resemblance of his work to an Escher drawing—stairs rising to platforms lower than themselves, doors leading outside that bring you back inside—is complete.

"Do not ask who I am and do not ask me to remain the same," he writes in the introduction to his one purely methodological work, *L'Archéologie du savoir*, itself mostly a collection of denials of positions he does not hold but considers himself likely to be accused of by the "mimes and tumblers" of intellectual life. "Leave it to our bureaucrats and our police to see that our papers are in order," he states. "At least spare us their morality when we write." Whoever he is, or whatever, he is what any French savant seems to need to be these days: elusive.

But (and in this he differs from a good deal that has been going on in Paris since structuralism arrived) the difficulty of his work arises not from self-regard and the desire to found an intellectual cult only the instructed can join, but from a powerful and genuine originality of thought. As he intends nothing less than a Great Instauration for the human sciences, it is not surprising that he is more than occasionally obscure, or that when he does manage to be clear he is no less disconcerting.

Originally published as "Stir Crazy," *New York Review of Books* 24, nos. 21 and 22 (26 January 1978). The book under discussion therein is as follows: Michel Foucault, *Discipline and Punish: The Birth of the Prison*, translated by Alan Sheridan.

Foucault's leading ideas are not in themselves all that complex; just unusually difficult to render plausible. The most prominent of them, and the one for which he has drawn the most attention, is that history is not a continuity, one thing growing organically out of the last and into the next, like the chapters in some nineteenth-century romance. It is a series of radical discontinuities, ruptures, breaks, each of which involves a wholly novel mutation in the possibilities for human observation, thought, and action. Foucault first referred to the "precarious splinters of eternity" these mutations produce as *épistémès* (i.e., "epistemological fields"), later on as historical *a prioris*, and most recently as discursive formations. Under whatever label, they are to be dealt with "archaeologically." That is, they are first to be characterized according to the rules determining what kinds of perception and experience can exist within their limits, what can be seen, said, performed, and thought in the conceptual domain they define. That done, they are then to be put into a pure series, a genealogical sequence in which what is shown is not how one has given causal rise to another but how one has formed itself in the space left vacant by another, ultimately covering it over with new realities. The past is not prologue; like the discrete strata of Schliemann's site, it is a mere succession of buried presents.

In such terms, Foucault sees European history cross-cut by three great fault lines separating what lies on the far side of them from what lies on the near by "pure distances" that are traversed by mere chronology—the blank, external seriality of events. The first of these fissures lies somewhere around the middle of the seventeenth century, and it divides a magical age from a classifying age. In the first period, that of Paracelsus and Campanella, things are related to one another by intrinsic sympathies and antipathies—wine and walnuts, death and roses—that God has stamped onto their faces for all to read. In the second, that of Linnaeus and Condillac, things are related to one another through the use of types and taxonomies—species and genera, speech parts and grammars—directly given in the presented arrangement of nature.

The second fissure occurs toward the beginning of the nineteenth century. It separates the tabular, classifying, Linnaean conception of how reality is composed—with everything in its row and column—from the wholly different one of Marx and Comte in which things are related to one another narratively—seen as foreshadowings and outcomes, causes and consequences. "History," rather than "Similitude" or "Order," becomes the master category of experience, understanding, and representation. And the third fissure, which Nietzsche, Freud, and Mallarmé presage, and which we are right now trying to find some way to live through, marks the beginning of the end of this temporalized consciousness and its replacement by some new, strange form of existence not yet completely in view. Foucault alludes to it, often obliquely, in such phrases as "the scattering of the profound stream of time," "the absolute dispersion of man," "the return of the masks."

To this conception of change by radical jumps from one frame to another, Foucault then adds another unusual notion, which, though it can be traced from the beginning of his work, has grown more and more prominent as he has proceeded. This is that all these *épistémès*, "discourse fields," or whatever, are not just shapes of thought but structures of power.

Whether they be images of madness, theories of pedagogy, definitions of sexuality, medical routines, military disciplines, literary styles, research methods, views of language, or procedures for the organization of work, the conceptual systems within which an age is immured define its pattern of dominations. The objects of oppression are not generalized entities like "the proletariat," but madmen, criminals, conscripts, children, machine tenders, women, hospital patients, and the ignorant. And it is not a faceless "ruling class," but psychiatrists, lawyers, officers, parents, managers, men, physicians, and *cultivés*—those the historical *a priori* empowers to set the limits of other people's lives—who are their oppressors. "Confinement," in all its particular, discontinuous forms, has emerged as the master obsession of Foucault's work. For all his radicalism (which is vehement and absolute), his history is neither of class struggle nor of modes of production, but of constraint: intellectual, medical, moral, political, aesthetic, and epistemological constraint; and now he writes at length on judicial restraint. In *Surveiller et punir*, translated here as *Discipline* (it should have been *Observe*) *and Punish*, he has found his appointed subject and has written his most forceful book.

II

Foucault begins his effort to unearth the genealogy of the prison, to expose the strata hidden beneath its present expression, at perhaps the most dramatic of his fault lines. This was the shift, between about 1760 and 1840, from the *âge de ressemblance*, in which torture and execution of criminals were popular spectacles, to the *âge classique*, in which the lives of criminals were regulated according to timetables in methodized institutions.[1] As his image for the first he takes Robert Damiens, a religious crank, who, in 1757, slightly wounded Louis XV with a knife. For his pains, his flesh was torn from him with hot pincers, his wounds salved with molten lead and burning sulphur, his body quartered by horses and some helpful butchers to detach the joints. What was then left of him (some who were there thought him still alive) was reduced to ashes and thrown to the winds, all in the public square before the Church of Paris.

As his image for the *âge classique* Foucault takes a set of rules drawn up for a "house for young prisoners" in Paris in 1838, rules in their own way hardly more humane than the punishments imposed in Damiens's time. The Code of 1838 organized the inmates' day into a minute by minute sequence of work, prayer, meals, education, recreation, and sleep, marked by drum rolls, ordered in squads, and enveloped in silence:

> Less than a century separates [the execution and the 1838 code]. It was a time when. . . the entire economy of punishment was redistributed. It was a time of great "scandals" for traditional justice, a time of innumerable projects for reform. It saw a new theory of law and crime, a new moral or political justification of the right to punish; old laws were abolished, old customs died out. "Modern" codes were planned or drawn up: Russia, 1769; Prussia, 1780; Pennsylvania and Tuscany, 1786; Austria, 1788; France, 1791, Year IV, 1808, 1810. It was a new age for penal justice.

Foucault then traces the many aspects of this great transformation. First, there is the disappearance of punishment as a public spectacle. In essence, this represents the decline of the body as the text upon which punishment was inscribed—on which the sentence was, as with poor Damiens, quite literally written. Public torture—*supplice* in French, which means something like liturgical torment, ceremonial pain—"made the guilty man the herald of his own condemnation." The power of the sovereign, and thus his rights, was made legible with racks and sulphur. As all crimes partook of some degree of *lèse majesté*, were a regicide in miniature, this "theater of hell" was one of the constitutive features of monarchic despotism; and when both the monarchs and public torture left the historical stage they left it together. Instead of the vengeance of princes came the protection of society; instead of the excitements of the scaffold, the quiet of the prison; for writing on the body, molding it to rule.

Most of Foucault's book is devoted to analyzing the systematization, generalization, and spiritualization of punishment, and its incarnation in the gray mass of the penitentiary—"the intelligence of discipline in stone." The social forces driving the changes—the heightened concern, in a Europe become urban, bourgeois, and parliamentary, with property crimes as against political ones; the labor discipline problems of nascent industrialism—get only passing attention. Foucault is not much interested in determinants and causes. He concentrates on the organization of what he calls a new economy of punitive power, an economy that had for its aim "not to punish less, but to punish better."

For all their apparent humanitarianism—to Foucault so much incidental music—the great penal reformers of the latter half of the eighteenth century, Beccaria, Marat, Bentham, etc., were basically concerned, he writes, to "insert the power to punish more deeply into the social body." After the Revolution,

"Society" replaced "Sovereignty" as the legitimacy that criminality challenged (and parricide replaced regicide as the ultimate crime of which all other crimes were little versions). The social body more than acquiesced in this shift, in which the main agency of penetration became the formal code. The power to punish was divided into articles and printed up in sectioned texts, and thus made less arbitrary, better defined, and more coherent.

Punishment was also made more pervasive ("no crime must escape the gaze of those whose task it is to dispense justice"); more empirical ("the verification of the crime must obey the general criteria for all truth"); more practical ("for punishment to produce the effect [this from Beccaria] it is enough that the harm that it cause exceed the good that the criminal has derived from the crime"); and more specific ("all offenses [and penalties] must be defined, . . . classified, and collected into species from which none of them escape, . . . a Linnaeus of crimes and punishments"). And, most portentous of all, punishment was made didactic:

> In physical torture, the example was based on terror: physical fear, collective horror, images that must be engraved on the memories of the spectators, like the brand on the cheek or the shoulder of the condemned man. The example is now based on the lesson, the discourse, . . . the representation of public morality. It is no longer the terrifying restoration of sovereignty that will sustain the ceremony of punishment, but the reactivation of the code, the collective reinforcements of the idea of crime and the idea of punishment. In the penalty, rather than seeing the presence of the sovereign, one will read the laws themselves. The laws associate a particular crime with a particular punishment. As soon as the crime is committed, the punishment will follow at once, enacting the discourse of the law and showing that the code, which links ideas, also links realities. . . . This legible lesson, this ritual recoding, must be repeated as often as possible; the punishments must be a school rather than a festival; an ever-open book rather than a ceremony.

Two questions, the central ones of his study, are then posed by Foucault. First, if we accept this shift to a tabular, taxonomical view of crime as an array of specific varieties of resistance to the natural order of society—crime as a catalogue of social perversities—how did the prison become virtually the sole mode of punitive response? And, second, since the prison did in fact become established as the punishing institution, what became of it after the onset of the historicizing *épistémè* during the last century? What has the modern persuasion, the one we are more or less still living with, or struggling against, made of the institution of prison?

The first question is all the more intriguing because it was not the intention of the classical reformers that the prison should become the nearly universal penalty for major crimes. On the contrary, they wanted the multiplicity of offenses to be matched by a multiplicity of punishments. Exile or transportation, corvée, branding, house or city arrest, reparation, fines, conscription, loss of various sorts of civil rights, various sorts of public shaming—"a whole new arsenal of picturesque punishments"—were, along with the more familiar torture and execution, to be part of a table of penalties connected to a table of crimes in an exact and visible logic of natural justice.

But in a few short decades, imprisonment (which had not before been an important mode of long-term punishment and was associated, like the Bastille, with tyranny and kings) came to replace them all to the point that one exasperated reformer could complain to the Constituent Assembly: "If I have betrayed my country, I go to prison; if I kill my father, I go to prison—every imaginable offense is punished in the same uniform way. One might as well see a physician who has the same remedy for all ills."

Foucault traces this unforeseen consequence of the new dispensation to its didactic force: the very existence of the legible lessons in the ever-open school book of the new codes imposed the need for a schoolroom (and a schoolmaster) to assure that they got properly learned. Minds were to be altered, and the prison became the machine for altering them. Jails, once dungeons where miscreants were kept while awaiting trial, occasionally to rot while doing so, now became reformatories where souls were reshaped and citizens made. The Walnut Street Prison, set up by (who else?) Philadelphia Quakers in 1790, was one of the first, most thoroughgoing, and most influential examples of what soon became the dominant model—"the house of correction," in which a combination of disciplined productive labor, a strictly organized, cot-to-mess-hall-and-back existence, and unceasing exposure to moral instruction was intended to "effect a transformation of the individual as a whole—of his body and of his habits by the daily work he is forced to perform, of his mind and his will by the spiritual attentions that are paid to him."

The notion that the scheduled life engenders virtue goes back at least as far as the monastery, but, Foucault argues, it was reconstructed in the late eighteenth and early nineteenth centuries, not only by the more avant-garde varieties of Protestantism, but by the rise of well-drilled armies, rationalized workshops, regularized schools, and routinized hospitals—"complete and austere institutions" all. Behind them all lay the attempt to render men orderly by keeping them in order, an effort that implied constant, detailed, aggressive surveillance, a tireless gaze alert to the least irregularities. The inspection, the examination, the questionnaire, the register, the report, the dossier become the chief tools of domination because they are the chief means by which those who maintain discipline keep watch on those who, supposedly anyway, benefit from it.

So far as the prison is concerned, these tendencies—the tabular view of order, the reforming view of punishment, and the view of power as surveillance—come together in that most chilling of eighteenth-century imaginings: Jeremy Bentham's Panopticon.

This "cruel, ingenious cage," in which all the occupants, each alone in his cell, invisible to the others, can be ceaselessly observed from a central tower—the prisoner totally seen without ever seeing, his guardian totally seeing without ever being seen—is not, Foucault says, a dream building. It is "the diagram of a mechanism of power reduced to its ideal form, . . . a figure of political technology." Though it was designed to reform prisoners, it could serve as well "to treat patients, to instruct school-children, to confine the insane, to supervise workers, to put beggars and idlers to work." Worse yet, whereas the classical age never quite managed actually to build it, the modern age, with a different conception of what criminality is and expanded resources for the scrutiny of human behavior, has very nearly done so.

If the Linnaean *épistémè* established the prisoner as a person to know, the succeeding *épistémè*—the sort of outlook we associate with Comte—provided the means for knowing him: "the human sciences." The criminal becomes the delinquent—not some hapless rogue who has merely committed a classifiable offense, but a historical person whose entire pattern of life has taken an aberrant course. His biography, his psychology, his sociology, even his physique or his head shape, all become relevant to knowing him, that is, to determining the causes of his behavior; and so toward the second part of the nineteenth century the age of the case history and of criminology was born. It was not the crime itself that was central now, or even, in the proper sense, the criminal; it is the system of forces that has conspired over time to produce a "dangerous person." Delinquency does not, like robbery, point to something irregular an individual has done; but, like perversion, to something unacceptable he has become.

The prison, once a place to await the torturer's attention, then a drill-ground for moral calisthenics, now becomes an institute for scientifically imposing normality on damaged lives. Or rather, the prison has this function added on to it, for here, as elsewhere in "archaeology," the later strata do not destroy the earlier ones but overlay them. The final edifice—what Foucault, to distinguish it from the dungeon and the reformatory, calls the "carceral"—is rather like one of those cathedrals that have been built up around the frame of a temple, itself erected on the stones of a sacrifice site.

"Criminology," that hybrid of psychiatry, sociology, medicine, pedagogy, political science, and social work, comes to form the field of juridical discourse, introducing yet another "new economy" of the punitive power—one essentially technocratic, a business of experts. The conception of law as command or statute is replaced by the conception of it as a norm. Judges, "as if ashamed to pass sentence," are possessed of "a furious desire . . . to judge, assess, diagnose, recognize the normal and abnormal and claim the honour of curing, . . . [to] pass 'therapeutic' sentences and recommend 'rehabilitating' periods of imprisonment." And, as this "immense appetite for medicine" and for "the chatter of criminology" spreads to everyone from the parole officer to the turnkey, the scholarly and the punitive meanings of the word "discipline" become ominously fused:

> [We see] the growth of the disciplinary networks [of the human sciences], the multiplication of their exchanges with the penal apparatus, the ever more important powers that are given to them, the ever more massive transference to them of judicial functions; now, as medicine, psychology, education, public assistance, "social work" assume an ever greater share of the powers of supervision and assessment, the penal apparatus will be able, in turn, to become medicalized, psychologized, educationalized.

But that's just the half of it. Once created, the carceral mode of punishment becomes "the greatest support" in spreading this normalizing power to the entire social body, creating what Foucault, excitement mounting, calls "the carceral archipelago." Here Foucault borrows an image he has not really earned and makes an equation that will not in fact balance out. "The judges of normality are present everywhere," he cries. "We are in the society of the teacher-judge, the doctor-judge, the educator-judge, the 'social worker' judge; it is on them that the universal reign of the normative is based."

In this new sort of "panoptic society"—one with many highly trained observers in many well-equipped towers keeping watch on an enormous variety of supposed delinquents—"the formation of. . . insidious leniencies, unavowable petty cruelties, small acts of cunning, calculated methods, techniques, 'sciences'. . . permit the fabrication of the disciplinary individual." We are far away now from "the country of tortures, dotted with wheels, gibbets, gallows, and pillories." And far away, too, from the chaste disciplines of Walnut Street. We are—Foucault's tone tightens to bitter rage—in "the carceral city" where "the prisons resemble factories, schools, barracks, hospitals, which all resemble prisons."

III

Perhaps. But the steady rise in rhetorical shrillness as one approaches the present raises the question of how securely Foucault, and the reader, can sustain an "archaeological" attitude toward an *épistémè* not yet buried, especially when he is so passionately determined to bury it. Politically committed to a continuous guerrilla war against the various islands of the carceral archipelago ("We must engage it on all fronts—the university, the prison, the domain of psychiatry—one after another, since our forces are not strong enough for a simultaneous attack"),[2] Foucault does not deal with the jails—schools, factories, asylums, barracks, hospitals—among which he lives in the same way as he deals with those he must reconstruct. The jails he lives among he wants to level, one by one, which may or may not be a good idea. But the making of ruins is a rather different sort of enterprise, involving rather different sorts of emotions and producing rather different sorts of perceptions, from excavating them:

> We strike and knock against the most solid obstacles [the "all fronts" passage continues]; the system cracks at another point; we persist. It seems that we're winning, but then the institution is rebuilt; we must start again. It is a long struggle; it is repetitive and seemingly incoherent. But the system it opposes, as well as the power exercised through the system, supplies its unity.

It is worrisome that such writing today reads less like café talk than it did even six short years ago. And one begins to suspect that we are faced with a not altogether simple, descriptive tracing of the genealogy of the prison through the various kinds of discourse that have characterized it, from Robert Damiens to Son of Sam. After so much uncovering of archaeological sites and fixing of sequences, we seemed to be faced with a kind of Whig history in reverse—a history, in spite of itself, of The Rise of Unfreedom.

Obsessed with the constraining mechanisms of modern life, Foucault has lifted them into a horrific figure for the whole of it—the panoptic society, the carceral city—and then sought to see what lies beneath such a fine monstrosity. Seen that way, the past appears as an ascending spiral of discontinuous, "humanized," but nevertheless more and more malefic power concentrations—"micro-fascisms," as someone has called them—eventuating, at length, in the horror we know. This horror is the state to which the past—which, according to Foucault, is not supposed to be able to produce anything but itself, and that in a sort of random walk—can now be seen to have somehow led. Like some constitutional liberal spying out the first, faint signs of modern liberty in the German forest or the Roman Law, Foucault finds the first, not all that faint, signs of modern constraint in the spectacle tortures of the Old Regime and the didactic disciplines of the *âge classique*.

What this demonstrates, of course, is that he has not escaped so completely from the vulnerable *épistémè* of historicism as he might like or imagine. The emerging contemporary *épistémè* that he characterizes as the "new metaphysical ellipse"—"a theatre of mime with multiple, fugitive, instantaneous scenes in which blind gestures signal to each other"—is not yet wholly here.[3] But perhaps like half-revolutions, half-escapes are enough, and will suffice. It is just such a half-escape, whatever he intended, that makes *Discipline and Punish* so fascinating. For although it puts the past at a great distance, showing it as caught in its own discourse, it also appropriates the past for its own current arguments. As with so many prisoners, of so many kinds, it is not getting out but wanting out that generates in Foucault a strange and special vision.

On Genet

I

Max Weber once said of a minor German poet, irregular, drifting, and a friend of his, who had gotten himself involved in some of the scruffier aspects of popular revolt, that God had led him into politics in a fit of malice. Literary figures, especially romantical ones, who involve themselves directly in the dirty-hands world of collective violence (as opposed to the much larger number who harangue meetings, disgorge newspaper articles, get up petitions, or display themselves in demonstrations) do not as a rule come off very well. The sort of person given to staging extravagant parabolical dramas or writing out involute private imaginings is usually at a bit of a loss among artisans of more practical fantasies; or, often enough, their victim. The danger of taking oneself too seriously or one's comrades in arms not seriously enough, confusing words with bullets or aestheticizing blood, is all too real.

Jean Genet, for our times perhaps the very epitome of the unnormalizable artist, vagrant, thief, prisoner, prostitute, homosexual, symbological playwright, autistical novelist, and possessor of a prose style his translator calls anarchic, subversive, bizarre, and metaphysical, would seem an excellent candidate for such disasters when thrown among two of the angriest political movements of the Sixties and Seventies—the Palestinian resistance in Jordan and Lebanon and the Black Panther uprising in the United States. If he is in addition, as Genet was when he wrote this episodic account of what he calls his "five years. . . lived in a sort of an invisible sentry-box from which I could see and speak to everyone while I myself was a fragment broken off from the rest of the world," old, dying, and emotionally played out, both fictional truth and factual accuracy appear to be in serious risk of dissolving into blur and grandiloquence. *Ex ante*, the thing looks dubious.

Originally published as "Genet's Last Stand," *New York Review of Books* no. 19 (19 November 1992). The book under discussion therein is as follows: Jean Genet, *Prisoner of Love*, translated by Barbara Bray with an introduction by Edmund White.

Ex post, it is, disconcertingly, a surprising success: the record of a shape-shifter at loose among fabulists. Although the text, constructed a decade and a half after the experiences it reports, is frequently difficult to follow, both because of his easy way with chronology (Genet does not seem to think that one thing flows from another, cause after cause, but that everything jostles together in a space of memory) and because the narrative sometimes wanders into the merest of free association (especially toward the end when, abjuring pain-killing drugs so as to keep his mind unclouded, his powers may have at last been weakening), his tale has a logic and direction that grows out of a strange, almost hallucinatory, sort of hyper-precision:

> None of the fedayeen ever let go of his gun. If it wasn't slung over his shoulder he held it horizontal on his knees or vertical between them, not suspecting this attitude was in itself either an erotic or a mortal threat, or both. Never. . . did I see a fedayee without his gun, except when he was asleep. Whether he was cooking, shaking out his blankets or reading his letters, the weapon was almost more alive than the soldier himself. So much that I wonder whether, if the farmer's wife [the mother of a friend, later captured and tortured, whom he had just visited, and who recurs, with her son, through the book as a kind of mnemonic obsession] had seen boys without guns coming towards her house, she wouldn't have gone indoors, shocked at the sight of young men walking about naked. But she wasn't surprised: she lived surrounded by soldiers.

Genet first went to the East Bank of the Jordan River in 1970, where, after the 1967 war, the Palestinians had dug into what they optimistically called "bases" but which actually were ramshackle, open-air squatter camps in and around established Jordanian villages and towns. He had been invited there, for reasons neither of them seems to have understood very clearly, by Yasser Arafat, who, just another authority figure, flaunting his head scarf as Hitler flaunted his mustache and Churchill his cigar, did not much impress him. This was the period of the increasing military pressure on the camps by King Hussein and his Bedouin and Circassian army, who appear in this narrative as far more vividly hated enemies than the more schematic, less reachable Israelis—a mini-civil war which ended with the destruction of the camps, the killing of many of their inhabitants, and the flight of most of the rest, mainly into Lebanon, in the famous, or infamous, "Black September" of 1971. Genet hung on, wandering amid the ruins ("age and weakness had given me immunity") through the following year, until he, too, was finally forced out.

This small knot of nondescript desert settlements, west of Amman, north of the Dead Sea, south of Golan, perhaps sixty miles across, was Genet's sort of place—a place marginal to everything and everywhere, where borders were but faintly dotted lines, the most recent deposits of local violence, where no one was really in charge, at least until Hussein showed the iron fist, and whose inhabitants, to the degree that this gathering of fugitives could even be called that, were, like him, extravagant, dauntless, outmatched, and doomed:

> The dream, but not yet the declared aim, of the fedayeen was clear: to do away with the twenty-two Arab nations and leave everyone wreathed in smiles, childlike at first but soon foolish. But they were running out of ammunition and their main target, America, was endlessly resourceful. Thinking to walk tall, the Palestine revolution was sinking fast. Training people to sacrifice themselves results not in altruism but in a kind of fascination that makes them jump off a cliff not to help but merely to follow those who have already lept to their deaths. Especially when they foresee, not through thought but through fear, the annihilation to come.

Genet less describes the activities of the fedayeen—most of which, so far as the violence goes, take place offstage for him, in ambushes and skirmishes he is unable to witness (the "young lions," as he calls them, those men with the guns between their legs, simply go off somewhere to engage Hussein's Bedouins, more occasionally the Israelis, and some come back and some do not)—or the development of the political situation (which he regards as "a shifting dream floating over the Arab world") than he attempts to evoke the tone of everyday existence in such a place at such a time and, even more important to him, to explore his strange, seemingly unbreakable attraction to it—his imprisoning "love." It is all anecdotes, images, personalities, fragments of dialogue; scenes and ruminations.

Take, for example, the counterfeit card players. At Ajloun, the base, a stone's throw from the Jordan, at which he spent the longest time (eight months), he meets, in the night into day depths of the Fast month of Ramadan, a local doctor of severe opinions:

> "I leave the fighters completely free. . . "
> "I should hope so."
> "The only thing I've forbidden is cards."
> "But why cards?"
> "The Palestinian people wanted a revolution. When they find out the bases on the Jordan are gambling dens they'll know brothels will be next."

But the fedayeen play, nevertheless. Or anyway they seem to. After the doctor, surfeited with soup and Qur'an chants, and bested in an exchange with Genet concerning who is more like Nero, Hussein or Adolphe Thiers, the scourge of the Commune, has gone off to bed,

> Two men came in. They were fighters, still quite young but with downy moustaches on their upper lips to show how tough they were. They

weighed one another up, . . . each trying to intimidate the other. Then they sat down facing one another, lowering themselves casually but stiffly on to the benches and hitching up their trousers to preserve a non-existent crease. . . .

The newcomer sitting next to me took his hand out of the left-pocket of his leopard trousers, and, with a movement at once very human and yet seeming to belong to some rare ceremonial, produced a small pack of fifty cards which he got his partner to cut. Then he fanned the cards out in front of them. One of the two swept them up and arranged them in a pack again, examined it, shuffled the cards in the usual way and dealt them out between the two of them. Both looked serious, almost pale with suspicion. Their lips were tight, their jaws set. I can still hear the silence . . .

The game began. Gambling . . . filled both their faces with greed. They were equally matched. . . . Around the two heroes, everyone tried to catch a brief glimpse of their swiftly concealed hands. Against all the rules the onlooker behind each contestant made signals to the player opposite, who pretended to take no notice. . . . One of the players dropped a card on the floor and picked it up so nonchalantly it reminded me of a film in slow motion.

I thought people would think he'd been cheating, imitating an "accident" familiar to card-sharpers. What little Arabic I knew consisted mainly of threats and insults. But the words *charmouta* ["whore"] and *hattai* ["degenerate"] muttered between the players' clenched teeth and lips gleaming with saliva, were quickly bitten back.

The two players stood up and shook hands across the table, without a word, without a smile.

But for all the intensity, the game was, in fact, unreal, a mocking pantomime put on for Genet's benefit. He compares it to an ironic Japanese feast he once saw called Obon, where the living caricature the dead, who have come back for three days to sit invisibly upon cushions, through deliberately clumsy actions (the children practice limping for weeks ahead), so as to say, "We are alive and we laugh at [you] the dead. [You] can't take offence because [you're] only skeletons condemned to remain in a hole in the ground."

The game of cards, which only existed because of the shocking realistic gestures of the fedayeen—they'd played at playing, without any cards, without aces or knaves, clubs or spades, kings or queens—reminded me that all the Palestinians' activities were like the Obon feast, where the only thing that was absent, that could not appear, was what the ceremony, however lacking solemnity, was in aid of.

It was, this game that was as idle as a ritual as it was empty as a game, an expression of despair:

> The fedayeen knew. The show they'd put on for me demonstrated their disillusion, for to play only with gestures when your hands ought to be holding kings and queens and knaves, all the symbols of power, makes you feel a fraud, and brings you dangerously close to schizophrenia. Playing cards without cards every night is a kind of dry masturbation.

This is the way in which the whole of Genet's account moves. Sudden turns from one thing to another. (In addition to the unexpected Japanese feast, he drops into the discussion a one-armed French general who also banned card games in Damascus when the French were in charge there, chess as the image of the cold war, and the grim handshake with which Australian tennis matches end.) He makes clear his intense concern with his own role in matters that seem radically external to him, detached and accidental. ("What am I doing here? If chance exists then there's no God, and I owe my happiness on the banks of the Jordan to chance. But though I may be here through the famous throw of the dice, isn't every Palestinian here by chance too?") His obsessive precision—about how people sit down, how they handle cards, how they look on—makes everything seem abnormally real. And the whole is held together by a subtle but pervasive atmosphere of blocked eroticism:

> The Syrians often let out the same cry as the shamming Palestinians when a one of swords [i.e., spades] or any of the same suit comes up. All except the seven are of ill omen: the one means excess, the two softness, the three distance, the four absence or loneliness, the five defeat, the six effort, and the seven . . . means hope, and it's the one card in the pack that's greeted with kisses. The eight means complaint, the nine masturbation, and the ten desolation and tears. . . .

All this is more mood than politics, or if it is politics it is politics of the most interior sort. Genet hardly refers to the issues involved, and then in a perfunctory, formulaic manner from which the energy of his prose departs altogether. "These were the Palestinians' enemies, in order of importance: the Bedouin, the Circassians, King Hussein, the feudal Arabs, the Muslim religion, Israel, Europe, America, the Big Banks. Jordan won, and so victory went to all the rest, too, from the Bedouin to the Big Banks." The Jews are "the darkest of peoples . . . a people whose beginning claimed to be the Beginning, who claimed that they were and meant to remain, the Beginning." Hussein is "something Glubb Pasha left behind on the throne," an ersatz Sun King with a taste for white skin and Lamborghinis. Israel, "imposing its morals and myths on the whole world, saw itself as identical with Power. It was Power."

These are barely ideas, and Genet, who was impervious to doctrine, is not really interested in them. What he is interested in is "Ferraj, Mahjub, Mubarak, and Nabila," all of them since "physically disappeared," "all of them about whom I know nothing and never shall know anything, except that they existed when I saw them and as long as they saw me and talked to me." Now, they are "too far away, too far away or too dead. In any case gone."

As he himself frankly realizes, Genet is, for all his empathy for the Palestinians' predicament, not so much a partisan ("My heart was in it; my body was in it . . . but . . . never the whole of myself") as a connoisseur of pure rebellion, of people like Saint-Just, the Panthers, the Baader-Meinhof gang (with whom he also entertained for awhile a private romance), and the fedayeen, who are "brief flashes against a world wrapped in its own smartness, . . . tracer bullets, knowing their traces vanish in the twinkling of an eye." Whether he would have found the Palestinians attractive, would have fallen in love with them, if they had been at all successful, if they had held off Hussein or reentered the occupied territories, if, to revert to his earlier image, they had not followed one another off the cliff in despairing sacrifice, might well be doubted:

> The gestures were genuine but the cards were not. Not only were they not on the table, but they weren't anywhere; it wasn't a game of cards at all. The cards were neither present nor absent. For me they were like God: they didn't exist.
> . . . [The fedayeen's] land—Palestine—was not merely out of reach. Although they sought it as gamblers do cards and atheists God, it had never existed. . . . The fedayeen's goal had been transformed into something impossible for them to imagine. Everything they did was in danger of becoming useless because they'd substituted the rehearsal for the performance. The card-players, their hands full of ghosts, knew that however handsome and sure of themselves they were their actions perpetuated a game with neither beginning nor end. Absence was in their hands just as it was under their feet.

However that may be, when Genet returns to his knot of settlements fourteen years later (he is, by then, seventy-four), his book nearly done and the cancer in his throat getting ready to kill him, what he finds is only the dull, worn aftertaste of capitulation—"a change for the worse trying to pass itself off as a change for the better." He wanders about trying to find traces of old friends or stories about what happened to them, largely without success. Hardly anyone remembers him. The stories are various and contradictory. A friend he has been told was killed turns out to be living quietly in Germany; his mother, that farmer's wife who had lived so happily among soldiers, cheered her son into battle, and wielded on occasion a gun herself now is weary, mistrustful, guileful, and dried up. He tries to breathe some of the romance back into things; he even speaks of the Pietà. But it is impossible. He creeps away, "almost on tiptoe, like someone leaving a room in which even the bed is asleep."

II

Genet's stay with the Black Panthers in the spring of 1970 just before his move to the Middle East is little more than a footnote to the rest. There are only a dozen or so pages about it scattered through the book, awkwardly inserted and flatly written. The biting humor of the Palestine section settles into juvenile jokes about elections and erections, the plangent eroticism into blunt vulgarity about genital bulges. One gets the sense that in America he was, and saw himself to be, more a trophy or a trotted-out celebrity (he refers to himself as an aged "waif" and as "White," "childish") than, as he was in Jordan, a pilgrim questing for connection. He spent, in any case, only a few months with the Panthers, giving speeches on their behalf at Berkeley, Stony Brook, and the University of Connecticut (though he had been in this country earlier as a French version of a gonzo journalist to cover the 1968 Democratic convention in Chicago), as opposed to his years living in the midst of the Palestinians, and in fact his relation to the party, its leaders, and to its cause, seems to have been rather tentative, as much bemused as anything else. It took him, he says, a long time to realize that George Wallace (whom he imagines was a senator) was a racist.

But the important point for him is that the Panthers provide, as Paris in 1968 did before them (when, so the story has it, he responded to rightwing student chants of "*Genet pédéraste, Genet pédéraste*" by appearing lighted on a balcony with his arms upraised), and the Palestinians after them, another forbidden border to transgress. He was always seeking out such borders—legal, moral, political, racial, sexual, and, perhaps most of all, as in the disorderly stream of wide-awake dreams that make up this book, literary—and crossing them in so visible a way as to make it impossible for the world not to notice. However uncertainly he understood what the Panthers were all about ("they were haunted by fears and fantasies I'd never known except in ironical translation"), he had no trouble at all grasping the concept of "in-your-face":

> The Whites' recoil from the Panthers' weapons, their leather jackets, their revolutionary hair-dos, their words and even their gentle but menacing tone—that was just what the Panthers wanted. They deliberately set out to create a dramatic image. . . .

And they succeeded. The theatrical image was backed up by real deaths. The Panthers did some shooting themselves, and the mere sight of the Panthers' guns made the cops fire.

Genet's whole career was consumed in taunting power in this way, except that he never fired anything except images, words, and unconscionable behavior; the more unequal the combat, the more certain the failure, the more he seemed drawn to it. By the time he got to Jordan the game was about up for him. He lived another sixteen years, producing a preface to George Jackson's prison letters, an apology for the Baader-Meinhof gang even some his defenders found hard to take, an inflammatory description, with bloated bodies and crucifixions, of the scene at Shatila, the Palestinian camp in Lebanon, after the massacres there in 1982. But in Jordan, and in this book, completed, if indeed it was completed, only weeks before his death, something more than drama and provocation appears—a quiet, almost diffident attempt to define a moment, and himself in that moment, in such a way that neither will be dismissible from history as oddity and aberration. The man Cocteau, who is supposed to have discovered him in the first place, called "The Black Prince of French Literature" seems in the end to have settled for witnessing. "I feel, now, like a little black box projecting slides without captions."

Ethnography in China

Among the Na, a tribal people hidden away in the Yongning hills of Yunnan province in southern China and the subject of the French-trained Chinese anthropologist Cai Hua's provocative new monograph, there is no marriage, in fact or word. Mothers exist, as do children, but there are no dads. Sexual intercourse takes place between casual, opportunistic lovers, who develop no broader, more enduring relations to one another. The man "visits," usually furtively, the woman at her home in the middle of the night as impulse and opportunity appear, which they do with great regularity. Almost everyone of either sex has multiple partners, serially or simultaneously; simultaneously usually two or three, serially as many as a hundred or two. There are no nuclear families, no in-laws, no stepchildren. Brothers and sisters, usually several of each, reside together, along with perhaps a half-dozen of their nearer maternal relatives, from birth to death under one roof—making a living, keeping a household, and raising the sisters' children.

The incest taboo is of such intensity that not only may one not sleep with opposite sex members of one's own household, one cannot even allude to sexual matters in their presence. One may not curse where they can hear, or sit with them in the same row at the movies, lest an emotional scene appear on the screen. As paternity is socially unrecognized, and for the most part uncertain, fathers may happen, now and again, to sleep with daughters. A man is free to sleep with his mother's brother's daughter, who is not considered any kind of relative, not even a "cousin." There is no word for bastard, none for promiscuity, none for infidelity; none, for that matter, for incest, so unthinkable is it. Jealousy is infra dig:

> "You know, Luzo [who is nineteen] has not had a lot of [lovers], but he
> has made many visits [his friend said]. This is because he only goes to

Originally published as "The Visit," *New York Review of Books* 48, no. 16 (18 October 2001). The book under discussion therein is as follows: Cai Hua, *A Society without Fathers or Husbands: The Na of China,* translated from the French by Asti Hustvedt.

the homes of beauties. In particular, he goes to visit Seno, a pretty girl in our village. Do you want to go [visit her] at her house?" he asked me.
"No! If I go there, Luzo will be jealous," I answered.
"How could I be jealous!" [Luzo] responded. "You can ask whomever you want. You will see that . . . we don't know how to be jealous."
"He's right!" his friend interjected. And to explain himself he added: "Girls [are available] to everyone. Whoever wants to can visit them. There is nothing to be jealous about."

Obviously, this is an interesting place for an anthropologist—especially for an anthropologist brought up on that King Charles's head of his profession, "kinship theory."

I

There are two major variants of such theory, "descent theory" and "alliance theory," and the Na, Hua says, fit neither of them. In the first, associated with the name of the British anthropologist A.R. Radcliffe-Brown and his followers, the "nuclear," "basic," or "elementary" family—a man, his wife, and their children—"founded as it is on natural requirements," is universal, and "forms the hard core around which any social organization revolves." The relationship between parents and children, "filiation," is critical, and out of it are developed various "jural," that is, normative, rules of descent which group certain sets of relatives together against others: lineages, clans, kindreds, and the like. "Families can be compared to threads which it is the task of nature to warp in order that the social fabric can develop."

In the alliance model, deriving in the main from the French anthropologist, and Hua's mentor, Claude Lévi-Strauss, "the institutionalized exchange of women" between families "by the alliance of marriage [is taken] to be the central point of kinship." The universality of the incest taboo, "a natural phenomenon," necessitates marriage and the creation of the "transversal [that is, affinal or 'in-law'] networks of alliances [that] engender all social organization."

Since the Na have no matrimonial relationship they falsify both theories. They neither form elementary families out of which a filiative social fabric can be spun, nor, though they have a variety of the incest taboo (an odd variety, in that with its father-daughter twist it does not exclude all primary relatives), do they form twined and expandable affinal networks, or indeed any networks of "in-laws" at all. "From now on," Hua proclaims at the end of his book, "marriage can no longer be considered the only possible institutionalized mode of sexual behavior." The Na "visit" demonstrates that

Marriage, affinity, alliance of marriage, family, [usually considered] essential to anthropology, . . . seem absent from this culture. The Na case attests to the fact that marriage and the family (as well as the Oedipus complex) can no longer be considered universal, neither logically nor historically.

This is a little grand, for there are other "institutionalized modes of sexual behavior"—concubinage, prostitution, wife-borrowing—just about everywhere, and whether the Oedipus complex is universal or not, or even whether it exists at all, is not dependent upon marital arrangements. But clearly, "the visit" is an unusual, perhaps—though one never knows what is coming next out of Papua, the Amazon, or Central Asia—a unique institution sustaining a most unusual "kinship system," its existence often regarded as impossible. It is a system in which the facts of reproduction (though recognized—the Na know where babies come from) are incidental and all ties are (conceived to be) "blood ties"—the entire house can be called consanguineous.[1]

The Na "visit," for all its fluidity, opportunism, and apparent freedom from moral or religious anxiety, is as well outlined a social institution, as deeply embedded in a wider social structure, as marriage is elsewhere. (The Na are Tibetan-style Buddhists, nearly a third of the adult men being monks, whose sexual practices, a handful of Lhasa-bound celibates aside, are the same as those of laymen.) This is clear from the exact and explicit terminology that marks it out:

> Society calls a man and a woman who set up this kind of sexual relationship *nana sésé hing*, which means people in a relationship of furtive meetings; the man and the woman discreetly call each other *açia* ["discreetly" because of the "incest" taboo against public references to sexuality where opposite sex consanguines may hear them]. The term *açia* is made up of the diminutive prefix *a* and the root *çia*. The Na add *a* to names and proper nouns to indicate intimacy, affection, friendship, and respect; *çia*, when used as a noun, means lover. The same word is used for both sexes, and as a verb it means literally to lie down and figuratively to mate, to sleep and to tempt. *Açia* means lover.
>
> A Na saying depicts those who are *açia* very well: . . . It is not enough to say that we are *çia* for it to be so, sleeping together once makes (us) *çia*.

The enactment of such a relationship shows the same detailed cultural patterning: it is not a matter of brute and unfettered physical desire, but of a modeled, almost balletic self-control. The rendezvous takes place in the bedroom of the woman around midnight. (A bit earlier in the winter, Hua says, a bit later in the summer.) The man comes in near-perfect quietness, does what he does (Hua is wholly silent about what that might be and about how the cries of love are muffled), and leaves at cockcrow, creeping as stealthily back to his own house. As men and women enjoy "complete equality" and are "in daily contact, in town, in the workplace, and elsewhere," either can make the first advance and either may accept or refuse:

> A girl might say to a boy, "Come stay at my house tonight." The boy might then respond, "Your mother is not easygoing." And then the girl might say, "She won't scold you. Come secretly in the middle of the night." If the boy accepts, he says, "Okay." If the boy refuses, he says, "I don't want to come. I'm not going to come over to sleep." In this case, no matter what the girl says, nothing will change his mind.
>
> When the man takes the initiative . . . he often uses the expression "I'll come to your house tonight, okay?," to which the woman responds with a smile or by saying, "Okay." Some come straight out and ask "Do you want to be my *açia*?" If a woman refuses . . . , she can use a ready-made formula: "No, it is not possible. I already have one for tonight." In that case, the man will not insist.[2]

There are other, more oblique ways of making one's wishes known. One can snatch away some personal object—a scarf, a pack of cigarettes—from the desired partner. If he or she does not protest, the tryst is on. One can shout from a distance, "Hey, hey, do you want to trade something?" If you get a "hey, hey" back, you exchange belts and fix an appointment. These days, Chinese movies—shown virtually every night, though they are imperfectly understood by the Tibeto-Burmese-speaking Na—are a particularly favored setting for putting things in motion:

> The young men and women purchase tickets and wait in front of the theater, getting to know each other. . . . One man can offer several women a ticket, just as one woman can offer a ticket to more than one man. Once a ticket is handed over, the man and woman move away from each other and only get back together inside the theater. During the film, the viewers talk loudly, often drowning out the sound from the speakers. If they have had a good time during the movie and reached an agreement, they leave discreetly to spend an amorous night together.

The "amorous night" itself may be a one-time thing. Or it may be repeated at shorter or longer intervals over the course of months or years. It may be begun, broken off for awhile, then begun again. It may be stopped altogether at any time by either party, usually without prior notice or much in the way of explanation. It does not, in short, involve any sort of exclusive and permanent "horse and carriage" commitment. But it, too, is, for all its fluidity and seeming negligence, carefully patterned—framed and hemmed in by an elaborate collection of cultural routines, a love-nest ethic.

When the *amant* arrives at the *amante*'s house, usually after having climbed over a fence or two and thrown a bone to the guard dog, he will give some sort of signal of his presence—toss pebbles on the roof, crouch at the woman's bedroom window (Hua says that every man in a village complex—four or five hundred people—knows the location of every woman's bedroom), or, if he is confident of being received or has been there often, simply knock on the front door. "In a household where there are women of the age to receive visitors [there may be several such on one night, and even a woman may have, in turn, more than one visitor], every evening after nightfall, the men of the house will not open the front door."

Usually, the woman who is waiting will herself open the door and the two will creep wordlessly off to her bedroom. If the wrong woman opens the door— a sister or a cousin, or perhaps even one of those "not easygoing" mothers— this causes little embarrassment: the man simply proceeds to the right woman's bedroom. During the encounter, the lovers must whisper "so that nothing will reach the ears of the woman's relatives, above all the men (especially uncles and great-uncles)."

No one can force anyone else in these matters. The woman can always, and at any time, refuse the man's entreaties and send him packing. A woman may never, in any case, visit a man; so if she is scorned she is just out of luck. A legend accounts for this virtually unique exception to rigorous symmetry of the system:

> When humanity originated, no one knew how to regulate visits. Aba-odgu, the god in charge of setting all the rules, proposed the following test: he ordered that a man be shut up in a house and that a woman be sent to join him. To reach the man, the woman had to pass through nine doors. At dawn, she had reached the seventh door. Then Abaodgu tested the man, who succeeded in passing through three doors. . . . Abaodgu [concluded] that women were too passionate [to do] the visiting. . . . The men [would have to] visit the women.

Hua goes on to trace out, methodically and in remorseless detail, the variations, the social ramifications, and the ethnographical specifics of all this, worried, not without reason, that if he does not make his arguments over and over again and retail every last fact he has gathered in four periods of fieldwork (1985, 1986, 1988-1989, 1992) his account will not be believed.

He describes two other, special and infrequent "modalities" of sexual encounter—"the conspicuous visit" and "cohabitation." In the conspicuous visit, which always follows upon a series of furtive visits, the effort to conceal the relationship is abandoned ("vomited up," as the idiom has it), mainly because the principals have grown older, perhaps tired of the pretense and folderol, and everyone knows about them anyway.

In cohabitation, an even rarer variant, a household that is short of women by means of which to produce children or of men to labor for it in its fields will adopt a man or woman from a household with a surplus to maintain its reproductive or economic viability, the adopted one becoming a sort of permanent conspicuous visitor (more or less: these arrangements often break up too). Among chiefly families, called *zhifu*, a Chinese word for "regional governor," successive relationships are established over several generations, leading to a peculiar household alternation of chiefship and a greater restriction on who may mate with whom.

Hua describes, analyzes, and redescribes larger matrilineal groupings, which are mere notational devices to keep descent straight, as well as the internal structure of the household—a matter of careful seating arrangements, ritual obligations, and double, male-female headship. He gives accounts of the physical construction of the house, of various kin-related feasts and gift exchanges, and of beliefs about procreation (the man "waters" the woman as rain waters the grass, an act of "charity" to the woman's household which needs children to perpetuate itself).

But in the end, "The visit . . . is essential and basic; it is the preeminent modality of sexual life in this society. . . . Everyone is forced to follow it, its practice being determined not just by individual will but . . . [by] societal coercion."

II

As one prepares to book passage for Yunnan, however, a troubling thought arises: Can all this really be true? No-fault sexuality? Multiple partners? No jealousy, no recriminations, no in-laws? Gender equality? A life full of assignations? It sounds like a hippie dream or a Falwell nightmare. We have learned recently, if we did not know already, to be wary of anthropological stories about obscure and distant people whose thoughts and behaviors are not just different than our own, but are some sort of neatly inversive, fun-mirror mockery of them: clockwork Hawaiian ritualists, murderous Amazonian hunters, immoralist Iks, "never-in-anger" Eskimos, selfless Hopi, complaisant Samoan maidens. Such stories may or may not be true, and argument, in most cases, continues. But if even the most famous bearer of tales out of China, Marco Polo (he has a passage in his *Travels* of 1298 vaguely alluding to Na promiscuity), is now accused of having never set foot in the place, can this bit of the world turned upside-down exotica escape suspicion?

So far as the harder facts of the matter are concerned, there would seem to be little room for doubt. Hua, now professor of social anthropology at the University of Beijing, was trained at the Laboratory of Social Anthropology at the Collège de France, and his book comes recommended by Lévi-Strauss, the founder of the Laboratory ("Dr. Cai Hua has done Western Anthropology a great service. . . . The Na now have their place in the anthropological literature") as well as by the former professor of anthropology at Oxford, Rodney Needham ("The ethnography is thorough and patently reliable, replete with valuable findings . . .").

Hua spent about two years among the Na, and, though himself a Han Chinese, he appears to have gained a good command of the Na language. He conducted systematic interviews in five villages (sixty-five households, 474 people— the total Na population is about thirty thousand), patiently constructing genealogies and tabulating *açia* relationships. (The female champion claimed 150 lovers, the male, 200—perhaps Abaodgu was, after all, mistaken.) He read through the extensive Chinese annals on the group, running back through the Qing (1644–1911) and Ming (1368–1644) dynasties to the, in this part of China, barely visible Yuan (1279–1368), as well as through mountains of more recent government reports and surveys. He traveled through the region, reviewed the (somewhat confused) anthropological literature on matrilineal systems, and looked at least briefly into all sorts of collateral matters: land tenure, migration, trade, ethnic connections, folk healing, chiefship, and the local penetration of national politics. There can be little doubt that he walked the walk.

And yet, something large, hard to define, and overwhelmingly important is missing from Na's brisk, professional, conceptually self-sealing account: there is an aching hole at its very center, an oppressive absence. A few hurried and abbreviated passing remarks aside, an anecdote here, an incident there, we hear little of the tone and temper of Na life, of the color of their disposition, the curve of their experience. There is nothing, or almost nothing, of individual feelings and personal judgments, of hopes, fears, dissents, and resistances, of fantasy, remorse, pride, humor, loss, or disappointment. The question that in the end we most want answered and the one most insistently raised by the very circumstantiality of Hua's ethnography—"What is it like to be a Na?"— goes largely unattended. We are left with a compact, well-arranged world of rules, institutions, customs, and practices: a "kinship system."

Can this be enough? "Na-ness" as a form-of-life, a way-of-being-in-the-world, is, whatever it is, a much wider, more ragged, unsettled, less articulated, and less articulable thing. It is a mood and an atmosphere, a suffusing gloss on things, and it is hard to describe or systematize, impossible to contain in summary categories. How are children, raised by those life-partner sister-brother pairs in those tight little consanguineous households thick with erotic pretense and incest worry, brought around to seeing themselves as tireless sexual conspirators—waiting bedside if they are women, stumbling through the dark if they are men? What does that do to their overall sense of agency? of identity? of authority? of pleasure? of trust? What does "gender equality" mean, what can it mean, in such a context?

What, really, does *çia*, which Hua so nonchalantly renders as "love" while never giving us even reported or secondhand descriptions of what goes on erotically, in beds or out of them, mean? No performance failure? no carnal inventiveness? no *folie*? no frigidity? no deviance? And what is all that business about "vomiting up" secret affairs and about mothers not being "easygoing"? The emotional and moral topography of Na life must be, surely, at least as unusual as their mating conventions and their adoptive practices. But of it we are afforded only the most general of senses; hints and glimpses, nervously brushed by en route to "findings."

Some of this inability—or unwillingness, it is hard to be certain which—to face up to the less edged and outlined dimensions of Na life may be due to what we have come these days to call Hua's "subject position." As a Han Chinese, brought up in what must be one of the most family-minded, most explicitly moralized, least unbuttoned societies in the world, studying as non-Han a society as it seems possible to imagine (and one located in "China" to boot) by using the concerns and preconceptions of Western-phrased "science," Hua has his work cut out for him. In itself, this predicament is common to all field anthropologists, even ones working in less dramatic circumstances, and there is no genuine escape from it. The problem is that Hua seems unaware that the predicament exists—that the passing of "Na institutions" through Chinese perceptions on the way to "doing the West a service" by placing them "in the anthropological literature" raises questions not just about the institutions, but about the perceptions and the literature as well.

In particular, the very idea of a "kinship system," a culture-bound notion if there ever was one, may be a large part of the problem. It may flatten our perceptions of a people such as the Na, whose world is centered more around the figuration of sexuality and the symmetries of gender than around the ordering of genealogical connection or the stabilization of descent, and turn us, as it does Hua, toward such worn and academical questions as the naturalness of the nuclear family, the function of residence rules, or the proper definition of marriage.

The "symbolic anthropologist" the late David Schneider (who, after a lifetime working on the subject, came to believe that his profession's obsession with "kinship," "the idiom of kinship," and "the kin-based society" was some sort of primal mistake brought on by biologism, a tin ear, and a fear of difference) said that "the first task of anthropology, *prerequisite to all others*, is to understand and formulate the symbols and meanings and their configurations that a particular culture consists of."[3] If he was right, then it may be that Hua's exact and careful account of the Na will be remembered less for the institutional oddities it assembles and celebrates than for the half-glimpsed cosmos it lets escape.

This is all the more saddening because, after centuries of resistance to efforts to bring it into line with what is around it—that is, Han propriety—that cosmos is now apparently at last dissolving. The pressures on the Na to shape up and mate morally like normal human beings have been persistent and unremitting. As early as 1656, the Manchurian Qing, troubled by succession problems among "barbarian" tribes, decreed that the chiefs of such tribes, including the Na, must marry in the standard way and produce standard sons, grandsons, and cousins to follow them legitimately into office.

The extent to which this rule was enforced varied over time with the strengths and interests of the various dynasties. But the intrusion of Han practices—virilocality (by which married couples live near the husband's parents), patrifiliation (making kinship through fathers central), polygynous marriage (i.e., involving several wives), written genealogies, and "ancestor worship" (the Na cast the ashes of their dead unceremoniously across the hillsides)—into the higher reaches of Na society provided an alternative cultural model, a model that the Na, for the most part, contrived to keep at bay. Members of chiefly families, and some of the wealthy commoners and resident immigrants, began to marry to preserve their estates and to secure a place in the larger Chinese society. But most of the population proceeded as before, despite being continuously reviled as "primitive," "depraved," "backward," "licentious," "unclean," and ridden with sexual disease. (The last was, and is, more or less true. "More than 50 percent of Na adults have syphilis . . . a significant percentage of the women are sterile . . . people are deformed. . . . The . . . population is stagnating.")

This cultural guerrilla war, with edicts from the center and evasions from the periphery, continued fitfully for nearly three hundred years, until the arrival of the Communists in the 1950s rendered matters more immediate.[4] The Party considered the tradition of the visit "a 'backward and primitive custom' . . . contraven[ing] the matrimonial legislation of the People's Republic of China . . . [and disrupting] pro-ductiveness at work because the men think of nothing but running off to visit someone." The Party's first move against the tradition was a regulation designed to encourage nuclear family formation by distributing land to men who would set up and maintain such a family. When this failed to have any effect at all ("the government could not understand how it was possible that Na men did not want to have their own land"), it moved on, during the Great Leap Forward, to a full press effort to "encourage monogamy" through a licensing system, an effort "guided" by the recommendation of two groups of ethnologists, who insisted that, "with planning," Na men and women could be led toward setting up families as economic units and raising their children together. Though this was a bit more successful—in Hua's "sample" seven couples officially married—it too soon ran out of steam in the face of Na indifference to the sanctions involved.

The small carrot and the little stick having failed to produce results, the Party proceeded in the period of the Cultural Revolution (1966–1969) to get real about the problem. Dedicated to the national project of "sweeping out the four ancients" (customs, habits, morality, culture), the People's Commune of Yongning pronounced it "shameful not to know who one's genitor is" and imposed marriage by simple decree on any villager involved in a conspicuous visit relationship. But this too failed. As soon as the cadres departed, the couples broke up.

Finally, in 1974, the provincial governor of Yunnan, declaring that "the reformation of this ancient matrimonial system comes under the framework of the class struggle in the ideological domain and therefore constitutes a revolution in the domain of the superstructure" (one can almost hear the collective Na, "*Huh?*"), made it the law that: (1) everyone under fifty in a relationship "that has lasted for a long time" must officially marry forthwith at commune headquarters; (2) every woman who has children must publically state who their genitor is, cart him off to headquarters, and marry him; (3) those who divorce without official sanction will have their annual grain ration suspended; (4) any child born out of wedlock will also not get a ration and must be supported by his genitor until age eighteen; and, (5) visiting, furtive or conspicuous, was forbidden.

This, supported by nightly meetings of the local military brigade and some collusive informing, seemed finally to work—after a fashion, and for a while:

> [The] District government sent a Jeep filled with marriage licenses to the People's Commune of Yongning. Ten and twenty at a time, couples were rounded up in the villages . . . and a leader would take their fingerprints on the marriage form and hand them each a marriage license. . . . [When] the day [for the ceremony] came, horse-drawn carriages were sent into the villages to provide transportation for the "newlyweds" to [Party] headquarters . . . They each received a cup of tea, a cigarette, and several pieces of candy, and then everybody participated in a traditional dance. The government called this "the new way of getting married."

It was new enough, but for the Na it was ruinous. "No other ethnic group in China underwent as deep a disruption as the Na did during the Cultural

Revolution," Hua writes in a rare show of feeling. "To understand the trouble this reform caused in Na society, it is enough to imagine a reform in our society, but with the reverse logic":

> During that period [one of Hua's informants said], the tension was so high that our thoughts never strayed from this subject. No one dared to make a furtive visit. Before, we were like roosters. We took any woman we could catch. We went to a woman's house at least once a night. But, with that campaign, we got scared. We did not want to get married and move into someone else's house, and as a result, we no longer dared to visit anyone. Because of this, we took a rest for a few years.

After the accession of Deng Xiao-ping in 1981, the more draconian of these measures—the denial of rations, the exposure of genitors—were softened or suspended, and emphasis shifted toward "educational," that is, assimilationist, approaches. In particular, the expansion of the state school system, where "all the textbooks are impregnated with Han ideas and values," is leading to rapid and thorough Sinicization of the Na. Today—or, anyway, in 1992—the school, assisted by movies and other "modern" imports, is accomplishing what political pressure could not: the withering away of "Na-ism":

> When students graduate from middle school, they must complete a form that includes a column requesting information on their civil status. Unable to fill in the blank asking for the name of their father, they suddenly become aware they do not have a father, while their classmates from other ethnic backgrounds do. Some of the Na students, usually the most brilliant ones, find a quiet spot where they can cry in private. . . . The message [of the school] is clear. . . . There is only one culture that is legitimate, and that is Han culture.

In China, as elsewhere, it is not licentiousness that powers most fear. Nor even immorality. It is difference.

PART II

Islams and the Fluidity of Nations

In Search of North Africa

Physicists, novelists, logicians, and art historians have recognized for some time that what we call our knowledge of reality consists of images of it that we ourselves have fashioned. In the social sciences this is just now coming to be understood, and then only imperfectly. The contribution of the investigator not only to the description and analysis of his object of study but to its very creation still tends to be obscured by the sort of mentality which regards the Human Relations Area Files, the Gallup Poll, and the US Census as repositories of recorded truths waiting merely to be discovered. In the arts, the unimplicated observer has been reduced to a minor convention; in the sciences to an unreachable limiting case. But in much of sociology, anthropology, and political science he lives on, masquerading as a real person performing a possible act.

Part of the reason for this failure, on the part of investigators otherwise only too self-conscious, to reflect on the way in which they first construct the objects they then inspect is that the issue has generally been confused with the not unimportant but rather less profound one of bias. Concealing private prejudices in public language is certainly an affliction of social scientific research; for some people, that, in fact, is its vocation.

But beyond the tired debates about "value neutrality" and the pious unmaskings of other people's *parti pris* is the more disturbing question which the unreliable narrator raised for fiction, the complementarity principle for physics, and *Rashomon* for common sense: if what we see is to a considerable degree a reflex of the devices we use to render it visible, how do we choose among

Originally published in the *New York Review of Books* 16, no. 7 (22 April 1971). Books under discussion therein are as follows: Ernest Gellner, *Saints of the Atlas*; William B. Quandt, *Revolution and Political Leadership: Algeria 1954–1968*; Paul Henissart, *Wolves in the City: The Death of French Algeria*; and Jean Duvignaud, *Change at Shebika: Report from a North African Village*. Films under discussion are as follows: *The Battle of Algiers*, directed by Gillo Pontecorvo, and *Ramparts of Clay*, written by Jean Duvignaud and directed by Jean-Louis Bertuccelli.

devices? Thirteen ways of looking at a blackbird are twelve too many for some-one who still believes that facts are born not made, and that differences of perception reduce to differences of opinion.

That they do not so reduce is apparent from a recent series of rather desper-ate attempts to get a sociological hold on the contemporary Maghreb—i.e., western North Africa—a part of the world which, resembling everything but itself (when Tocqueville first saw Algiers it reminded him of Cincinnati), has an unusual capacity for inviting the application of standard notions about how societies work, and then defeating them.

Academic monographs, social realism documentaries, and belletristic es-says compete to develop a representational form in which Maghrebi society can be caught and communicated. The first result of the dawning realization that though society doubtless exists independently of the activity of sociolo-gists, sociology does not, is a proliferation of genres. The second, still so faint as to be scarcely visible, is the development of the sort of radically experimen-tal attitude toward modes of representation that set in so much earlier else-where in modern culture.

As would be expected, the academic studies—*Saints of the Atlas* and *Revolu-tion and Political Leadership*—are the least affected, in both senses of that term, in this way. Gellner and Quandt are old believers. For them, there is still an object "out there," like Everest, on the one hand, and on the other, a set of analytic abstractions, developed by scientists, designed to describe it. Research consists of the empirical investigation of the adequacy of the abstractions to the constitution of the object. And scientific works are systematic presenta-tions of the results of research.

The document makers, whether in films, such as *The Battle of Algiers*, or magazine prose, as in the book *Wolves in the City*, are, if anything, even more bound to the notion that social reality is presented to them directly and that the main thing is to look at it with sufficient care and the appropriate attitude. But they are at least aware that some artfulness—the simulation of a Forties newsreel for Pontecorvo, Newsweek-Marches-On dramatization for Henis-sart—is necessary to convey the look of it to others.

Only Duvignaud (and, apparently, his cinematic translator, Bertuccelli) knows that the artfulness comes in very much earlier and very much more profoundly. His portraits of North African village life, both in his book and in the quite different, even contrasting, ways of *Ramparts of Clay*, the film made from it, are at base fictions, stories he has told himself and now recounts to others. There is not much left in Duvignaud's "inventions based on life" of the im-maculate perception view of scientific understanding, and nothing at all of the relaxing notion that the world divides into facts.

North Africa doesn't even divide into institutions. The reason Maghrebi society is so hard to get into focus and keep there is that it is a vast collection of coteries. It is not blocked out into large, well-organized, permanent groupings—parties, classes, tribes, races—engaged in a long-term struggle for ascendancy. It is not dominated by tightly knit bureaucracies concentrating and managing social power; not driven by grand ideological movements seeking to transform the rules of the game; not immobilized by a hardened cake of custom locking men into fixed systems of rights and duties.

These features, which loom so large elsewhere in the Third World, are, of course, present on the surface of life. But it is only surface. Anyone who takes them for more (as do most foreign observers, but hardly any domestic ones) finds the society constantly coming apart in his hands. Structure after structure—family, village, clan, class, sect, army, party, elite, state—turns out, when more narrowly looked at, to be an *ad hoc* constellation of miniature systems of power, a cloud of unstable micro-politics, which compete, ally, gather strength, and, very soon overextended, fragment again.

The social order is a field of small, pragmatical cliques gathering around one or another dominant figure as he comes, more or less transiently, into view and dispersing again as, largely traceless, he disappears. The cliques are somewhat more stable in the Moroccan High Atlas or the Tunisian steppe than they are in Algiers, but the difference is only relative. The social partitions of North Africa are everywhere movable and incessantly moved.

Gellner's reaction to the difficulties such constant rearrangement of loyalties poses for social description is to perceive a fixed and well-formed ground plan half-hidden beneath it. And as his object of study is a Berber tribe (the Ahansal), his training is in British social anthropology, and his conception of social order is organismic, the plan he perceives is genealogical.

According to Gellner, for all the maneuver and conspiracy, blood is still thicker than water. Whatever the surface irregularity of social life, it is played out within a grid of kinship relations which both contains it and gives it meaning. The famous Semitic proverb, "Me against my brother, my brother and I against my cousin, my cousin and I against the stranger," crystallized into a nested set of lineages and clans, is the basic organizing principle of Ahansal society:

> [O]ne might ask whether . . . in fact the society is not much more fluid than the neat tree-like patterns of group genealogy and alignment would suggest. Such a conclusion would be quite mistaken. . . . [Genealogical] organization displays a set of alignments, ratified not merely by custom, sentiment and ritual, but more weightily by shared interests which provide the baseline for alliances and enmities, for aid and hostility, when

conflict arises. Calculation, feeling, new interests, diplomatic ingenuity may at times cause the final alignments to depart at some points: but the initial and fairly strong presumption is that allegiances of tribe and clan will be honored, and that other inducements must have been operative if they were not so honored.

The trouble is that such "inducements" seem almost always to be "operative." "Final alignments" seem to depart not just at some points but at most. One could get about as far, possibly even further, with understanding North African society, Gellner's somewhat special sample of it included, with the principle, "My cousin and I against my brother, the stranger and I against the whole lot of my horse-thieving relatives."

Kinship alliances do play a role in North African social organization, especially in rural settings, but there is nothing particularly privileged about them. To raise them to the "constitutional" level of fundamental laws occasionally transgressed is to reduce the actual flow of North African social life to a collection of special cases arbitrarily explained. This is what happens to Gellner, as the surface of his initially so finely modeled book breaks up into a catalog of fragmentary observations. As he proceeds, the "neat tree-like patterns" become harder and harder to perceive, until at the end they seem overwhelmed altogether by "calculation, feeling . . . interests . . . ingenuity," and matters trail off into a series of one-thing-after-another descriptions of particular facts about particular settlements, groups, and even individuals—micropolitical situations.

The book as a whole gives a picture of an overplanned enterprise getting instructively out of hand. And although, from one point of view, this is testimony to the fact that Gellner is acute enough to rise above his principles, from another, it suggests that the best way to solve the intricacies of North African society is not to descend upon it with a finished theory looking for an instance.

Yet, as Quandt's book on the Algerian revolution strives to show, scientific opportunism doesn't work very well either. Rather than proceeding with some organized set of prior principles to see how they fare in the world of facts, Quandt describes, in more or less everyday, "common sense" language, the social process he is investigating—the evolution of the Algerian political elite from the outbreak of the revolution in 1954 to the consolidation of the Boumedienne regime in 1968—and then puts together *ad hoc* categorial schemes and generalized hypotheses to order and explain it.

This makes for more flexibility than Gellner's approach has; one feels less caught in a conceptual cage. But it also makes for more eclecticism. Although the schemes are inventive and the hypotheses more or less unexceptionable, they don't do much more than restate the fact that rivalry is as pervasive among the Algerian elite as among a Berber tribe—a restatement made in phrases fashionable enough in Cambridge and Santa Monica to permit Harold Lasswell and Daniel Lerner to pronounce them, in their Foreword to the book, "the nascent language of the policy sciences."

The language, alas, remains nascent, not to say embryonic: it is all banalities and promises. Quandt explains the fragmentation of the Algerian elite by the fact that its members entered it at different points in the development of nationalism and thus have different conceptions—"liberal," "radical," "revolutionary," "technocratic"—of the nature of politics. He explains political instability by the fact that men seeking power naturally strive to attract as wide a variety of supporters as possible, while men arrived in power, when payoffs have to be made, seek, equally naturally, to narrow their base to a "minimum winning coalition," thus creating disappointments, resentments, and lasting enmities as superfluous backers are cast off. And he explains why government tends to be ineffective by the fact that the Algerians generally are marked by a high level of distrust, an exaggerated sense of honor, and a chronic resentment of authority.

There is probably some truth in all of this, even if only of the kind we get in statements like "Opium puts you to sleep because it has dormitive powers." And, like Gellner, Quandt assembles a good deal of useful information. But one would expect, somehow, the *scienza nuova* to come to something more, and to a firmer conclusion than,

> . . . Algerian leaders may eventually either create an authoritarian regime, unresponsive to the people, or a relatively open political process which permits considerable mass participation. One result of extreme elite instability has been that few irreversible choices have been made as to the nature of the political system, and from this situation stem both the liabilities and promises of Algerian political development.

In short: "Where there's life, there's hope."

In any case, where the monographs draw blueprints of North African society in order to represent the form they profess to find within its motion, the documentary realists construct strong narrative lines, rigorous dramatic progressions—well-told tales—toward the same end. Both the film *The Battle of Algiers* and the book *Wolves in the City* are, in form at least, social thrillers, with historical personages as protagonists, historical events as scenes, and historical outcomes as morals. They gain their aura of factual immediacy and natural revelation—the sense that truth is being delivered neat—by depicting life as better plotted than it really is: its meaning is written, self-declaiming, directly on its face.

This is not in itself an argument against them, any more than schematicism is, as such, an argument against Gellner or Quandt. Pontecorvo's film projects a powerful, and so far as one can see not inaccurate, view of what the beginning of the end of French Algeria was like, and Henissart's book, a certain weakness for melodrama aside, a vivid view of what the end of the end of it was like. The story is savage in both cases, but heroic and romantic in the first; mean and romantic in the second.

The limitations of such storytelling are clear: anything the surface flow of social life—the actual events of 1956-57 and 1960-62—can't somehow be made to say can't be said. Once you've projected the story line—the ironic confrontation of the French General Massu's *résistance d'hier* and the Algerian Ben M'Hidi's *de demain*; the mindless violence in frantic search of direction which hummed about the aloof General Salan, a man who seems as mysterious as a Buddha—you are stuck with it, and the chance of the medium not so much becoming the message as impoverishing it grows very real.

In *The Battle of Algiers*, this leads to a view of what held the casbah insurrection together that is excessively Leninist, emphasizing the role of the revolutionary elite. There is a failure to penetrate the cacophony of diverse personal alliances and personal rivalries, to say nothing of personal motives, that was the FLN then. Nor does the film even recognize that there was such a cacophony rather than the neat pyramid of guerrilla organizations which the figure representing Massu draws, like some war college instructor, on the blackboard, and which the film, intent on keeping the drama defined, accepts for fact.

In *Wolves in the City*, where attention to the native population is absent altogether (apparently because Henissart knows nothing about it, but perhaps also because to include it would destroy the narrative line), it leads the story to a view of the OAS as a gang of desperadoes. The way in which the OAS grew out of and was integrated into the pattern of European life in colonial Algeria is almost completely obscured, sacrificed to the detail of surface realism. Though Pontecorvo's film is a far finer achievement, a masterpiece of sustained tone, both works share a similar defect: intensely concerned to be interesting to Westerners, they make what they describe seem too familiar. Lacking the courage to be dull, they can go only so far in presenting to us a social reality not our own.

Not that dullness itself, as opposed to the willingness to risk it, is of any use. What makes Jean Duvignaud's work so much stronger than the monographs and documentaries is his awareness that the passage from the experiences the outside observer has when confronted by North Africa to those the North African has while living there is a complex and treacherous one, and that unusual means are necessary to negotiate it. This obsession with the difficulty of merely seeing what is before one's eyes (and having seen it, communicating it) does render both his book *Change at Shebika* and the film *Ramparts of Clay*, which is based on it, somewhat trying to the patience. The book is a field diary including sociological homily turned worriedly in upon itself; the film a *tableau vivant*, a movie which barely moves at all. Neither logical elegance nor narrative force is Duvignaud's talent, nor for that matter is erudition or descriptive precision. But a sense for the elusiveness of the ordinary, in sociologists a rarer talent, is.

Change at Shebika is the record of an out-of-doors teaching project of the sort so many American students are just now urging upon their schools. Duvignaud, then (1960–65) Professor of Sociology in Tunis, selected a number of university students—fifteen over the five-year period—to take with him, in small groups, a few days or weeks at a time, to what, even for North Africa, is a rather beaten-down, end-of-the-world village.

The students were all New Tunisians—highly Westernized, highly ideological, highly urban. Only one had ever been south at all, and she as a tourist; and though ten had peasant grandparents, only three still had rural ties of any significance. The professor, a man in his early forties, was a Parisian intellectual struggling to reconcile ideas from Lévi-Strauss, Sartre, and Jacques Berque. Apparently without more than a superficial knowledge of Islam, Arabic culture, or North African history (it is not entirely clear from the text, but he seems not even to speak Arabic), he was animated by an intense desire to educate the Tunisian elite to the deficiencies of their own view of their own country. And, finally, the objects of all this hope and attention were a small band of impoverished share-croppers, plus their wives and children—about 250 people in all—fumbling with the shards of a dismembered tradition in a marginal economy deteriorated and getting worse.

The object of Duvignaud's book is thus not social description as such. He makes a claim, in a methodological appendix, to have produced a "total Utopian reconstruction" of Shebikan village life, invoking, among others, Flaubert, Joyce, Hermann Broch, and Truman Capote as models. ("If Balzac and Dickens were alive today, they would be sociologists.") But, in fact, his portrait of that life is anecdotal, unsystematic, and more than occasionally stereotyped.

Nor is its object directed social change. Duvignaud wants to understand how change occurs in a place like Shebika, but, aside from inflicting himself and his students upon them, he did not attempt to intervene in the villagers' lives. He is not concerned with drawing up plans or instituting programs, but with causing mentalities to alter—those of his students, those of the Shebikans, and, though (curiously) he doesn't explicitly say so, his own.

In this, he regards his micro-experiment as strikingly successful:

The five years that we spent in Shebika were, both for the villagers and for the researchers from the city, a truly phenomenological experience of change. That is, the fundamental mental categories by which each side had conceived of change, if they had conceived of it at all, underwent a modification directly as a result of the study. A project on change became . . . an example of change itself. For the phenomenologist, who argues that the conceptual reality that actors present is perhaps the most fundamental form of social life, this is a dramatic experience. A village which had lost . . . its collective identity, gradually became the subject of change and of a history, a history that lay mostly in the future.

One student, angered by the "irrationality" of local customs, finds himself drawn, simply because the villagers are so evasive about it, into an investigation of the local saint shrine, and though he doesn't find out very much about it, he does find out a great deal about why the villagers are so determined that he should not. Another, a girl, breaks under the strain of resisting her father's wish that she advance her education in Paris, as befits the daughter of a nationalist hero and high civil servant, instead of scrambling about in "this scorpion's nest." A third is paralyzed by the gap between what the villagers expect him to do for them and what he can do for them, which is essentially nothing.

On the village side, the disturbance is even more profound. A young girl, an orphan servant, dazzled by the example of the girls from Tunis, teaches herself to read and dreams of going away with the researchers; but, when she expresses the dream, the other women pronounce her deranged and crush her spirit. A picture essay on the village in a mass magazine, prepared by the team, finds its way back, giving the villagers their first look at themselves from outside and enlarging, rather beyond reality, their sense of their importance in the world. The men of the village, employed by the government to cut stone for what they think is the repair of their houses, stage a protest when they discover that they are cutting it for the construction of a building to lodge civil servants and gendarmes coming through on inspection tours. This was the first collective political action any of them can remember occurring in the village.

The students grew more "realistic," Duvignaud says, the village more "purposeful." The first threw off the technocratic optimism of the Tunis elite for a juster appreciation of the gap between political plans and social realities; the second was "called. . . out of a state of passive mediocrity and bitterness into a consciousness of its own existence . . . discovered its own identity, and . . . the expectation of change grew sharper and more impatient than ever." Thus, microscopically and tentatively, was begun the process of inner transformation that, generally and decisively, will have to occur if Tunisia is to become what it pretends to be, dynamic:

> Shebika's latent dynamism is not to be doubted. On the contrary, its people have a greater capacity for creating new social structures and making practical adjustments to them than do the dwellers in the industrial suburbs of the cities. The expectation and frustration felt by the people of Shebika, and their dramatic display actually led to broad possibilities of creation . . . Shebika is a "social electron," which, if it is given the tools, can create a new situation quite on its own.

This is encouraging, but it all sounds, if one may say so, a bit American. It is a powerful picture, this bringing to earth of the children of privilege and stirring the life of a sleeping village; and the picture is sensitively and imaginatively drawn as Duvignaud searches through the fine details of events for the faintest traces of dynamism. But is it true? Are the changes real, the dynamism genuine? Or has sentiment born of commitment merely made it seem so? Interestingly, the film *Ramparts of Clay* suggests that Duvignaud himself may not be so sure. For the film, tracing over some of the same events, gives a picture not of inner dynamism and purposeful change, but of passing, quite ordinary tremors in a fundamentally immobilized society.

In the film, the presence of the researchers has disappeared altogether. Shebika is rendered as hermetic and self-absorbed. The orphan girl's rebellion, the stonecutters' protest, the disappearance of a lone salt digger in the mountains are presented imagistically—the old women spattering the girl's face with sheep blood; the stonecutters standing up after three days of soundless protest to reveal the corpses among them; the horse of the salt gatherer returning alone. They are mere occurrences in a basically steady flow of life, like those small whirls of dust that are always blowing up for a few seconds in the steppe and then, as suddenly, dissolving. The rhythm of the film is largo, the angle of vision external, as from the helicopter shown photographing the girl dissolving into the steppe as it rises out of Shebika in the final scene. Even the alteration of title suggests the reversal of emphasis on fixity and a closed-in quality from openness and change.

The film is beautifully done, greatly courageous in its determination to risk boring most people for the sake of informing a few. Nor is it, finally, so much a contradiction of the book from which it was developed as a part of it, a complement to it. Diary and tableau comprise, in a sense, a single work. This is one movie where you must also read the book, not only on the pain of mere incomprehension, because the film is made in a kind of pictorial shorthand, but because together they suggest, better than anything else I know, not only

how difficult it is to understand North African society, but some of the paradoxes that understanding must contrive to contain.

For that society is both full of motion and also barely moving. And, willing
as very few sociologists are to experiment with forms of representation, Duvignaud, powerfully aided by Bertuccelli, has managed, for all his limitations as
a scholar, to make us see precisely this.

Mysteries of Islam

What is Islam? A religion? A civilization? A social order? A form of life? A strand of world history? A collection of spiritual attitudes connected only by a common reverence for Muhammad and the Quran? Any tradition which reaches from Senegal and Tanzania through Egypt and Turkey to Iran, India, and Indonesia, which extends from the seventh century to the twentieth, which has drawn on Judaism, Byzantine Christianity, Greek philosophy, Hinduism, Arabian paganism, Spanish intellectualism, and the mystery cults of ancient Persia, which has animated at least a half dozen empires from Abbasid to Ottoman, and which has been legalistic, mystical, rationalist, and hieratic by turns, is clearly not readily characterized, though it all too often has been.

Marshall Hodgson, who was chairman of the Committee on Social Thought at the University of Chicago until his tragic death at forty-seven in 1968, and whose masterpiece, now finally published, represents the only serious attempt in English to address the phenomenon of Islam whole and entire, calls it a "Venture," and that will perhaps do as well as anything. The task, which Hodgson, who was a passionate Quaker, attacks with the combination of erudition, chronic querulousness, and resolute common sense characteristic of that persuasion at its best, is to discover what sort of venture it is.

His first move is to rescue Islam from its Western scholastics, the Arabists; his second is to rescue it from its own, the ulama, or Muslim religious leaders. The Arabist bias, a product of nineteenth-century European orientalism, views the early Arabic period, the years of the founding at Mecca and Medina, as defining the true faith. It regards subsequent developments, Persianate, Sufist,

Originally published in the *New York Review of Books* 22, no. 20 (11 December 1975). Books under discussion therein are as follows: Marshall G. S. Hodgson, *The Venture of Islam: Conscience and History in a World Civilization, Vol. 1: The Classical Age of Islam*; Marshall G. S. Hodgson, *The Venture of Islam: Conscience and History in a World Civilization, Vol. 2: The Expansion of Islam in the Middle Periods*; and Marshall G. S. Hodgson, *The Venture of Islam: Conscience and History in a World Civilization, Vol. 3: The Gunpowder Empire and Modern Times*.

Spanish, Mongol, Indic, or whatever, as derivative at best, decadent at worst. For the Arabists Islamic culture is identified as "culture appearing in the Arabic language," and Syriac, Persian, or Greek cultural elements are treated as "foreign," though they formed in fact the ancestral cultural traditions of the vast majority of the peoples who comprised the classical Muslim communities.

The notion—supported often enough by racist ideas, occasionally by curious theories concerning monotheism and desert landscapes, sometimes merely by a too philological approach to the world—that Islam is the expression of "the Arab mind" has proved extremely difficult for even leading scholars to get around, much less the general public, for whom it has become by now a received idea. That such a notion makes, even for the medieval period, more than three-quarters of the world's Muslim population somehow peripheral to their own faith does not seem to be considered much of an argument against it. Islam is a religion that was made in Arabia from Arabian visions and then, hook or crook, impressed upon others.

The ulama bias, which the orientalists, and as a result of their influence the rest of us, incorporate into the Arabist one, Hodgson calls "Shariah-mindedness," after the term for Islamic religious law. Again, everything properly Islamic proceeds from the pristine period of Mecca and Medina, when faith, law, custom, and political authority are conceived to have been completely fused through the person of the Prophet and the pronouncements of the Quran. All later Islam is seen as an effort, at most marginally successful, to maintain this ideal condition throughout the whole of the Muslim world. And the vehicle of this effort is the law, a set of explicit, unambiguous prescriptions constructed on the basis of reports concerning the Prophet's actions and jurisprudential interpretations of the Quranic prophecy.

The ulama, as the guardians of this conception of what Islam should be— an undivided community of free individuals strictly observant of the codified commands of God—have thus been the carriers, as well, of a distinctive religious outlook: a rigorist, moralistic, rather literalist, and pragmatical legalism. Hodgson is no more concerned to deny the enormous importance of the ulama idea over the centuries than he is to discount the Arabian heritage; but he is concerned to question, and fundamentally, the identification of it as the essence of Islam, the orthodoxy by which piety is weighed and fidelity measured. Like Arabism, Shariah-mindedness has been but one element, and not the most important, in a various and irregular spiritual tradition.

To develop a more realistic conception than the Arabist-legalist one of what the Muslim venture has been all about Hodgson constructs a distinction between "Islam" as "what we may call a religion," and "the overall society and culture associated with that religion" which he wants to call "Islamicate." This term, like a number of others he coins ("agrarianate," "cited," "technicalistic"), probably hasn't much of a future; but it does enable him to separate those aspects of the Muslim world which have directly to do with the relations of man and God from those which do not. The line is not sharp, but if one is to define the role of Persian literary traditions, Turkic political structures, or Greek scientific concepts in what, in another coined term, Hodgson calls Islamdom, and to avoid having to talk about Islamic irrigation systems, Islamic languages, or Islamic sex habits, some such distinction is necessary.

"Arabic" for Hodgson then becomes a cultural strain in a general Islamicate civilization in which Persian, Berber, Spanish, Turkish, Mughal, Hausa, or Malaysian are others. Shariah-mindedness becomes a particular orientation in a general Islamic religiosity in which Sufism, Shiism, Wahhabism, rationalism, and modernism are others. Hodgson's theme is therefore the interaction of the Islamic and the Islamicate within Islamdom (the part of the world "where Muslims and their faith are recognized as prevalent and socially dominant") across the centuries, and the shapes of conscience which that interaction has created. It is a theme he sustains clearly, and continuously, through fifteen hundred pages of the most intricate descriptive argument.

He divides the career of Islam and Islamicate culture into six major phases:

1. the foundation of the tradition in the midst of pagan Arabia in the seventh century;
2. the initial political and cultural development, from about 750 to 950, of that tradition—the civilization of the high caliphates at Damascus and Baghdad;
3. the eleventh- and twelfth-century spread of that civilization throughout the central Islamic lands, the so-called Middle East, plus, at that time, Spain;
4. the Mongol explosion of the fourteenth century—Tamerlane and all that—which at once invaded this newly formed culture sphere and, joining it, introduced into it a powerful new principle of political organization, the military patronage state;
5. the foundation, from 1500, after the Mongol lesson had been absorbed and the Mongol dynamism exhausted, of the early-modern Muslim states, the "gunpowder empires"—Sufavid, Mughal, and Ottoman; and,
6. the reaction of the Muslim heritage, Islamic and Islamicate alike, to the "technicalistic" world the West produced after 1789.

It is a vast panorama, with a cast of thousands continuously in motion, and if Hodgson wobbles a bit (and sometimes more than a bit) when he gets west of the Nile or east of the Oxus, the over-all effect is magisterial: he handles with equal sureness Ghazali, Al-Farabi, Arabic poetry, Persian miniatures, Shii sectarianism, Sufi ecstasy, nomadic militarism, urban mercantilism, Syrian land tenure, the triumph of Ataturk, and anti-Zionism.

The view that emerges from this welter of detail—he has a half-dozen pages on young men's clubs in medieval Syria, another half-dozen on Mamluk city planning, and at one point he goes on about Muslim iconoclasm and modern art—challenges the commonly accepted version of Islam as a narrowly exclusivist creed combining fanaticism, fundamentalism, and xenophobia in equal proportions. For Hodgson Islam has been as broadly catholic a religion as the world has seen, making a place within itself for virtually every sort of spiritual orientation it encountered in its spread along the midline of the world. The Islamicate impulse has been indeed the stronger and Muhammad's community has become more what its history has made it than what its dogmas projected.

Even the founding period along the Western edge of the Arabian peninsula was much less of a parochial, corner-of-the-world affair than later commentators, for reasons of their own, have represented it. Mecca was far from a camp in the desert. It was the crossroads of two of the most important trade routes of the seventh century, one from the Gulf of Aden to the Mediterranean, the Suez of the time, and one from Abyssinia and East Africa to Iraq, Iran, and central Eurasia. Wedged in thus between the Sasanian Empire—Zoroaster, Mani, the Magi, and sacred monarchy—and the Eastern Roman Empire—Hellenism, iconolatry, and the ecclesiastical spirit—it was exposed as well to Judaism, gnosticism, and the oratorical "moralism" of Bedouin nomads. Muhammad drew on all of these in articulating his prophecy.

When during the course of the seventh century and the three following, Islam spread through Syria, Mesopotamia, Iran, and the western Mediterranean, this initial cosmopolitanism was permanently reinforced. By the time Al-Ma'mun was caliph in Baghdad—that is, after 813—the eclecticism of Islamicate civilization and the diversity of Islamic faith were indelible characteristics. Greek science and Mazdean occultism, Arabic grammar and Persian poetry, Syrian mercantilism and Iranian absolutism, Medinan traditionalism and Iraqi chiliasm, were all entangled, together with a *Thousand and One Nights* folk tradition of jinn and marvels. The result was a promiscuous melange even the most militantly reformist movement has never been able to sort out again.

But it was, in Hodgson's view, the period after the classical caliphate lost its dominant position in the new international civilization that had been launched under its auspices and before the Mongol incursion—that is, between the mid-tenth and the mid-thirteenth centuries—which was the definitive one for both the religious and cultural dimensions of Islam, and to which he devotes by far the longest, the most original, and the most deeply felt section of his book. It was then that three crucial developments took place. First an international political order was formed "which tied the world of Islam together regardless of particular states." Secondly, a distinctive social structure, centering around a dominant class of urban notables and local garrison commanders, a complex organization of craft and trading guilds, and that shining triumph of male narcissism, the harem system, appeared through the whole Islamic world. Finally, and most fundamentally, a radical spiritual revolution, emerging at once from above and below, transformed the entire cast of Muslim piety and with it the civilization it supported: Sufism. All this occurred at the axial time in Islamic history, the creation of "the true House of Islam." What comes before is viewed by Hodgson as having been an aggressive, ultimately successful struggle to build; and what comes after as a defensive, ultimately unavailing effort to maintain.

Sufism, which Hodgson, who otherwise is finicky to the point of obsessiveness about definitions, rather nonchalantly glosses as "mysticism," thus emerges as the critical historical category in his interpretation of the Islamic venture. It is the bridging idea that connects North African saint worship with Indian illuminationism, Shii esotericism with Sunni populism, tenth-century cosmologizing with nineteenth- and twentieth-century reform mongering, the Aristotelianism of Ibn Sina with the Platonism of Suhravardi and the Bergsonism of Iqbal. Therefore much depends—almost everything really—on the skill with which he characterizes Sufism as a phenomenon and deploys it as an idea.

Defining Sufism too capaciously would blur historical reality to the point where the specifics of Islamic faith and Islamicate civilization dissolve into a kind of generalized milk-and-water piety, half-religious, half-aesthetic; while if Sufism is too restrictively defined, the result will be strained attempts to force Islam's diversities into a single mold, a new orthodoxy to replace legalism. With the cautionary Arabist-Shariah example before him, Hodgson only occasionally succumbs to the latter fate, as when he tries to make Indic conceptions of divine kingship an outgrowth of Sufi notions of the perfect man. But perhaps because he is so concerned to avoid the narrowness of the Arabists (and because of his own notions of what, behind all variations in style and custom, true spirituality really is—a clarified inwardness that shines outward as love), he is not as successful in avoiding the former. His is, in the end, a rather tamed sort of Islam, a mild, poetic, unaffected religion of experience and fellowship constantly harassed by petty formalists, bigoted ideologues, crude tribesmen, and ambitious soldiers.

For Hodgson, Sufism is, first and foremost, an intellectual tradition, a conceptual mysticism. For all the dervish-whirling and God-is-Great chanting of the brotherhoods, for all the radical populism that animated its rise, and for all the vapors and superstitions that gathered about it, it projected an organized picture of reality fit to stand comparison with its major competitors for the mind (and thus, for this scholar-pietist, the soul) of the reflective Muslim. In the Middle Ages, these competitors were mainly Greek rationalism, Persian symbology, and, once again, Semitic legalism. Far from being a mere outburst of ragged emotion against these towers of methodical thought, Sufism for Hodgson was their proper rival—indeed, in the end, their master.

With such a perspective, the key figure, the man who made Sufism respectable both intellectually and religiously, and thus secured its place at the center of medieval Muslim culture, becomes inevitably Al-Ghazali, who died in IIII. Ghazali combined, in a curious and fateful way, Augustinian doubt-torn probings of the limits of faith with a Thomistic urge to reconcile conflicting spiritual trends. He integrated reason, revelation, law, and experience in the Islamic tradition by making the last, in the form of Sufi mysticism, the guarantor of the other three. Speculative, dialectical thought on the Greek pattern, to which he had given his early allegiance, and which he never could bring himself wholly to abandon, could not provide certainty; the doctrines it produced were correct, but the Greek methods could not prove them so. Muhammad's Prophecy had been a genuine irruption of the divine into the world, and by far the greatest of them; but mere knowledge of that fact, learned from traditions, texts, and schoolmen, could not provide the certainty of faith either. Nor could the Islamic law; built on the Revelation it must on pain of heresy be scrupulously obeyed, but it was merely the outer face of faith, not its inner substance. Only gnosis—if that is how one ought to translate the Sufi *macrifa* ("cognition," "intellection," "experience," "realization," "conversance")—provided more than reasons for belief but belief itself:

> [The historical, legal, and philosophical doctrines] that would verify the presence of the Prophet must be capped by [another] ingredient . . . some touch of prophesying itself. One must be able to perceive the ultimate truth, in however slight a measure, in the same way the prophets perceived it, in order to verify definitely that they were prophets—just as one must be in some slight measure oneself a physician to judge of physicians. One must know what it is, to have not merely knowledge about the truth but immediate acquaintance with it as prophets had. . . .
>
> This lay in the Sûfî experience. . . . Ghazâlî interpreted prophecy not as an unparalleled event but . . . as a special natural species of awareness which merely took its most perfect form in Muhammad. This awareness was of the same sort as the Sûfîs gained, though of a much higher degree. Hence Sûfîs were in a position to recognize full-scale prophecy when they saw it. . . . Though the Prophet was long since dead, a touch of prophecy was always present and accessible in the community. . . .

The intellectual foundation of Ghazâlî's mission, then, was an expanded appreciation of Sûfism. Kalâm [dogmatics] was relegated to a secondary role; and the most valuable insights of Falsafah [Greek-style philosophy] . . . were subsumed into a re-valorized Sûfism, which now appeared as guarantor and interpreter of even the Shar'î [legal] aspects of the Islamic faith.

It was through this Sufist process that, first unselfconsciously and then more and more explicitly, "the international Islamicate social order" formed between 950 and 1250 (Ghazali coming at the exact midpoint of it) developed, bringing popular piety, Shariah-mindedness, and courtly high culture into uneasy but stable balance. On the one hand, Sufism evolved an elaborate metaphysics, centering around images of light, love, and the perfect man; on the other, it gave birth to a flexible yet intricate form of social organization—the tariqah brotherhoods—based on long, spread-out chains of teacher-disciple relationships. A civilization that threatened to break into separate parts as it spread east toward India and Southeast Asia, north into the Eurasian steppes, and west to Spain and North Africa found a new and stronger principle of integration to replace that of the vanished Caliphate, in a "comprehensive Sûfî spirituality. . . supported by high intellectual sophistication."

Poetry, urban organization, state formation, class structure, architecture, and trading institutions all took form—the styles, alleys, veils, and arabesques we now associate with Islamicate culture—under the aegis of a new cosmopolitanism, "tolerating wider differences in tongue, and welcoming all that was Muslim from anywhere," so long as it connected in some way to "the ultimate spiritual criterion of the mystic, the sense of inward taste [of the divine]."

Yet, it is not, somehow, entirely convincing, this Sufi-ized (and Persianized) view of Islam's triumphant Middle Ages. For it makes them, as some views of our own medieval period also do, seem held together by a vague but constant religiosity suffusing all things, a religiosity both hard to define ("mysticism" will simply not do when it has to cover Moroccan miracle-workers, Anatolian poets, and Punjabi cosmologists) and difficult to connect in any exact way with the enormously varied institutional life it supposedly governed. Life in Hodgson's work seems organized by a mood, and though the mood was doubtless there, and powerful, there is an imprecision in such a way of seeing things that makes one wonder whether analyzing the Islamic venture largely by such mega-concepts as "Arabism," "Shariah-mindedness," "Islamicate," "mercantilism," "the mid-Arid zone," "agrarianate," and "Sufism" is not likely to lift the entire enterprise, despite the piling on of immense weights of descriptive detail, a few feet off the ground.

The vast dimensions of the subject—Islam, religion and civilization, everywhere and always—to some degree require the historian to work with such diffuse and panoramic ideas. But that his analysis must be based on them exclusively, or very nearly so, is less clear. Nor is it clear whether such concepts, or they alone, can bring one to the heart of such a phenomenon as Islam, close to the immediacies of its historical experience. Hodgson, thorough, scrupulous, and concrete to a fault—nothing he argues is left without supporting evidence—goes about as far toward elucidating the course of Islamic history as anyone probably can, and surely further than anyone has before him. But even he seems blocked by the very sweep of his categories, condemned to see the progression of Islam in the reduced middle distance, half montage, half silhouette.

The problem becomes all the more acute as, the great age over, Hodgson moves forward to confront less a coalesced "world civilization" than a tumbled collection of rival states and clashing cultures. When the history of "Islamdom" can no longer be represented as moving toward the crystallization of an inner ideal, but only as struggling to keep an achieved one alive, the weakness of Hodgson's broadly framed integrative concepts in grasping its irregularities grows apparent. His touch loses something of its delicacy. In part, this is doubtless because he died while working on the final sections of this book and never had a chance to revise them. But it is also true that as the historical record becomes more circumstantial, events become more visible and eras less so; and so a direct challenge is posed to what is perhaps Hodgson's central methodological premise: that the character of a civilization is defined by its most general features.

For the Mongol period around the fourteenth century, about which not all that much is known anyway, the challenge can be deflected. The Mongols, with their towers of skulls and their horseback adventurism, shook the Sufi synthesis but they did not shatter it, and they ended by joining it. Their main contribution to it was the organization of government "as a single massive army," with the monarch as its commander in chief. His camp, wherever it lighted, was its headquarters, and privileged military families its officer corps, the whole governing apparatus riding arrogant and self-contained above the established forms of social and cultural life.

By the next period, this political revolution—"the military patronage state"—came to fruition in a set of independent and quite disparate early-modern "gunpowder empires"—Ottoman, Safavid, and Mughal—dominating respectively the western, central, and eastern regions of the Islamic world. Hodgson notes that "by 1550 a major blow had been dealt to the cosmopolitan comprehensiveness of Islam" by the formation of these more effectively organized armed soldier states. But he evades the issue this presents to his enterprise and treats them descriptively (this is the one part of his work that seems potted—standard summaries from standard sources), trying, vaguely and half-heartedly, to see in them a last, defensive expression of the medieval pattern.

With the modern period, between 1800 and 1950, there is no plausible way to represent matters as still in some form of Ghazalian balance. Here the incongruity between Hodgson's notion of what a civilization (and within a civilization, a religion) is and the facts of Muslim life, as Muslims lead it, becomes intensely apparent. He is forced toward the uncomfortable suggestion that the Islamic venture is just about over, an expired vision destined to persist as a nameless ghost haunting its literary remains:

> . . . Islam as an identifiable institutional tradition may not last indefinitely. It is a question, for Muslims as for all other heirs of a religious heritage, how far any creative vision for the future . . . will depend on preserving and developing the heritage; and how far it will depend on escaping the inhibiting effects of the wishful thinking and even the grand (but partial) formulations of truth which the heritage seems to impose. It is possible that eventually Islam (like Christianity already in some circles) will prove to have its most creative thrust by way of the great "secular" literature in which its challenge has been embedded, and will move among its heirs like a secret leaven long after they have forgotten they were once Muslims. Persian poetry will not die so soon as the disquisitions of [law] or [theology]. And Persian poetry may eventually prove to be as potent everywhere as among those who use language touched by the Persianate spirit, and so by Islam.

So Hodgson's book ends with the end-of-Islam, except for its legacy of moral aestheticism. He foresees an Islamless Islamicate that can coexist, in the modern "technicalistic" world, with the religionless Christianity so popular "in some circles" when Hodgson was writing, and so *vieux jeu* now in those same circles, which now are fascinated by popular beliefs and festal celebrations. Perhaps such a view is the final outcome of trying to inflate Sufism into a comprehensive interpretative category with neither well-drawn edges nor a well-located center. The diversity of Islamic religious viewpoints remains; Qaddhafi's desert camp fundamentalism and Sadat's Cairene eclecticism do as much to divide as connect them. And, though it is not much more attractive to me than it is to Hodgson, the great power of Shariah legalism persists. So too does the diversity of institutions and cultural traditions within Islamdom: the Berbers and Malaysians both regard their sharply different social systems as properly Islamic.

One might be in a better position to understand and evaluate such phenomena if one's idea of what Islam is and has always been were closer to

Wittgenstein's notion of a "family resemblance." We think we see striking resemblances between different generations of a family but, as Wittgenstein pointed out, we may find that there is no one feature common to them; the resemblance may come from many different features "overlapping and crisscrossing." This sort of approach seems more promising than one that sees the history of Islam, as Hodgson's does, as an extended struggle of a gentle pietism to escape from an arid legalism. A picture of the Islamic venture derived from "overlaps" and "crosscrosses" would be less ordered and less continuous, a matter of oblique connections and glancing contrasts, and general conclusions would be harder to come by. But it could leave us with a history less orchestrated than Hodgson's, and more immediate.

Yet his is, for all that, a magnificent achievement: a clear, comprehensive, beautifully researched, and, above all, profoundly felt account of a great spiritual tradition, a monument both to the faith of Muslims and to his own. For once, the cliché applies: no one seriously interested in Islam can ignore this book. Muslim illuminism has found a powerful scholarly voice, and its echoes will be with us for a very long time.

The Last Arab Jews

At the close of World War II there were about a half-million Jews living in North Africa; today there are about 20,000, and those are submerged, partially and uneasily, in the anonymizing mercantilism of the largest cities. (Of Morocco's perhaps 15,000, more than half are in Casablanca, and virtually all of the rest in Marrakech, Rabat, Meknes, Fès, and Tangier; of Tunisia's 3,500 or so, about two-thirds are in Tunis.) Where once there were scores of integral Jewish communities long in place, socially self-enclosed, and culturally self-regulating, only two remain: Hara Kebira, "The Big Village" (pop. 804), and Hara Sghira, "The Little Village" (pop. 280), on the small offshore island of Jerba in southern Tunisia, fifty miles from the Libyan border.

The Last Arab Jews is an anthropological portrait of these two communities based on fieldwork carried out in them during 1978, 1979, and 1980. The researchers are, however, not anthropologists, but historians, one Canadian-born American, one Tunisian-born French, one an economic historian, one a social historian, one a medievalist, one a modernist, and, what is perhaps particularly important in this part of the world, one a man and one a woman. Between them they provide a brief but vivid overview of all the major aspects of local life—economic, political, religious, familial—and set it against the background of a long, half-mythicized past and the prospect of a short, dissolving future. Written in dispassionate, even subdued, tones, with the summary empiricism of the ethnographer, it is nevertheless a moving account, if only because these last of the last are quite probably just that, the concluding phase—"no more forever," as an earlier account of the final days of an Algerian settlement was entitled—of an ancient and, for all its vicissitudes, extraordinary civilization.[1] There were 4,000 Jerban Jews at the end of the war; had they grown at the rate of the general Tunisian population they would now be

Originally published as "The Ultimate Ghetto," *New York Review of Books* 32, no. 3 (28 February 1985). The book under discussion therein is as follows: Abraham L. Udovitch and Lucette Valensi, *The Last Arab Jews: The Communities of Jerba, Tunisia.*

15,000, not 1,000. "The Jerban communities are amputated and their ability to reproduce themselves as a collective unit is in serious question. Outside Jerba . . . it might not [I would say, certainly would not] be possible at all."

In the eyes of the Jerban Jews, their island within an island (more than 80,000 Muslims—Ibadis, Malikis, Hanafis—live variously around them) is a sort of diaspora Holy Land, "the antechamber," as they put it, "of Jerusalem." The main synagogue, called "The Marvelous," and long a major pilgrimage site for North African Jews, is considered to date from the destruction of the first Temple in 586 BC. Kohanim (priests), fleeing there from the disaster, carried with them (so it is said) a door and some stones from the ruined sanctuary which they incorporated into the new structure, making it something more than an ordinary synagogue, if not quite yet a true temple. (Until recently, The Little Village, where the Marvelous Synagogue—it is only one of no fewer than seventeen in the two settlements—is located, was apparently inhabited exclusively by Kohanim.)

A metal wire, rather like a clothesline, runs from rooftop to rooftop around the perimeter of the villages, turning them into a sacred space forbidden to outsiders. A second such wire marks off the marketplace in the village square as an equally explicit secular space, "a place of work and of exchange with Muslims . . . off limits for [Jewish] men on the Sabbath, as it is every day of the week for [Jewish] women." The villages are "theocratic republics," meticulously regulated by hair-splitting rabbinical judges who become such by popular recognition, as well as centers of rabbinical learning of a particularly strict, purity-obsessed variety. "Building a wall around the Torah," a wall as much to keep Jews in as non-Jews out, is the driving force of collective life. "Being Jewish," as the authors well say, "[is] a full time activity."

Thus, in one sense, the Jews of Jerba live in the ultimate ghetto: a minority community, cast into a metaphysical exile "from which [it] can expect nothing but misery and slavery until the day of redemption," and one so closed in upon itself—the women moving between the household, the male-free courtyard, and the ritual bath; the men between the neighborhood, the female-free synagogue, and the market square—as to seem a kind of social time capsule, a fixed pattern of life buried in a suspended history. Yet the paradox is, if it is indeed a paradox and not merely the way such things are ordered in this odd corner of the world, that the Jerban Jews are as Maghrebian, in their fashion, as the hardiest Muslim, and as rooted in Tunisian culture. Whether or not they are in the "antechamber of Jerusalem," whether or not they are *Juifs en Terre d'Islam* (as the simultaneously published French edition is rather more ominously titled), these are "Arab" Jews, and they take about as much of their character from their surroundings as they do from their faith.

It is not merely that the language of everyday life is Arabic; or that the men, most of whom are merchants or craftsmen, venture beyond the local market to practice their trades; or that household organization, sexual division of labor, demographic structure, and even, religious symbolism aside, marriage customs, legal forms, aesthetic preferences, educational practices, and ideas of gender, approximate those of the surrounding population; or that the style of personal behavior has about it the air of catch-as-catch-can that marks political and economic life from the Rif to the Western Desert. It is that, on Jerba as else-where in this region of rather bits-and-pieces culture, social existence has long been divided. One part of life takes place behind social walls so high that no outsider can see over them, a world of veils, endogamy, and dietary customs; the other takes place in the noon light of radical cosmopolitanism, a world of bar-gains, contracts, and pragmatic friendships. Muslims and Jews, Arabs and Ber-bers, tribesmen and townsmen, white men and black men, have lived for as long as we have records at once carefully set apart and carelessly tumbled together.

For Jews, this cultural doubleness—monoform communities in polyform societies—was, of course, both extreme and essential to their continuing sur-vival. The decline of this duality under the loyalty-fusing imperatives of mod-ern nationalism—assimilate or emigrate—has rendered their situation not only difficult, as it has always been, but unworkable altogether. That the older pattern has been maintained in Jerba beyond what has proved possible else-where—which is perhaps what most intrigues Udovitch and Valensi—is in part owing to its remoteness, in part to the relative moderation, as these things go, of Muslim Tunisians and of their political leadership.

But mostly the survival of the old pattern is a result of the unusually intense development of the behind-the-walls life of the two settlements. Jerban Jews have been able to resist both Frenchifying Tunis and Zionizing Israel, to the degree that they have, because they have constructed inside their wire and around their synagogue a vitality to hold them there.

The forms of this vitality are manifold. Some concern matters having to do with home and hearth, such as a hyper-moral, and hyper-private family life, an exhausting round of yearly, weekly, daily, and even hourly rituals, and elab-orate (and elaborately segregated) patterns of male and female sociality, all of which Udovitch and Valensi record in some detail. But the most important, because taken together they represent an extraordinary florescence of civic Judaism—extraordinary not just for North African, or "oriental," communi-ties, but for the Diaspora generally—are the rabbinical supervision of public life, the annual pilgrimage centered on the founding synagogue, and the writing and publishing of scholarly books. Jewish Jerba is, or anyway has for centuries considered itself to be, not just a repository of an uprooted universal culture awaiting historical redemption, but also, and it would sometimes seem at least as passionately, a capital of a dug-in provincial culture.

Rabbinical supervision, which almost everywhere else in the Maghreb was challenged by the power of secular elites, was here so marked that the Jerbans conceive of their history as a sequence of wise and wonder-working rabbis guiding a spontaneously observant, freely obedient people. (Udovitch and Valensi, in their anxiety to rebut stereotypes of religious authoritarianism, perhaps accept this conception a bit too much at face value, as they do a number of accounts the Jerbans give of themselves.) Education, the administration of justice, and even the evolution of local custom, took place, and still does, under the watchful eye of one or another such rabbi—responsa upon responsa, judgment upon judgment, homily upon homily.

The pilgrimage, a week-long event a month after Passover, celebrates a number of things at once—the founding of the Marvelous Synagogue by the refugee Kohanim, the memory of a mysterious, radiant girl who appeared one day on its site and whose body a fire failed to consume, and the lifting of an ancient plague upon the death of some particularly holy rabbis. It involves an extended candle-lighting and vow-making procession in and around the synagogue, headed by an enormous menara ("a hexagonal pyramid, skillfully mounted on three wheels") symbolizing the five levels of beings from the twelve tribes through the great rabbis and biblical personages to God. A number of (even) less orthodox activities also take place, such as leaving a raw egg on the spot where the mysterious girl's body was found to ensure the marriage of an unmarried woman within the year. At the height of its popularity in the nineteenth century, the pilgrimage drew huge crowds of Jews (and a fair number of Muslims, to whom the place is also magical) from all over North Africa. Even today people come, or more properly come back, from as far away as Rome, Montreal, or Paris to re-create "for the duration of a week, a religious element . . . [in] lives which have been deprived of it."

The publishing of scholarly books, moreover, which began in Jerba only in this century (though works written by Jerbans, rabbis and learned laymen alike—but not by women, all of whom until quite recently were illiterate—were published well before that in Leghorn, Tunis, and Jerusalem), has produced more than five hundred printed works, from prayer books and law manuals to volumes of religious poetry and Talmudic commentary. Written in Hebrew or in Arabic with Hebrew characters, these books were distributed throughout Jewish North Africa, a "level of literary productivity [which], with the exception of such specialized communities as academia, may be unprecedented." "The colonial authorities and the Jewish notables of Tunis" charged that Jerba was "a 'backward' community kept in 'abjection and ignorance by their rabbis who were stubbornly opposed to any progress.'" But Jerba's claim to be the moral center of Maghrebian Jewry was neither ill based, nor, from the point of view of cultural survival, ill advised:

> Far from being ignorant, the Jerbans were offering resistance—at times silent and at times quite vociferous—to any challenge to their own values. The fact that they are still there today proves that, in this particular contest, they prevailed.

So far. If the end seems near, it is not because the Jerbans' sense of "their own values" or the institutions they have devised to maintain them have weakened. Rabbinical leadership remains strong, even if today's rabbis are perhaps not so impressive as yesterday's. The pilgrimage continues, even if it now sometimes seems as much a tourist event and commercial festival as a religious observance. The books go on being published, even if now there are only two presses where once there were five. The problems are on the other side of the wall, where the Jews, their red Tunisian skullcaps worn, as always, toward the back of the head to distinguish them from the Muslims, who wear them, as always, forward, no longer find it so easy to participate in the scuffling give-and-take of public-square life.

The main setting in which this change in the beyond-the-wire rules of the game can be seen to be taking place is that most *plein air* of Maghrebian institutions: the bazaar. "Virtually all able-bodied adult males" of the Jewish community "are involved [in the bazaar] as sellers, producers or financiers." It is "the locus of the most frequent and varied contact between Jews and Muslims"; the place where the lines of cultural demarcation "are most fluid and permeable"; "the arena in which important aspects of identity, self-image and mutual perceptions are defined and enacted."

During the eighteenth and nineteenth centuries Jews controlled most parts of the bazaar, not just in their own community, but in the leading Muslim town on the island, Houmt Souk. Itinerant Jewish traders and artisans circulated as well to the scattered Muslim villages, peddling petty manufactures, buying up agricultural products, serving as carpenters, harness makers, tailors, tinsmiths. In the present century all this activity began, at first slowly, then more and more rapidly, to diminish, until in recent years the confinement of Jewish traders and craftsmen to a few specialized occupations, largely reserved to them, has become extreme. In 1902, about 40 percent of the Jews were engaged in one or another sort of general commerce (textiles, foodstuffs, tobacco), another 40 percent in a wide variety of traditional crafts (cobblers, bucket makers, embroiderers, scribes), and 15 percent in the specifically Jewish trade of jeweler (often combined with moneylending).

In 1978, about 10 percent were in commerce, 20 percent in traditional crafts (mostly tailors), and 60 percent in jewelry and/or moneylending. What Udovitch and Valensi call "the gold rush," but what might more aptly be called "the gold imprisonment," has reduced what was once a varied and across-the-board trading community, reaching, if not without tension, into all parts of the general society, virtually to the status of an occupational caste. About half the Jewish labor force is now employed in the jewelry trade, and the proportion is growing; nearly 80 percent of the young men entering the labor market are choosing careers in it. The cosmopolitan side of Jewish life—in which if they were not precisely like everyone else, they were at least among everyone else, striking deals and forming alliances—is dissolving. And with it is dissolving the sense—theirs and that of their neighbors—that, distinctive as they may be, they belong where they are.

Of course there are many reasons for this progressive extrusion of the Jews from the larger life of Jerba. The influx of mass-produced consumer goods has caused the disappearance of most traditional trades. The rise of motor transport has rendered the itinerant peddler on his donkey obsolete. The improving educational level of the majority population has enabled it to dispense with Jewish commercial know-how. The general tendency to rationalize and integrate the Tunisian economy has made personal, face-to-face ways of doing business increasingly vulnerable to impersonal ones between firms and customers. But clearly the critical factor, entwined with these and with the entire course of postcolonial history, is the appearance of exclusionary nationalisms in the Middle East, and of states only marginally less so to go with them. "Staying on" as a Tunisian Jew, like doing so as an Arab Israeli, is an increasingly difficult thing to manage.

The signs are everywhere and getting clearer. The Jerban municipal council has officially renamed Hara Kebira—"The Large Village"—As-Sawani, "The Gardens," a Jerban Jew wrote Udovitch and Valensi in 1981 after they had left the island.

> When I asked [a Muslim official] why [the change was made], he responded that it was its proper name. The name Hara Kebira is to be erased and not to be remembered or mentioned anymore. . . . I thought to myself: We Jews, who reached this place long before them, who have a history of more than two thousand years here, not only are they seeking to push us out, but they are even conspiring to erase our past and the names of famous Jewish places from history.

Two years earlier, in 1979, a new synagogue, about to be inaugurated, was burned, presumably by arsonists. The Jews, comparing the event to the destruction of the Temple, fasted and mourned, and eighteen months later reconsecrated it.

We still recall that terrible night [the same correspondent wrote] in which the Torah was burned and the ark was laid waste . . . and we were helpless, unable to save them. We still remember the magnitude of the disaster which occurred. We all stood dumb-struck, confused and trembling in the destroyed synagogue. Thanks be to God . . . the synagogue and the arks were repaired, and the people contributed scrolls of the Torah. And on this night all of us, from the youngest to the oldest, stood rejoicing. It was a joy and gladness for the Jews. This was but a small restitution for that which happened—may it never happen again, amen.

The future, however, will bring what it will bring; and Udovitch and Valensi are not exactly sanguine.

Given that the [Tunisian] state is neither pluralist nor secular, and given that the Jerban Jewish communities are not prepared to accept a process of secularization which would condemn them to extinction, any integration into the dominant society and culture is [now] unthinkable. . . .

[But] if they leave the island, [they] would also have to abandon their language, their costume, their elaborate system of local customs, their educational system, and . . . their history.

In the meantime, Udovitch and Valensi have told the community's story, well and fairly. If, as seems likely, it turns out to be its epitaph as well, it is anyway an appropriate one, plainly eloquent.

House Painting: *Toutes Directions*

I

In late February of 1986, a week or two before the massive joint celebration of the 25th anniversary of Hassan II's accession to the Moroccan throne and the 10th of his launching of the Green March in the Sahara (the March actually took place in November of 1975, but it was ritually assimilated to Coronation Day for this milestone occasion), the municipal council of a small city in the east-central part of the country issued a decree. Henceforth, the color of all buildings in the city was to be beige: *crème*, in the French redaction, *qehwi*, in the Arabic. Paint could be obtained at designated outlets.

Compliance with this decree was, as one would expect, very far from complete, and the city, Sefrou, 28 kilometers due south of Fez, of which it is in many ways a miniaturized version, remains in fact more white than anything else, and when not white, pastel. But, as one would not expect (at least I did not), the decree was, among certain sorts of people and in certain sections of the city, immediately and completely obeyed: brightly colored, variegated house façades, some of them masterpieces of design bravura, were painted over during the course of a day or two, into a dun homogeneity—*la vie urbaine officielle*. Behind this event, trivial in itself and of very uncertain permanency of effect, lies a long and far from trivial story, political and cultural at the same time. The changing shape of the city, its changing class and ethnic composition, the changing relations between it and its hinterland, it and its economic base, it and its governing elites, it and the national power, and most critical of all, the changing, and diversifying, sense of its inhabitants as to what *citadinité*—that French word that translates so awkwardly into English but so readily, as *mudaniyya* ("belonging *to* and *in* a city," as Mohammed Naciri has put it), into Arabic—really means, were all caught up in a bitter and many-sided

Originally published as "*Toutes Directions*: Reading the Signs in an Urban Sprawl," *International Journal of Middle East Studies* 21 (1989): 291–306.

debate, a debate about what a proper "Islamic city" ought to be, how it ought to feel, what it ought to look like.

Driven on by the controversies swirling about the assumptions, or supposed such, of "Orientalism," the debate in scholarly circles over "The Islamic City"—whether there is such a thing; what, if there is such a thing, is "Islamic" about it; and how much, if there is such a thing and we can isolate what is Islamic about it, its religious character matters in terms of how if "really" works—has quickened in recent years. The exaggeration of the uniformity of city life throughout the Islamic world, the idealized quality of descriptions of that life, which are overly dependent upon a few models and upon theories in place since Ibn Khaldun, the tendency to see such cities against the background of European norms, and the ahistorical, hypertextual conception of Islam as a social force within them, have all come in for severe attack. The very idea comes now with a question mark welded to it.

Be that as it may, surely there has been a good deal of constructing of chimeras, imagined entities that never were, in scholarly work on North African and Middle Eastern cities. Just as surely, there has been, in such work, a great deal of genuine discovery that ought not to be discarded simply because it proceeded from *Weltanschauungen* not now in favor. But the important point is that whatever the status of the idea of an Islamic City is in scholarly discourse, Orientalist or otherwise, it is very much alive in the minds, and in the discourse, of workaday Muslims—urbanites and countryfolk, masses and elites alike; and, in fact, is made even more alive by the enormous transformations cities are now undergoing in the Islamic world. "A certain idea of a city" becomes, if anything, more vivid and more absorbing as it becomes harder and harder to see it in the disordered sprawl of modern life. The Islamic City grows increasingly significant as a notion and an aspiration, or perhaps merely significant in a different way, as the conditions for its existence become more precarious, disparate, and difficult to realize.

There is by now scarcely a city or town in the whole of the Middle East, however ancient, that presents a historically coherent face to the world. This is, of course, true to some extent throughout Asia and Africa, but it seems especially characteristic of Arabo-Islamic cities (and certainly of Moroccan ones, certainly of Sefrou), because new city forms tend less to replace old ones, update them, or absorb them into themselves, than to grow up around them, leaving the old ones more or less intact. *Mudun, mudun judād, villes nouvelles, habitations spontanées . . . clandestines . . . periphériques,* are all in place at once, like remains from different floors of a multiply occupied archeological site. The urban landscape is not merely various, as are all such landscapes, it is disjunct. It is within such a landscape of diverse orderings that point in divergent directions that the discourse—popular, political, and itself multiple—about the Islamic City, a discourse of buildings and institutions, façades and ideologies, street nets and public services—the semiotics of mudaniyya—takes place.

"Semiotics" has become a bit of a red-flag word, and often enough one of uncertain reference as to what is meant by it changes and proliferates. My use of it is simply Saussure's original one, "the science of the life of signs in society," without further commitment either to the formalistic varieties of it that have grown up in the structuralist tradition or to the scholastical ones that have grown up in the Peircian. Wittgenstein's view that thought (feeling, belief, construction, judgment) is a public activity, carried on not in "the head," "the heart," or some other gossamer private place but in the *plein air* world by means of sign systems—that meaning arises in use, and use is social—is the grounding notion; the rest must come from descriptive analysis. And though the signs involved are, so far at least as human beings are concerned, predominantly linguistic, they are not exclusively so: images, numbers, melodies, gestures, and, in the case at hand, objects of the built environment (or, for that matter, the unbuilt) interweave with words, and words with them, to produce the web of perceptions we weakly call "experience." The semiotics of urban life, in the Islamic world or anywhere else, is but the interpretation of that life in terms of the expressions in which it traffics.

In the history of Sefrou, and most vividly in its recent history, all these concerns come together: the progressive disarticulation of the urban landscape as the city grows; the intensified concern with the idea of the Islamic City as a governing norm; the increasing difficulty of defining such an idea and such a norm in the context of the progressive disarticulation and the sense, therefore, that the idea, and thus perhaps even Islam itself, is endangered; the "reading-in" (or, to adapt a phrase of Richard Wollheim's, the "seeing-in") of all this into the physical appearance of the city; and the emergence of it into sharp social, economic, cultural, and most specifically and consequentially, political contestation as these changes proceed. Municipal decrees about what color houses should be, hardly critical themselves, catch up, as gestures do in such an emblematic environment, a lot of themes.

Sefrou, this thousand year old town of, in 1984, some 40,000 to 50,000 inhabitants, set amid olive groves in the watered piedmont that separates the great Fez-Meknes wheat plain from the sheep and strip-farm Middle Atlas, is hardly representative, in the statistical sense, of Morocco, much less of North Africa, the Middle East, or the Muslim world. Nor, though it includes within it almost all the elements of a classic medina in their classic forms—mosques, walls, baths, impasses, bazaars, fountains, caravansaries, shrines, citadels—is it any sort of ideal type of Islamic city. Its use is neither as a sample of something nor as an epitome of something, but as an instance of something: a case in point. The value of looking hard at it and what has been happening to it recently is that of all instances: after doing so one may see in other instances matters otherwise occluded. Examples instruct, they do not prove.

II

In 1911, on the eve of the Protectorate, the city of Sefrou was about 10 hectares in size, contained possibly 6,000 people, of which nearly half were Jews, and consisted of the walled old city of passages and impasses; the *medina qadīma*, an impacted Jewish quarter; the *mellāh*, in the dead center of it; and a city citadel area, also walled, the *qal'a*, just above it.

A decade later, in 1922, with the Protectorate at last firmly in place, and the city officially municipalized, Lyautey style, it was 13 times as large—about 130 hectares—and consisted of the old areas plus a new Arab quarter, laid out on a gridiron plan just outside the walls, and a French villa area, with shaded gardens and serpentine streets, in the hills above the citadel. In 1944, toward the close of the Protectorate, the municipal boundaries were expanded again, to 380 hectares (the population now was 18,000, less than a third Jews, getting on toward 1,000 French), the added area being more "new medina" quarters plus some extra-mural marketplaces.

And there they stayed until 1982, when a Socialist government, recently and almost accidentally come to power and facing a new election, suddenly, amid intense controversy, some of it physical, more than tripled the city's official size to about 1,200 hectares so as to bring within its political ambit the "peripheral," "illegal," "alien" (*berrāni*) settlements that had sprung up with stunning rapidity during the previous decade, and whose votes they saw as theirs. This was a social revolution (or an attempt at such, for in the event it failed) through municipal redefinition.

In this deliberate, stage-by-stage augmentation of the city to 120 times its original extent (and about 9 times its population) over the course of some 70 years, its modern cultural genealogy can be seen, as one after another form of life, European, Euro-Moroccan, country Moroccan, comes to occupy some part of its site, distributed around its traditional Arab and Judeo-Arab medina core. Some of these forms of life—the French, the Jews—have largely disappeared, or at least the populations that introduced them have. ("We have lost both our brains and our pockets," one old-line Sefruwi said to me.) Others, country Moroccans, mostly Berber-speaking, mostly rude, have only recently appeared with very much force. ("The city used to eat the countryside," the same man, a long-time construction entrepreneur of no little weight, said, "now the countryside eats the city.") And it is this final, final to date, addition that may, in the end, prove the most transformative. Since the Socialist in-gathering, the citizenry of Sefrou is more than half half-urban.

To simplify a complex situation, but to do so precisely in the way Sefrouis themselves for the most part simplify it when trying to make sense of what is happening to them, the explosion of rural immigration has divided the city into two major categories, conceptually at least (and what is more important, rhetorically), quite distinct: "Real Sefrouis" (*ṣefrūwī ḥqīq*) and "Outsider Se-frouis" (*ṣefrūwi berrānī*).

Real Sefrouis, who sometimes also refer to themselves, in a kind of bilin-gual pun, as *ṣefrūwī carré*, "Sefroui squared" (i.e., *ṣefrūwī-ṣefrūwī* in the *nisba* system of social labeling that prevails here), are, or claim to be, descendants of families who have been present in the city, if not since its founding—and some claim even that—at least for a very long time. Arab-speaking, they are mostly land holders, merchants, professionals, or, increasingly, civil servants, and though they come in all classes, from the abject poor to the crocodile rich, the unusually compact city elite—social, political, economic and cultural alike—is drawn from among them, and long has been.

The Outsider Sefrouis are the in-migrants. (Sefruwi berrani, another nisba, which also has the force of "stranger," "alien," or "foreigner," is not a contradic-tion in terms, but an emphatic, and, like sefruwi hqiq, a contested, rhetorical classification.) Heavily, though not exclusively Berber-speaking, and in any case mostly at least partly bilingual in Arabic, they live on, in diverse propor-tions, returns from recently sold-off rural farms, remittances from relatives working in Europe, and casual labor, casual trade, and, to an uncertain extent, casual crime.

Both sides of this divide are, thus, at once very new and very old. And it is between them—diffuse, heterogeneous aggregations rather than true groups, or even factions—that the economic, political, and cultural contestations of public life, always intense in this masculinist, power-candid world, take place more and more often.

The Real Sefrouis, about a third of the Muslim-Jewish-French population at Independence, about a third of the (larger) City Muslim/Country Muslim one now, live almost entirely outside the old city core. The lower and middle classes have been moving into the gridiron quarters abutting the walls since the 1940s. Since the 1950s, the elite, which, anchored as they were in secluded family alleyways, were slower to abandon the medina, have taken over the vil-las of *les quartiers chics* (or, in another pointed bilingual pun, *sheikhs*) left empty by the departed French. The same elite, the bulk of whom belong to some seven or eight large local families, have inherited the municipal admin-istrative apparatus, strengthened their economic position, especially in land holding, transport, and construction, and related themselves to the Monarch as "king's men," much as their fathers had related to the Protectorate government as *notables indigènes*. During the Independence struggle itself, their grip was briefly shaken by the power of upstart nationalist leaders, mostly from the Muslim reformist party *Istiqlal*; but it was soon restored as the Monarchy, reasserting its ascendancy, reasserted theirs. By the 1963 municipal elections, they were back in place; the same men, with the same interests, the same resources, and the same understanding of mudaniyya: Arabo-Islamic "cityhood."

On the Outsiders side, the peripheral settlements they created so explosively in the 1970s and 1980s are not crowded "bidonville" shack areas, of which Sefrou has virtually none, but disorderly expanses of substantial stone, brick or concrete-block houses, generally urban in type, set haphazardly (and illegally) on the landscape: uninvited suburbs.

Significant migrations from the countryside began immediately after Independence in 1956, but they were largely absorbed into the popular quarters of the old city that were left vacant by townsmen moving into the extramural sections, away to larger cities, or in the case of the Jews, to foreign countries. After 1970 or so, when the *exode rural*, as even monolingual Sefrouis call it, grew from a stream to a torrent, such absorption into established structures was no longer possible. The new settlements sprang up, house by house; first, in the barren, unstable limestone areas above the city, and then, more disturbingly, in the *huerta* (Spanish for "orchard")—the irrigated olive groves that, forming the city's aesthetic frame and providing a fair amount of its income, have been for centuries the sign of its "oasis" felicity—below it. And where the earlier migrants had been mostly landless poor, attracted to the city out of necessity and the hope of somehow scraping by in its darker corners, the later ones were people who, though hardly well-to-do and with no real economic base in the city or any prospect of one, were, from their alienated farms and their European remittances, not uncapitalized. The dwellings they built—sizable structures, designed to be noticed and to last—show it.

This phase of the transformation of Sefrou thus changed more than its social composition. It changed, as the earlier phases had not (or not more than marginally), its aspect, air, demeanor, look. What was once a chiseled jewel set in a paradisian garden was now a sprawling, disorganized, anything but jewel-like *bourg*, another French word everyone in the city seems now to know.

III

This socioeconomic transformation of Sefrou from a highly defined administrative, commercial, and cultural complex—an urban solidity in a tribal flux—to a diffuse conglomeration of buildings, people, activities, and institutions, fully permeable to the life ways around it, was bound to issue eventually in political expression, even in a traditionalist monarchy still resistant to electoral politics. When the ratio of urban population to rural in the region goes from about 1:4 to nearly 1:2 in 20 years; when real city property values increase more than 5 times (and in the unbuilt-up areas, 10 to 20) in the same period; when, as a rather broad guess, three-quarters of the huerta (half of which in any case belongs to two percent of the population) has already been built over, and the process is accelerating; when probably two-thirds of the buildings in the town, the bulk of them without water or electricity, many of them without road access, and all of them without sewers, have been built since 1960; and when a large flow of funds (exact figures, or even inexact ones, are unavailable) from wage work in Europe is going to finance this construction boom in a city otherwise economically stagnant if not declining, the established power structure, no matter how long it has been in place, how firmly it is reinforced by central authority, and how culturally legitimized it is, is going to be put under something of a strain.

The extent of this strain became suddenly apparent in the municipal council elections of 1976, when that structure, in fact, cracked. The representatives of the traditional elite, who had monopolized the council since Lyautey set it up in 1913, were summarily turned out, and the Moroccan Socialist party, never before much of a factor, won, to everyone's astonishment including its own, three-quarters of the seats. Though the council, hemmed in on all sides by bureaucratic and police control in a system euphemistically called "tutelage," *la tutelle*, is quite limited in its capacity to act on its own, it is, simply by virtue of being a popularly elected body in a local government otherwise centrally appointed, the main expression of locally rooted power balances. The dramatic displacement from it of the sons and grandsons of the men who traditionally manned it, a public humiliation of some consequence, inaugurated, therefore, a kind of Prague Spring in Sefrou: a period (7 years as a matter of fact) at the end of which an unexpectedly opened door was, amid rising tension, outside pressure, and a certain amount of mere violence, relentlessly and, so it seems, definitively, re-shut.

This odd interregnum, a populist moment in a paternalist system, was made possible by the Monarchy's practice, inherited from the Protectorate and further perfected, of using municipal elections as a form of public opinion polling—*sondage*. Elections are, in general, controlled, but at each one, certain places are allowed a more or less free rein in order to bring political realities into open view. How does the land lie? Who must be dealt with? The next time, this relative freedom disappears and other places get a chance to have a less fettered vote. In 1976, it was Sefrou's turn to experience sondage democracy. In 1983, the experiment was over, and the Sefrou elite was thrust bodily back into office. Not a single Socialist was returned. The party collapsed as a local force. Its main leaders left the city.

But however brief and however beset by utopianism, factionalism, and civil service foot-dragging (but not by Marxist ideology, which played little or no role), the Socialist interlude brought the question of what sort of city Sefrou should be into heightened relief. The displacement of the Real Sefroui *a'yān* notability, the extension of the city boundaries (and thus of legitimacy and city services) to include the Outsider Sefroui settlements, and the vigorous attempt on the part of the council to increase its freedom of action vis-à-vis the central administrative apparatus (that is, to weaken la tutelle), challenged not just traditional privileges and traditional exclusions, but also, if inadvertently, the idea of the Islamic City within whose frame such privileges and such exclusions were defined. Setting out to make a local social revolution, an enterprise in which they more or less totally failed, the Socialist "new men" made, rather against their own inclinations, at least the beginnings of a cultural one. They left the material economy about as they found it. They left the symbolic economy—the figuration of city space—thoroughly transformed.

What the Socialist interruption interrupted was neither the directions of change that had, well before its advent, gripped the city, and which continue to advance now that it is over, nor the structure of social inequality that, even during its tenure, sharpened and solidified. It interrupted the way in which these directions and inequalities were represented and perceived. By enfranchising the Outsider population, not just legally (which, in a traditionalist tutelle state, does not matter all that much) but morally (which, in such a state, especially if it is Muslim, matters a very great deal) the Socialists reinforced both the in-migrants' determination to be included within the body of the city and inscribed in its landscape; and, perhaps even more powerfully, the Real Sefrouis' determination to set the criteria—lifestyle criteria in the first instance, attitudinal, in the second—upon which such inclusion rests. It is the clash of those determinations (what are the signs of mudaniyya now?) that has become the nerve of social struggle.

IV

Shortly before the double celebration I mentioned earlier of his quarter century as king and his decade as Saharan commander, Hassan II gave a speech in his palace at Marrakech—broadcast on the state radio and television—to the association of Moroccan architects and city planners: "un véritable cours d'architecture et d'urbanisme," as the royalist newspaper *Le Matin du Sahara* had it.

Morocco has been marked at each great period in its history, he said, by an architectural originality. One recognizes immediately the monuments and buildings of the Idrisi, Almoravid, Almohad, Sa'adi, and 'Alawi periods. Each dynasty (the first of these, semi-mythical, is 8th century A.D. and supposedly the period when Islam arrived and Fez was founded; the last is Hassan's own, which arose in the 17th century) has stamped its epoch with its style. Now, however, a decline has set in. All sorts of ill-designed and ill-constructed buildings are appearing haphazardly around our ancient cities. Garish European-style houses, vulgar and ostentatious, are proliferating in the wealthy quarters. The classic form of the Moroccan Islamic city, the flower of our cultural greatness, is disappearing into a nondescript, alien sprawl.

For example, he said, take Sefrou. Not long ago it was a lovely little place, with its gardens, its walls, its mosques nestled at the foot of the Middle Atlas— a beautiful expression (he called it a jewel) of the authentic Moroccan tradition. Now it had become shapeless and ugly (*laide*, though he was speaking Arabic). Faced with the prospect of a doubling of our housing capacity by the year 2000, it is necessary to construct "Moroccan for the Moroccans." We must give to our works a national character; preserve, amidst modernization, that which is beautiful and authentic; conserve (as apparently Sefrou has not) the spiritual identity, Muslim and Maghrebian at the same time, of Moroccan architecture and urban form. As the *Le Matin* report pointedly concludes: "One understands from this that His Majesty, Hassan II, whose reign is one of the most glorious and the most productive of our History, wishes to leave his mark, as brilliantly as he has politically and economically, through an original architecture, modern and authentically Moroccan, in a word through an architecture."

The King's *cours*, singling out Sefrou before the entire country as an egregious case of un-Moroccan, un-Islamic urban blight, shook, as might be imagined, the reinstalled royalist city council quite severely, especially as it was followed almost immediately by an official reprimand and a command to "do something" by Accession Day from the provincial governor at Fez. But, in fact, it merely brought to a boil a process of cultural confrontation already well underway in the city.

The dismay of the Real Sefrouis at the city's physical transformation had grown to enormous proportions during the Socialist period, producing a litany of moral complaint, class resentment, and aesthetic nostalgia; a self-conscious effort to recreate the institutions of a properly Muslim city was begun. The traditional office of *muḥtasib*, a sort of combination religious preceptor, moral policeman, and market administrator, once extremely powerful but fallen into almost complete disuse, was restored to political prominence in 1982 during the bitter struggle that returned the old guard to power. A long-time traditionalist leader (and, as an 'Alawi sharif, a distant relative of the king) was appointed to it, and promptly indicted the Socialists as "atheists." A very large, classically styled mosque—built by the state and called the Hassan II—was completed just outside the walls, replacing the old grand mosque (which was itself refurbished) in the medina as the official city mosque, and the muhtasib was also designated as its Friday sermon-giver. Other classically Muslim offices—the *nāẓir*, administrator of religious properties; the *qāḍī*, religious judge; the *'ādel*, notary; the *muqqadem*, quarter chief; the *amīn* craft head—were similarly reemphasized as canonical features, signs if you will, of a genuinely Islamic city. Public baths, public ovens, neighborhood prayer houses, market fountains, and other traditional civic institutions were renovated, and an outburst of rather demonstrative private mosque building by leading notables occurred.

At the same time as this cultural, or religiocultural, revivalism was developing on the Real Sefroui side (and much of it was essentially cosmetic—the muhtasib's power over moral or economic life is marginal at best; religious courts are very restricted in scope; craft heads are advisory elders, not guild chiefs), a counter-assertion, in a vocabulary at once similar and rather different, was taking place on the Outsider Sefroui side.

The Outsiders' self-assertion as authentic city people (*madanī*), their determination to move from the margins to full inclusion in urban society grew steadily more intense, and was fed by the Socialists' reach toward them, their swelling numbers, and their sense of being treated as barbarian intruders, morally unwelcome and materially neglected. (The term they usually use to indicate their move from the country to the city is not the Real Segrouis' exode rural, which makes them sound like tattered refugees, but *hijra*, the Arabic at once for emigration and immigration, and, of course, for the Prophet's move from Mecca to Medina that inaugurated the Muslim Era.) And this determination, the determination to complete their hijra, is also most emphatically expressed in an architectural idiom, a rhetoric of mosques and houses and, most especially—and most surprisingly—façades.

Façades are surprising or, perhaps at the deeper level of embodied meaning toward which we are reaching, unsurprising, because, as has often been remarked, classical medina houses are turned radically inward. They present to the public streets and alleyways a uniform and (a chastely decorated door occasionally aside) extremely subdued face: whitened walls and small, grilled windows well above eye-level. It is in interior courts, gardens, and reception rooms, brocaded women's quarters, mosaic fountains, and carpeted tea salons, that status display takes place. From outside, a rich man's home and a poor one's look hardly different; within, they contrast as a palace to a hovel in their decorations, furnishings, and use of space. Certainly, this is true in Sefrou; not only in the Medina proper, where there are virtually no external markings at all and a street looks like a solid wall, irregularly punctured with narrow entryways, but in the immediate extramural quarters as well, where one does not know (at least if one is a stranger) prior to entry whether one will be confronted by a cave or a jewel box. And it is this, perhaps the most charged domain, certainly the most intimate, of urban imagery that the Outsiders in their sprung-up suburbs have completely reversed. They have turned the city house, semiotically, inside out.

The houses the Outsiders have built are, as mentioned, mostly substantial stone and concrete structures, many of them quite large and arranged haphazardly, given their "illegal," thus opportunistic siting, along rutted paths and tracks. Within, most of them are strikingly bare. Indeed, they are often virtually empty—large spaces with but an isolated bed or a forlorn table and chairs. Most of their owners' capital is sunk in the structure itself and in the hyper-inflated land on which it is built, and the absence of city services (water, electricity, sewage, roads) in any case limits what can be done: there are no reflecting pools or back-lit divans here. It is on the exterior walls that display occurs. Almost all these houses are very brightly painted in bold, primary colors—reds, yellows, greens, blues, even now and then purples, oranges, and pinks—garishly intermixed, and a great many are further decorated, sometimes in an all-over fashion, with designs based on traditional craft motifs—especially ones taken from carpets and textiles, and to some degree from potter, leather work and female face-tattoos.

The general term for these flamboyant façades (which, as they tend to be four-walled, are perhaps more exactly referred to as envelopes) is the French *fantasia*, the term used for the famous horsemanship and powder-play displays of tribal Moroccans; like those displays, they are public demonstrations of individual force. They are, as everyone recognizes, both the Outsiders, who produce them, and the Real Sefrouis, who wish to erase them, statements: claims, announcements, arguments, demands.

The edict that the façades were to be painted over in civilized beige was thus more than the council's response to the necessity to "do something" visibly and quickly before Accession Day. It was a move in what has become a quite self-conscious politics of signs.

Turning their houses inside-out, the Outsiders seemed to threaten to turn Sefrou as a whole inside-out; to make its colored peripheries, not its decayed core, its defining feature. The aesthetic and moral reaction by the Real Sefrouis to the façades as offenses against mudaniyya was, if anything, more passionate than their concern with the intruders' material claims, which they felt able enough to hold at bay. Where the Socialists had sought to accommodate the Outsiders' demands for inclusion in urban society by legally incorporating them into the municipality, the notables sought to make them—now that they were, alas, so included—at least look like proper urbanites. Sefrou, the council said, should be "The Beige City," as, say, Marrakech was "The Red City."

The upshot was, in fact, a bit of a compromise. Most of the Outsiders did paint over their houses (the peripheries changed color almost overnight), in exchange for an implicit recognition of them as proper urbanites, entitled to proper municipal services such as water, roads, electricity and the like, not illegal squatters who ought to be (and occasionally have been) bulldozed away.

This compromise in deference to the king, if that's the proper word for it ("bargain" might be a better one), has hardly ended the confrontation. It has merely moved it onto a new plane of discourse, one in which the issues are represented as being between various interests within the city, not between it and aliens gathered along its edges. This can be seen in a remarkable letter in the Istiqlal Party newspaper, *Al-'Alam*, dated February 15, 1988, from a resident of Sefrou's largest, fastest growing, and most energetic peripheral settlement, Dhar bin Seffar.

One of the most astounding things is the scarcity of drinkable water in Sefrou, though it lies at the foot of the Middle Atlas. This fact is one of the paradoxes that leave the observer in perplexity trying to answer a clamor of questions. We do not need to remind our citizens of what the Atlas Mountains represent for Morocco in general as a reservoir of water for our country.

Here we reach the subject of this correspondence, which we publish on behalf of the families living in the quarter Bin Seffar, who request, through it, that the big problem of drinkable water be attended to and that the needs of about 2,500 people be met.

This quarter does not have more than a single fountain, toward which its inhabitants rush early in the morning in order to grasp a few drops of its watery generosity [*jūd*].

We do not speak here of the long lines, of the long waiting, of the fights that arise among the waiting people . . . .

What the residents are asking for is for the opportunity of benefiting from the drinkable water to be given to all without discrimination, especially as it has been observed that those in charge of the distribution favor certain sides [factions, parties] against others. That is clear from their giving the privilege of obtaining water to some residents and neglecting the others.

The residents of the quarter request from the members of their municipal council, who poured promises upon them during the election campaign [against the Socialists], to stop this favoritism and consider all the residents as equals, no difference between this one and that one, but only in light of his acts in the service of the general interest.

What these humble people request is nothing more than the simplest of human rights: just some water to quench their thirst, and they will not upset [alarm, threaten] anyone! They want only water . . . !?

V

The sovereign division in Western thought between Meanings and Materialities is, like the very similar and derivative one between soul and body, perhaps overdue for retirement, certainly for revision. Meanings of any value in human life are inevitably sunk in materialities. Materialities that bear on that life in some practical way inevitably do so within a webwork of sense and expression. "Symbol" versus "reality," "form" versus "content," "the world as experienced" (perceived, interpreted, understood) versus "the world as thing" (object, cosmos, causal manifold) are hardly more useful for framing accounts as to how matters stand with the "Islamic City" than is "mind" versus "matter." A "figure of space" (to adopt a phrase of Steven Mullaney's about Elizabethan London) in which "topography tends to recapitulate ideology," and ideology to transform topography into a "legible emblem," an "icon of community," a "social text," the "Islamic City" would seem not easily divisible into its force as a sign and its significance as a force.

Though local in its impact and parochial in its concerns, the struggle in Sefrou between 1976 and 1986—over different concepts of how a city should look, how and by whom it should be governed, who should live in it, what its life should be, where its center should lie, its expanse be segmented, its boundaries be placed—was nevertheless part of a far more general process with far wider implications. Not only are the images of "cityhood" "citadinité" and "mudaniyya," around which dispute pivoted, widely distributed throughout the Middle East, but the effort to rework the landscape of urban life so as to give it anew an intelligible form is also part and parcel of the similar reworking, now almost everywhere evident, of the umma's understanding of the *toutes directions* world in which it is these days enmeshed. Reading the signs in urban sprawls (something nearly as difficult for the inhabitants of them as it is for external observers) is a necessity for anyone who would not get lost in them, left adrift—baffled, clumsy, angry, and powerless.

To change the face of a city (or the façade of a house) is to change the way those who live in it understand it and to put under pressure the cultural frames by which they have been used to understanding it and the terms of which they have been used to living in it. Auden's famous phrase about "a new form of architecture / a change of heart" is more than a poetic figure. What is happening to the "Islamic City"—and not just in Sefrou—is what is happening to "Islam." It is losing definition and gaining energy.

On Feminism

I

The intrusion, advance, spread, import, insinuation—word choice is important here, exposing world views, projecting fears—of feminist thought into just about every aspect of contemporary cultural life is by now entirely general. Literature, philosophy, sociology, history, economics, law, even linguistics and theology, are engulfed in fierce and multisided debates over the relevance of gender difference, gender interest, and gender prejudice to this or that issue or to the shape of the enterprise overall. But nowhere has the reaction to efforts to move such concerns to the center of attention stirred deeper disquiet than in that last redoubt of impersonal reason, natural science. Sexing science, or even scientists, makes everyone, even those most passionate to accomplish it, extremely nervous.

The worry is, of course, that the autonomy of science, its freedom, vigor, authority, and effectiveness, will be undermined by the subjection of it to a moral and political program—the social empowerment of women—external to its purposes. A physicist determining the spin of a particle, a neurologist tracing the circuitry of vision, or an evolutionist isolating the mechanisms of phyletic change is likely to find such pronouncements as "a sexist society should be expected to develop a sexist science" or "science . . . is not sexless; she is a man, a father and infected too" to be silly at best, lunatic at worst, and in either case deeply threatening to the centuries of long struggle to examine the workings of nature free of the distortions of wish and prejudice.[1] Objectivity—logic, method, knowledge, truth—is what science is about; the rest is romance and special pleading.

Unfortunately, or fortunately, depending upon where one's loyalties lie (and both unfortunately and fortunately if, as is increasingly the case, one's loyalties

---

Originally published as "A Lab of One's Own," *New York Review of Books* 37, no. 17 (8 November 1990). Books under discussion therein are as follows: Nancy Tuana, editor, *Feminism and Science*; Londa Schiebinger, *The Mind Has No Sex? Women in the Origins of Modern Science*; and Donna Haraway, *Primate Visions: Gender, Race, and Nature in the World of Modern Science*.

are divided), this radical contrast, inherited from the ancients, between "knowl-edge" (episteme) and "opinion" (doxa) has been breaking down, not merely as between "science" and "non-science," but, more fatefully, within "science" it-self, for at least thirty years. Thomas Kuhn's enormously influential *The Struc-ture of Scientific Revolutions*, first published in 1962, with its reconceptualiza-tion of scientific change as consisting in an episodic succession of professional dominant thought frames rather than a step-by-step advance toward reality, truth, and the cloudless vision, is usually considered the watershed work. But since Kuhn's book appeared, there have arisen, one hard upon the next, a series of even more headlong revisionisms. In the sociology of science there has been a so-called strong program, determined to examine science as through and through a social and cultural phenomenon, like capitalism, the papacy, astrol-ogy, football, or easel painting. In the history of science there has been a stress on "who is to be master," in which power struggles among research groups, institutional interests, organizational imperatives, disciplinary elites, profes-sional reputations, and policy concerns are seen as shaping the evolution of scientific thought. In philosophy there has been "antifoundationalism," the rejection of fixed "methods," permanent "principles," and inherent "essences" in favor of multiple perspectives, intellectual genres, language games, rhetori-cal styles, and practical outcomes. Pluralism, contingency, pragmatism, ma-neuver. If it is not the case that "anything goes," at least many things do, and none of them is beyond remark.

This movement toward what is most often termed a "social constructionist" conception of science has hardly gone unresisted by those for whom "the world" or "nature," "the way things actually are," is the beginning and end when it comes to knowing. (Alasdair MacIntyre, the moral philosopher and general objector to how we think now, has announced that he won't rest until the last proponent of the strong program is strangled in the entrails of the last expert in the theory of metaphor.)[2] But as it has gained momentum, amounting by now to something of an avalanche, this general movement has cleared the way and provided the model for feminist criticism. If, like everything else cultural—art, ideology, religion, common sense—science is something ham-mered together in some place to some purpose by partisans and devotees, it is, like everything else cultural, subject to questioning why it has been built in the way that it has. If knowledge is made, its making can be looked into.

Feminist looking, still tentative, limited, and internally troubled, has, since perhaps the mid-Seventies, been driven forward by a critical (and also much debated) bit of social constructionism within feminist thought itself: the dis-tinction of gender from sex—of what it is culturally to be "a woman," "a man," "a gay," "a lesbian," or whatever from what it is biologically to be "female," "male," "hermaphrodite," or whatever.[3] If "woman" and "man" are historically situated social categories, like "black" or "Norwegian" or "communist" or "middle class"—or like "astronomer" or "gynecologist"—then asking whether science is "a man," or anyway "masculine" (the mode word now—Virginia Woolf would have hated it—is "androcentric") is no more unreasonable than to ask whether football or the papacy are masculine. It may, however, be a good deal harder to answer.

II

The uneven and extremely miscellaneous collection of papers, originally published in a journal of feminist philosophy called *Hypatia* and brought together as a sort of progress report by Nancy Tuana, manages to touch on most of the matters impeding an answer to the questions I have posed without getting very far toward resolving any of them. Framed by nervous, questioning titles ("Is There a Feminist Method?" "Can There Be a Feminist Science?" "Is the Subject of Science Sexed?" "Is Sex to Gender as Nature Is to Science?" "Where Are We Now and When Can We Expect a Theoretical Breakthrough?"), the book is an anthology of dilemmas, conundrums, puzzlements, and worries, which, taken together, give an arresting picture of great intellectual commotion without much in the way of a definitive sense of where it is that it might be heading.

Part of the problem is simply the multiplicity of concerns gathered together under the feminism-and-science rubric. Sue V. Rosser, in her opening "overview," a cascade of names, citations, and one-line summaries, lists six: the transformation of training methods and academic curricula to attract more women into the sciences; the historical understanding of the obscured and denigrated role of women in the development of modern science; the sociological investigation of the current status (improving, but still disadvantaged) of women in science; the feminist critique of male-biased scientific enterprises (sociobiology, brain research, intelligence testing, biochemistry); "feminine science" (Do women—Barbara McClintock, Rosalind Franklin—do science differently from men?); and "feminist theory of science" (Is objective, "gender-free" science possible? Is its pretense a sham?). Six, seven, ten, or a dozen—it hardly matters: this is not a field, or even a program. It's a tumble of possibilities out of which something or other may somewhere come.

That in itself is perhaps only to be expected in an enterprise that is, as Rosser rightfully insists, just now getting seriously under way. But the diffusion of aim and the tone of bafflement that accompanies it ("How do you speak to scientists?" "What do we mean by truth? What can we possibly mean?") do not spring merely from growing pains; they arise from deep intractabilities buried within the task as such. Putting together a critique of the fictions and illusions surrounding "womanhood" and a mode of knowing claiming to "[limn] the true and ultimate structure of reality" poses rather more problems than moralized and power-conscious "emancipatory theory," the saving hope of all these essays, can easily meet.[4]

In the best of the essays, this sense of impasse is everywhere apparent. Sandra Harding's examination of the question whether there is, as a number of people have suggested, a distinctive feminist method of research (consciousness-raising, organismic thinking) that can be used as a criterion to judge the adequacy of research designs, procedures, and results—a question to which she answers a resounding, well-argued "no"—ends with an apology to her colleagues for disappointing them in this matter and a suggestion that they give up trying to regrind "the powerful lenses of scientific inquiry" and console themselves with the more practical task of swinging them around to feminist concerns.

Helen Longino, asking the even broader question of whether there can be a feminist science in any sense at all, also offers a doubled answer: "no," if by feminist science is meant an "expression and valorization of a female sensibility or cognitive temperament"—complex, interactive, holistic, and "soft"—for there is no such sensibility or temper; "yes," if the social conditions—"the making of money and the waging of war"—under which science is now being prosecuted by the androcentric powers-that-be are changed to something less thrusting, manipulative, instrumental, and "hard." Here, too, one can eat one's cake as a detached scientist and have it as a partisan. "While remaining committed to an abstract goal of understanding," to "the science one has learned and practiced," we can choose "to whom . . . we are accountable in our pursuit of that goal, . . . to the traditional establishment or to our political comrades."

This formulation—Curie in the lab, Sanger in the agora—seems a bit easy, and in the most searching, and the most tangled, piece in the volume, Evelyn Fox Keller is unwilling to settle for it. Though engaged in the same enterprise as Harding and Longino—separating the defensible idea of a feminist science from the chimera of a feminine one—Keller, author of a much discussed biography of the Nobel prize winner Barbara McClintock, *A Feeling for the Organism*, resists the notion that the separation is to be made by dividing science into its technical and its moral parts, into methods, which are gender free, and their deployments, which are not.[5]

Keller wants to affirm both the autonomy of science as an account of "nature" and the force of "gender ideology" in shaping that account. Caught between feminist interpretations of her McClintock study as a manifesto for an alternative, "female science," and arguments from working scientists that, since many male scientists have "a feeling for the organism," McClintock's sex is irrelevant to her work, Keller wants to find a "middle ground" from which she can avoid so polarized a choice. But her efforts to do this involve such a tortuous string of on-the-one-hands and on-the-others ("science does not and cannot mirror nature"; "it [is] necessary to shift the focus . . . from sex to gender"; "neither nature nor sex can be named out of existence") that the best she can come up with is imagined discourse:

> We need a language that enables us to conceptually and perceptually negotiate our way between sameness and opposition, that permits the recognition of kinship in difference and of difference among kin; a language that encodes respect for difference, particularity, alterity without repudiating the underlying affinity that is the first prerequisite for knowledge.

Intractability and impasse, the feeling of not knowing which way to turn, stays, behind the brave front of new codes and symmetric expressions, rather firmly in place.

III

Quite possibly, the way out of this wilderness of question marks lies not in waiting expectantly for a Theoretical Breakthrough, but in describing what happens when the imaginings of gender and those of science actually encounter one another in salons, guilds, schools, and academies. This is what Londa Schiebinger does in her fine account of the vicissitudes of women scholars in the scientific revolutions of the seventeenth and eighteenth centuries. Her book is neither a "compensatory history," countering a "great man" story with a "great woman" one, nor a "different voice" plea for the celebration of female intellect; nor is it but another somber chronicle of male injustice. It is a beautifully detailed portrayal, alternately amusing, astonishing, dismaying, and painful, of "how real men and women participated in [early modern] science" and what difference it made—to them, to science, and to our general idea of sexual difference. Feminism put to work.

Schiebinger's general strategy is not as such particularly original. Like most intellectual historians these days, of science, literature, or anything else, she places both thinkers and their ideas within the social setting—she calls it "the institutional landscape"—in which they appear, get noticed or ignored, are taken up and celebrated or discounted and driven toward the margins of serious life. The tendency in early modern science to make women and their work peripheral, to constrain them within very narrow circuits of thought and reputation, was something some people (mostly, but not exclusively, men) did and other people (not always unwillingly) suffered. "The persistent effort to distance science from women and the feminine" was just that: an effort. "Science was itself part of the terrain that divided the sexes."

Schiebinger begins her mapping of this terrain with a survey of the status of women in the institutions—national universities, Renaissance courts, Enlightenment salons, royal academies, artisan guilds—within which early modern science arose. The universities, recently evolved from medieval monasteries, were, the Italian ones in part aside, completely closed; the courts, their martial swagger set off with humanist learning, were a bit more open, but only as after-dinner conversation shops for philosophical ladies; the salons were run by clever and ambitious women, but mainly in the service of male careers; the academies, except again, and again in part, for the Italians, did not elect women. In the guilds women could engage in a certain amount of underlaborer science—anatomical modeling, plant sketching, calendar making—but received little in the way of credit for it.

It is something of a wonder that female scientists existed at all. It is even more remarkable that those who did were impressive enough to induce redoubled efforts to keep them firmly away from the center of things. "Being a Woman," Margaret Cavendish, the duchess of Newcastle, a "natural philosopher" in the vein of Hobbes, Gassendi, and Descartes, and located by marriage at the edge of their circle, wrote in 1663, ·

> [I] Cannot . . . Publickly . . . Preach, Teach, Declare or Explane [my works] by Words of Mouth, as most of the Famous Philosophers have done, who thereby made their Philosophical Opinions more Famous, than I fear Mine will ever be . . .

The rest of the book consists, then, in a tracing of the efforts of able women (Cavendish herself, who was something of a pistol, the physicist, and *amie de Voltaire*, Madame du Châtelet, the quietist etymologist Maria Merian, the craft astronomer Maria Winkelmann) to get, if not famous, at least anyway properly recognized, and the mounting obstacles thrown in their path by the heightening of sexual contrast, the growing acceptance of a masculine image of science, and, most critically, the triumph, by the time of Kant, Comte, and Claude Bernard of "complementarian," separate spheres—men are thinkers, women helpmates—view of gender relations.

The story is neither simple nor without its surprises and ironies. There are male naturalists attacked by lady salonnières for femininity of style; women anatomists constructing female skeletons with reduced skulls, exaggerated pelvises, and ostrich necks; passionate rationalists going on about women's "beautiful understanding" which "can leave Descartes's vortices to whirl forever without troubling itself about them"; royal astronomers turning their sisters into trained and adoring "puppy-dog" assistants; botanical dons questioning the seriousness of women amateurs or "those men who resemble women"; male feminists urging women scientists to ground their work in "practical matters"; female feminists urging them to remain unmarried. Schiebinger moves through this harlequin material with authority, fairness, and appropriate scorn, and she proves her case:

> Science and femininity share an intimate history, shaped as they both have been by similar social, political, and economic forces. By burying gender in science, European culture lost part of its past.

IV

But that was then, and this is now. To see the workings of gender in the making of science, and the workings of science in the making of gender, as they proceed these days, when it is not so much salons and academies, or even universities, as research teams, invisible colleges, mass media, think tanks, large machines, and state agencies that form the "institutional landscape" of science, it is necessary, perhaps, to have a well-defined case of a recently evolved and rapidly changing field, which strikes a chord in the culture and is receptive to women. For this, primatology, the systematic study of apes and monkeys, is virtually ideal; a sheer gift for someone, like the critical biologist cum cultural historian Donna Haraway, whose aim it is to monitor the traffic between images of nature and ideologies of sex.

All the ingredients are there. In the first place, though fascination with non-human primates stretches back to at least the eighteenth century (when Monboddo thought orangutans could play the harp and Buffon sketched them erect with walking sticks), systematic empirical inquiry—taxidermy, laboratory colonies, field studies, cinematography—really starts in earnest only in the 1920s and 1930s, and mainly in the United States. Its history is visible. Second, the "monkeys is the craziest people" similarity of chimps, gorillas, baboons, and so on to ourselves in looks and behavior gives them enormous popular force as images of the not-quite-human: unsettling near-men, comical, childish, primitive, lewd, who leave us uncertain whether to put them in cages or teach them language. Third, the evolutionary cousinship of monkeys, apes, "fossil men," and human beings makes the description of simian physiology, psychology, and social life seem, to the hard Darwinian, the ground plan of our own, a baseline sketch of what it is, *in esse* and generically, to be a "Man." And fourth, for a number of reasons not altogether clear (its late appearance? the need for husband and wife teams in field research? its upper-class ambiance? its back-to-nature tone?), women have become unusually prominent in primatology—some indeed, Jane Goodall, Dian Fossey, world-famous.

Haraway, who in addition to being a biologist and a historian also aspires to a prophetical role, sweeps into all this laying about her with great abandon— "Monkeys and Monopoly Capitalism," "Teddy Bear Patriarchy," "Apes in Eden, Apes in Space," "Women's Place Is in the Jungle" are some of the chapter headings—in a prose style that seems to have been gathered from the sky. But in the end, in four hundred pages that might better have been half that, she manages to raise, in one way or another, most of the relevant issues (and nearly as many that are not so relevant) and construct a warts-and-all account of the formation of a science amid the push-and-shove of modern culture. Not everything in *Primate Visions* is either true or fair, and a lot of it is outright odd. Yet, however diffusely, the story gets more or less told; however oracularly, it generally informs. What is surprising is how conventional a story, under the postmodern gloss and the barricade sloganizing, it turns out to be.

The plot is essentially linear and thoroughly whiggish. In the 1920s and 1930s primatology was complacently patriarchal, with its great white hunters and stuffed gorillas, breeding colony laboratories and sexological field studies. In the immediate postwar period, the extraordinarily rapid expansion of paleoanthropological fossil-man studies in Africa, the rise of the so-called "New Physical Anthropology," and, a bit later, the appearance of sociobiology (plus a certain amount of advanced grantsmanship and celebrity making), set in place a scientifically armored image of "Man the Hunter" that swept all before it. In the past decade or two, women primatologists, most of them trained in one or another of these enterprises but increasingly animated by feminist concerns, have begun to resist the peremptoriness of all this and move the field in more enlightened, and less settled, directions. Not up from the ape. Up from masculinism and the single view.

It is, in any case, not the plot, but what it tells us about how we think about things, and how wrong we are in doing so, to which Haraway would have us attend. And it is here that her work will most provoke those for whom science is reality-driven and everything else is something else—ideology, folklore, poetry, metaphysics—for she denies any fundamental distinction in kind between what is said in the dry, "this-is-your-captain-speaking" voice of disciplinary expertise and what is said in the charged, all-too-human tones of the general culture. According to Haraway, the "discursive fields" within which primatology formed—public museums, university laboratories, experimental field stations, jungle safaris, academic summit meetings, National Geographic Society television specials, space shots, East African fossil sites, textbooks, popular tracts, press reports, science fiction, Tarzan movies—determine what it is as much as its methods, its theories, or its factual claims:

Monkeys and apes, and human beings as their taxonomic kin, exist on the boundaries of . . . many struggles to determine what will count as knowledge. Primates are not nicely boxed into a specialized and secured discipline or field. . . . Many kinds of people can claim to know primates, ... [and the] boundary between technical and popular discourse is very fragile and permeable. . . .

Some of the interesting border disputes about primates, who and what they are (and who and what they are for), are between psychiatry and zoology, biology and anthropology, genetics and comparative psychology, ecology and medical research, laboratory scientists, conservationists and multinational logging companies, poachers and game wardens, scientists and administrators in zoos, feminists and anti-feminists, specialists and lay people, physical anthropologists and ecological-evolutionary biologists, established scientists and new Ph.D.'s, women's studies students and professors in animal behavior courses, linguists and biologists, foundation officials and grant applicants, science writers and researchers, historians of science and real scientists, marxists and liberals, liberals and neo-conservatives.

This is social constructivism with a vengeance. So broad a focus naturally makes for clutter and a general air of blur and distraction. Is there anything that does not relate? (Perhaps not: Haraway brings in the science fiction writer Octavia Butler's "xenogenic" fetus with "five progenitors . . . from two species, at least three genders, two sexes, and an indeterminate number of races," deep-reads a Hallmark greeting card showing a midget King Kong being sexually harassed by a gigantic blonde, and announces, "I have always preferred the prospect of pregnancy with the embryo of another species.") But more than that, it makes for the possibility of discussing a large number of matters at great length and vast detail without sustaining an argument or arriving at anything that resembles a determinate conclusion. Everything is flourish, irony, gesture, and suggestion.

This loose-limbed way with things is not without its advantages, some of which Haraway well exploits. Her description of the boy's-book atmospherics of the Africa Hall of New York's American Museum of Natural History, "dedicated," by the likes of J.P. Morgan, W.K. Vanderbilt, and Teddy Roosevelt, "to preserving a threatened manhood" in the face of "prolific bodies of . . . new immigrants" is a fine satiric turn. Her picture of infant monkeys huddled at the bottom of a stainless steel "well of despair" designed by the experimental psychologist Harry Harlow to "reproduce the. . . utter hopelessness [of] human depression" is an unforgettable image of scientific sadism. And her account of Sherwood Washburn's creation at Berkeley of a human origins program emphasizing the "ape-beneath-the-skin," with which about every important field anthropologist has at one time or another been associated, is a model example of how academic empires get built these days. But when it comes, eventually, to establishing her own thesis—"Primatology Is a Genre of Feminist Theory," a "Politics of Being Female"—her lack of method fails her. The genre doesn't appear, the politics remain unformed.

The fifteen or so women primatologists whose work Haraway reviews in some detail show hardly more in common than a tendency to be interested, among other things, in female animals, mothering, and sexual receptivity. One is concerned with sexual difference in time and energy budgets among baboons; another with reproductive strategies among female langurs; another with the importance among chimps of female gathering as against male hunting. Lemur intelligence, the emotional lives of gorillas, chimpanzee tool making, and the application of sociobiological notions of sexual competition to the evolution of womanhood all attract attention. Feminist primatology is "characterized by tensions, oppositions, exclusions, . . . not a series of doctrines, but a web of intersecting and frequently contradictory commitments."

So, indeed, is the whole of science. Haraway's account of "politics" comes to little more than a demonstration that women primatologists know one another, attend the same conferences, draw at times on one another's work—that is, form "networks." How these networks function, how they differ, if they do, from scholarly networks in general, and what effect their existence has on women primatologists' sense of themselves as scientists, remains obscure. Nor does there emerge some way of working and "discoursing" distinctive enough to look like a "genre" of anything, much less, as Haraway sometimes seems to suggest, a radical reworking of biology, anthropology, and our conception of nature. That may perhaps be the case. But it will take more than insistence to persuade the dubious to think so.

V

The feminist critique of science is clearly launched, and as clearly struggling. It seems unlikely either to melt away or turn everything upside down, but to become an abiding feature of intellectual life—ragged, various, and unignorable. Part of the scene.

Just how it will develop, which of the paths it has uncertainly set out upon will prove productive and which will run out into circular chatter, and even what subjects—the social status of women in science, the nature and significance of sexual difference, the role of gender in shaping inquiry—will turn out to be central is wholly unclear, and looks to remain so for a while to come. In the long meantime, the theoretical searching of Harding, Longino, and Keller, the artisan scholarship of Schiebinger, and the polemical vision building of Haraway exist, along with a number of other ventures, side by side, not so much clashing as looking warily across at one another and wondering, nervously, how it will all fall out.

How it will all fall out depends most critically on how the tension gets resolved between the moral impulses of feminism, the determination to correct gender-based injustice and secure for women the direction of their lives, and the knowledge-seeking ones of science, the no-less-impassioned effort to understand the world as it, free of wishing, "really is." No one, it seems, is anywhere near to doing that. But the issue is joined, and it will not soon disappear.

Indonesia: Starting Over

I

Indonesia has been one of the most remarkable development success stories in the last third of the twentieth century. In the mid-1960s, it was one of the poorest countries in the world, with a per capita income below that of many African and South Asian countries. It had experienced little economic growth for thirty years, it was on the verge of hyperinflation, it was engulfed in political turmoil, and it had begun to disengage from the world community and economy. Living standards were stagnant and about two thirds of the population lived in abject poverty. . . .

No one at that time would have dared to imagine—much less to predict—that just thirty years later Indonesia would be regarded as a dynamic "tiger" economy, and a member of that most exclusive club, the World Bank "East Asian Miracle Economies." The notion that Indonesia's economy would expand six-fold over this period, and that according to World Bank projections it could become the world's fifth-largest economy by the year 2020, would have appeared preposterous in the gloom of 1964-66. Yet that is precisely what has occurred in these three decades: economic growth has been among the highest in the world, and it has been accompanied, with a lag, by striking improvements in social indicators.

—Hal Hill, May 1997

[Very] suddenly and unexpectedly, everything collapsed [in Indonesia] in the latter half of 1997 . . . in the onslaught of the Asian financial crisis. The extent of the turnaround is nothing short of astounding. Economic output is expected to contract by about 15 percent, after expanding 8 percent in 1996 and 5 percent in 1997. The single-year

Originally published in the *New York Review of Books* 47, no. 8 (11 May 2000).

collapse in growth is among the largest recorded anywhere in the world in the post- World War period. Millions of Indonesians, many just surviving over the poverty line during the good times, have lost their jobs. Food production has been disrupted. . . . Prices for many export commodities. . . have fallen on world markets. Investors, both foreign and domestic, have fled to safer havens. The banking system is moribund and thousands of firms are facing the prospect of bankruptcy and closure.

—Steven Radelet, September 1998[1]

Since Indonesia's sudden reversal of fortune, globalism interrupted, a great deal more has happened there than capital flight, currency collapse, and a tripling of the poverty rate. The regime has changed twice—the regime, not just the government—once abruptly, in a spasm of violence, once glacially, with troubled and unnerving hesitation. The first time, in late 1998, Suharto, the architect, or anyway the godfather, of both the expansion and the collapse, walked away amid wild disorder—race riots, looting, bloody clashes between students and the army, Jakarta on fire, Surakarta ransacked—leaving B.J. Habibie, his just-appointed crony vice president, haplessly behind to sort through the ruins. The second time, a protracted, vastly complicated, ultimately indecisive, but, so it seems, fair and open national election (ninety million voters, forty-eight parties, seven hundred electors) ended last autumn with the midnight designation, by a half-dozen *arriviste* kingmakers, of Abdurrahman Wahid as the new president. An ill, erratic, nearly blind religious intellectual, he had been written off by almost everyone as too frail to serve.

In September, the ex-Portuguese enclave of East Timor, half of a very small island out on the edge of the archipelago, was at last allowed to separate after thirty years of on-again, off-again resistance to annexation, only to be laid waste by Indonesian-armed irregulars, whose savagery brought on a worldwide outcry, an Australian-led UN intervention, the human rights attentions of Mary Robinson, and, just possibly, a revanchist problem for the future. Local violence, some of it ethnic, some of it religious, some of it merely criminal or entrepreneurial, has broken out all over the archipelago, from Aceh and Kalimantan in the west to the Moluccas and New Guinea in the east, leaving hundreds dead, thousands in flight, the government at a loss, and the neighbors—Malaysia, Singapore, the Philippines, and Australia, who have minorities (and refugees) of their own who might like to see things generally rearranged—worried.

The army, its leadership divided and threatened with prosecution for war crimes in East Timor and elsewhere, is demoralized, resentful, disprivileged, cherishing enemies, weighing possible strategies. The press has been freed and reenergized: books are no longer banned. Suharto, ill and demonized, is housebound, as incommunicative as ever; and the country's most famous political prisoner, the radical nationalist novelist Pramoedya Ananta Toer, is out and about, giving interviews, accepting tributes, and counseling the youth. Oil looks good again, inflation is down, exports have recovered a bit, bankrupts are regrouping, growth has advanced to zero.

At the same time, militant Islam, NGO environmentalism, populist xenophobia, neoliberal utopianism, Christian apologetics, and human rights activism have all grown markedly in volume, visibility, and the capacity to bring on mass rallies, mobs, and marching in the streets. Factional party politics have returned with a vehemence and complexity not seen since the early Sixties, when Sukarno's "guided democracy," designed to keep him in power for life, collapsed in conspiracy and slaughter. It is a mixed and unsettled, fluctuating picture, without center and without edge—resistant to summary, hard to hold in place. As virtually everything has happened, it seems that virtually anything might; and it is impossible to tell whether all this stir and agitation—what the Indonesians, with their usual gift for verbal camouflage, have come to call *reformasi*—is the end of something or the beginning of something.

What it might be the end of is the political impulse that set the country in motion in the first place. Along with India, Egypt, and perhaps Nigeria, Indonesia has been a prototype of the "emerging," "developing," "post-colonial" country—crowded, splayed, capriciously bordered, and the product of a world-historical shift in the distribution of sovereignty, selfhood, and the power to act. Officially established at the end of 1949, after four years of intermittent warfare against the Dutch, and nearly forty of agitation before that, the country took shape during the heyday of third world nationalism—Nehru, Chou, Tito, Nkrumah, Mussadegh, Nasser; Dien Bien Phu, the Battle of Algiers, Suez, Katanga, the Emergency, the Mau Mau.

By now, this period—call it "Bandung," after the famous gathering of nonaligned, "emerging forces" leaders that Sukarno ("I am inspired . . . I am absorbed . . . I am crazed by the Romanticism of Revolution") staged there in 1955—is not even a living memory for most of the population. Its concerns are faded, its personalities simplified; the obsession that obsessed it, and to a fair extent subsidized it, the cold war, has been summarily called off. But the doctrines that were developed then, and the sentiments that accompanied them, continue to shadow the country's politics. A half-century old this coming winter, and just emerging from thirty-two years of business-card autocracy, Indonesia still projects itself as a triumphalist, insurgent, liberationist power.

The question that engages the more reflective Indonesians, and particularly the older ones who have been through it all and seen what it comes to, is of course how far this master idea, with its slogans, stories, and radiant moments, remains a living force among either the country's elites or its population, and how far it has become just so much willed nostalgia—declamatory, a pretense, worn, and seen through, cherished if at all by Western romantics and political scientists. Certainly the history of the country, which has tended to be one of grand promises and grander disappointments in quickening alternation— large plans, large collapses—would seem to militate against the continuing hold of Bandung-size expectations. Neither Sukarno's "old order" populism nor Suharto's "new order" paternalism (the differences between them have been much exaggerated by the partisans of both—their contrasts were mainly in style and presentation, and to some degree in disciplinary reach) was able to impress an identity and a transcending purpose on the society as a whole, to make of it an integral community, real or imagined.

"The Nationalist Project," the construction of an aroused and self-aware people moving as one toward spiritual and material fulfillment—"An Age in Motion," so the tag says—has become increasingly hard to formulate in be-lievable terms, much less to pursue and carry out. The shaken country that was delivered first, *faute de mieux*, to the unfortunate Habibie in the spring of 1998 (his presidency lasted seventeen months, plagued by confusion and scandal), and then, *in camera*, to the improbable Wahid, had lost more than its bank balance, its equilibrium, and its international reputation. It had lost the power of its history to instruct it.

II

The man who is expected to correct all this, to right its economy, calm its politics, restore its confidence, reset its course, clear its conscience, and im-prove its image, as well as, perhaps, to entertain and distract it, is a fifty-nine-year-old veteran politician whom virtually everyone seems to have met (in-cluding me: a decade ago, I spent four days closeted with him and a few of his allies in a rest house near Bandung discussing, no less, the future of Islam in Indonesian politics), most seem to have liked, and almost all seem to have underestimated.

Known universally as "Gus Dur," his honorific childhood nickname ("Gus" means "handsome lad"), Wahid was born and grew up at the very center of Javanist Islam and Javanist Islamic politics—his grandfather's famous religious boarding school, or *pesantren*, fifty miles southwest of Surabaya. His grandfa-ther, a personage and a personality, as well as a renowned Koranic scholar, founded the country's largest Muslim organization (it may, in fact, be the larg-est in the world), Nahdatul Ulama, in 1926—in part, at least, to counter the growth of secularist nationalism, and to strengthen the hold of vernacular piety against modernist innovations flowing out of the Middle East. The tolerant, open, somewhat traditionalist, somewhat inward "Javanese Islam" he represented continues to the present as a major social and religious force. Wahid's father, in the loose, inexplicit sort of way in which power is passed in the *pesantren* tradition, inherited the school, the stature, the program, and the organization; he was the country's first minister of religion, and a broker of consequence in Sukarno's ideological spoils system, distributing jobs to petitioners in the vast and shambling clerical bureaucracy that to this day regulates mosques, marriages, benefactions, and religious courts.

Wahid, after traveling, studying, and getting himself known in Cairo, Baghdad, and various countries in Europe for a while in the mid-Seventies, returned to become a widely read columnist at *Tempo*, the country's leading, and later suppressed, news magazine, and to found Forum Demokrasi, an elite ginger group whose criticisms of the establishment drove the government to near-murderous distraction. He also took over the reins of the Nahdatul Ulama organization, which he then promptly separated from the counterfeit political party ("Development and Unity") Suharto had concocted to contain it.

If close-up, been-through-the-mill experience, as well as patience, agility, humor, and a refined sense of timing, is what Indonesia needs, Gus Dur, who is the closest thing to a machine politician the country has, could be the man. Compared at various times to Peter Falk's Columbo, the Javanese shadow-play buffoon Semar, Chaim Potok's lapsed rabbi Asher Lev, Ross Perot, Yoda, and (by his defense minister) a three-wheel Jakarta taxi, Wahid would seem well equipped to weave his way through the densest sort of lunatic traffic.

That much, surely, he demonstrated in his oblique, arduous, and—when we consider what he had to overcome to undertake it—brave and tenacious trek to the presidency. When the electoral process (which was rather more of an enormous, and enormously complicated, straw poll designed to assess the general state of popular opinion than it was a proper selection mechanism) began in late 1998, Wahid was in the hospital, just beginning to recover from the second of the two diabetic strokes that had put him in a coma; he had already been damaged in one eye by diabetes, and blinded in the other. Aside from him, there were four leading candidates, thrown up by the convulsions of the previous two years, and off and running: Habibie, the sitting president, an establishment satrap trying desperately to look like a new broom; Megawati Sukarnoputri, Sukarno's daughter, a reclusive and taciturn, rather standoffish suburban matron, whom an unexpected and uncharacteristic series of strategic blunders on the part of Suharto had transmogrified into a popular hero; and Amien Rais, an ambitious and mercurial Muslim intellectual and sometime college professor who had studied theology and political science at

both Notre Dame and the University of Chicago and who had played a leading role in arousing the students in the last stages of Suharto's collapse. Then,
in the extra-party, shadow-state style of the Indonesian army, there was General Wiranto, its hesitant and unconfident and soon to be infamous chief of
staff.

Other suggestions and possibilities surfaced from time to time. Among them
were the Sultan of Yogyakarta; a Berkeley-trained neoliberal economist; the
head of Golkar (i.e. "Functional Group"), Suharto's parliamentary party and
political arm; and one of Wahid's oldest and, up to that point anyway, closest
friends. But for the whole eleven months the lumbering drama took to unfold
these five were the dominant players, and they remained so to and through its
quite operatic, vertiginous end.

For most of the campaign, indeed until a few half-hours before Wahid
squeezed his way in through the narrowest of spaces, the leading candidate, far
and away, was Megawati. Despite her heritage and the lingering charisma of
her father's name—particularly strong in Java, where power is supposed to
pass supernaturally and act thaumaturgically—she was a newcomer to Indonesian high politics, having lived the smooth and upholstered life of a society
wife until a spectacular collision with Suharto, which she had neither sought
nor wanted, and did not quite know what to do with once it occurred, turned
her overnight into the reluctant vehicle of popular outrage.

Seeking, apparently, to test the limits as the general, ill and recently be-
reaved of his wife, began to stumble a bit, one of his concocted political parties—"Indonesian Democracy," which was designed to contain the nationalist
left—installed Megawati as its titular head in December 1993. Suharto, to whom
she must have seemed like the ghost of insurgencies past, wildly overreacted,
trying forcibly to replace her with an army-backed puppet. When that failed,
leading to a breakaway of the party and the movement of university students
into the streets crying for Suharto's head and for his children's fortunes, he sent
soldiers and para-militaries to take over Megawati's Jakarta offices and arrest her
supporters. In July 1996, this produced what turned out to be the most consequential "affair" of his regime: thirty or so killed, a hundred-odd arrested,
scores of stores, houses, and vehicles burned. This, though no one knew it yet,
was the end of the beginning of the end of his rule. Megawati, startled and
swept along, was established as the people-power heir apparent, Indonesia's
version, culturally reedited, of Cory Aquino.

Despite the divine-right regality which never deserted her and in the end
undermined her, Megawati's campaign was an over-the-top, quasi-revivalist, in-
your-face affair: frenzied mass rallies, revolutionary symbolism, hypernationalist
sloganizing, and a certain amount of putsch-in-the-works and street-tough
threats—all of which may have frightened as many people as they attracted,

while scholars and journalists talked of civil war and the return of the repressed. Wahid, more or less recovered from the worst of his illness, formed a party of his own and set up an odd, on-again off-again, arms-length alliance with her.

The Islamic right, without a champion of its own or much of a program beyond moralism and xenophobia, attacked Megawati as not really a Muslim but some sort of Javanist Hindu, beholden to Christians and Chinese, possibly a crypto-Communist, and, anyway, a woman. She avoided the press, issued only the vaguest of policy statements (she had been against independence for East Timor and for a pegged rupiah, but she soon glided noiselessly away from these positions). She spoke, she said, with her dead father daily. In the event, after a half-year or so of this, she got a bit more than a third of the vote in the June 1999 elections for the National Assembly, which is convened every five years to designate a president. Habibie, who, ostensibly anyway, was Golkar's candidate and particularly strong outside Java, got a bit more than a fifth; Wahid and his party, whose appeal was localized, a bit more than a tenth; and Rais, who had been expected to do much better, given his popularity with educated Muslims and the Jacobin role he played in the last days of Suharto (whom he called, *inter alia*, "a rabid dog, biting everything," and volunteered to replace immediately), got something less than 8 percent. The stage was set for some serious politicking.

The details of the maneuvering, the alliances, the horse trades, the betrayals, the flatteries, the ear-whisperings, and the pirouettes that took place during the final three days of the "election"—i.e., the opening days of the National Assembly in October—remain, for the most part, both obscure and contested.[2] What is clear is that Megawati was out of her element, and Gus Dur was in the very thick of his. Unwilling, or unable, to cut deals and exchange favors, and apparently convinced that having roused the masses and "won" the election, she could not be denied, she lost every scrimmage at every stage, until in the end only Wahid, who had allied himself with just about everybody else in turn as the process unfolded, was left standing. (Rais, with Wahid's support, became head of the Assembly. Habibie's man in Golkar, a Sumatran named Akbar Tanjung, was induced to desert his boss and, with Wahid's support, became speaker of the Parliament. Wiranto, with Wahid's, as it turned out, retractable support, lobbied vigorously for the vice presidency.) "Wait until next time," Wahid is supposed to have told Megawati, kindly, one imagines: "You need more experience."

When Wahid's selection was announced on October 20, the reaction on the part of Megawati's supporters, who were as convinced as she was of her moral right to the presidency and the illegitimacy, deceitfulness, and corruption of everyone else, was enormous. Violence erupted all over the archipelago.

In Bali, where her campaign had begun and her support was perhaps the most passionate (she won 80 percent of the vote there), trees were felled across all the roads, a government office was burned, and youths attacked a dormitory where Timorese refugees were being held awaiting their repatriation. Plans were laid to attack the Muslim quarter, the so-called *kampong jawa*, which, had they been carried out, might well have convulsed the entire country. In Jakarta, a large downtown hotel where a huge crowd had gathered throughout the night to hear the outcome was immediately trashed, and angry protesters, weeping and screaming, spilled out into the city. It looked as if the promised civil war, or anyway a sidewalk coup, was at hand.

Wahid instantly changed course, turned away from Wiranto, and appointed Megawati as his vice president. He told her to go on radio and television and calm her followers, which she immediately did, saying, "I am your mother. You are my children. Return to your homes." And, in what, in some ways, was the most startling twist in the whole twisting drama, only slightly more startling than her acquiescence in her own eclipse, they promptly and efficiently obeyed—put away their placards, packed up their revolution, and walked quietly away. Bali was cleaned up in the course of a few hours; it was as though nothing at all had happened. Jakarta remained calm, if shaken. The eruptions elsewhere—in Surabaya, Medan, South Kalimantan, the off-coast islands of West New Guinea—soon fizzled out into scattered clashes. Whether all this was, as some began to call it, a move toward freedom, democracy, maturity, and the free market, or simply another turn in a very old wheel, there clearly was, at last and for the moment, a more or less legitimate, more or less open, more or less consensual government in place.

III

The great question remaining is, can the government in fact govern? Almost everything about the Wahid presidency, not just the President himself, breathes of the temporary, the ad hoc, the fragile, the jerry-built. Brought into existence by a thrown-together coalition of power brokers who have known one another too long and too well, confronted not by a single crisis but by a flood of them, and lacking very much in the way of either popular backing or a worked-out program, the new regime is reminiscent of nothing so much as those of the Naguibs, Barzagans, and Kerenskys of the world: distracted, scuttling, more or less well-meaning place-holders in a historical process preparing to run over them. Wahid, or his government, may turn out to be less evanescent than theirs, more consequential, or even more capable of defending its interests. That is at least one prospect insofar as one can speak yet of Wahid's actually having a government, as opposed to just a role (only a few of his cabinet members are his own choices; most are the result of what he himself called "a cattle auction" among the politicos who put him in power). It is clear by now that betting against Gus Dur is a bit of a mug's game. But he has, to put it mildly, a lot to do, and not much beyond his wits and, some say, his supernatural connections to do it with.

The problems facing him are diverse and urgent, each clamoring for immediate attention before they reach, severally or together, a point of no return. They cannot be listed as items for an agenda, because there is no way to put them into a logical sequence of importance and priority. But they fall, more or less, into three broad categories. First (but not, as foreign businessmen anxious to get back to foreign business tend to assume, necessarily foremost) there is the need to reignite the local version of the transnational economy that, between 1977 and 1997, added nearly $400 billion to the GDP, made a few people rich and a fair number middle class, and turned Jakarta, where upward of 70 percent of the activity was concentrated, into a forest of grandiloquent high-rises.

Second, there is the need to rein in and reprofessionalize the army, to halt and reverse the vast expansion of the functions and powers, legitimate, illegitimate, and outright criminal, that it achieved, first under Sukarno, who brought it into the world of commercial management when he dispatched the Dutch and confiscated their properties, then under Suharto, who fashioned it into a furtive para-government extending the hand of violence into the smallest and most distant corners of civil society. And third, there is the need to respond to an enormous increase in the power of regional, ethnic, racial, and religious forces, most of them not entirely new, entirely unified, or entirely clear in their aims, but all of them newly excited about their development possibilities now that the dominance of Jakarta has weakened and threatening to dismember the country and turn it into a Balkan nightmare.

When we try to sum up the Indonesian crisis in this compound, multiplex way, its most striking characteristic, the one that makes what happens there seem so broadly instructive, is that the immediate and the fundamental are thoroughly tangled up together. The restless surface—the street demonstrations, the regional killings—lies very close to the settled bottom—Muslim/Christian religious division, the political ascendancy of Java and the Javanese. The most pressing issues are at the same time the most far-reaching. Quick fixes, such as reallocation of revenue among regions, and lasting changes are so tightly linked that transient adjustments—a change of provincial boundaries, the dissolution of a government department—have general and enduring resonance. There is no small policy. Tactics are strategy, tinkering is planning, repair is reform, and however ad hoc and pragmatic particular actions may seem to be (and Gus Dur's are both, plus antic, mystifying, offhand, and unpredictable), they are responses to a good deal more than the fragility of the rupiah, the command structure of the army, or the stability of the outer provinces.

Whatever the fate of what some enthusiasts are already calling "the Wahid revolution" and others, less entranced, "what-the-hell-ism" (*biarin-isme*, for the cognoscenti), the path by which it arrives there, and what happens to it en route, should tell us a great deal about what can happen and what cannot, and not just in Indonesia or the post-heroic, post-colonial world, but in the dispersed, border-less, McDonaldized, and networked "global civilization" supposedly in the making.

So far as the revival of the neoliberal market economy is concerned—if that, amid the corruption, the waste, and the imaginative misuse of resources, is what it was in the first place—even the quick fixes and the transient adjustments are but scarcely begun. The relatively speedy recovery that the smaller "tigers," Thailand, Malaysia, Hong Kong, and South Korea, have experienced has as yet to take place in Indonesia, by far the largest among them. Unemployment is rising, production is flat, and there is little sign of a return of departed capital or departed capitalists, from wherever it is that it, or they, may now be resting, hiding, or beginning a new life.

But the deep-lying issues that any move toward recovery, however hesitant, however slight, immediately uncovers are already, not two hundred days into Gus Dur's term, subjects of heated, what-side-are-you-on political struggle. Every cabinet reshuffle, or rumor of one, every budget recalibration, however modest, every policy proposal, even the most technical or circumstantial—to allow a foreign bid on a state-seized company, to shift ministerial control over a bankrupted bank, to remove a Suharto-era businessman from his Suharto-era business, to renew a standing contract with an American mining company— gives rise to a loud, Aesopian debate which only seems to be about the matter at hand. The real division is over a deep and unresolved, possibly unresolvable, foundational question: How open, how borderless, how transnational an economy do we really want? How "global," how "developed," how "market rational" can we be, should we be, dare we be?

This may seem to be nothing more than the familiar opposition between those who see transparency, trade, and market freedom as the beginning, the middle, and the end of everything, and those who wish to replace what Sukarno fifty years ago called (just before he demolished it, and elections with it) "free fight liberalism" with policies more sensitive to cultural conscience and national feeling. But though free trade and protectionism, comparative advantage and import substitution, foreign capital and domestic ownership remain the poles between which the arguments and accusations move, the experience of the last thirty years has changed the sense of what is at stake in the debate.

Having known, now, both the joys and costs of extravagant market expansion and the pains and spin-offs of extravagant market collapse, the Indonesian elites, and a good part of the populace as well, are concerned less with trying to isolate the country from storms of "high," "late," "global," "footloose," or "advanced" capitalism than they are with enabling it to survive and move forward in the face of them.

There is, as the saying goes, no other option on offer than connecting the national economy to the IMF-WTO-Davos world being put together in the banks and boardrooms of New York, Tokyo, Frankfurt, London, Paris, and Geneva. The trick, if there is one, is somehow to ride out, even perhaps somehow to profit from, what no less a neoliberal than Paul Volcker has called the inevitable train wreck that occurs when grand, unregulated, high- velocity capital flows collide with weak and rickety national economies.[3] Economic nationalism still lives in Indonesia, so do "Asian values," and there are even some relics of the theory formerly known as Marxism lying about. But their promises of empowerment, authenticity, justice, and moral shelter, just yesterday so beguiling, ring increasingly hollow.

The same general picture, the persistence of familiar threats and the inadequacy of familiar remedies, appears in the other matters of immediate concern: the role of the army and the integrity of the state. So far as the army goes, the problem is simple enough on the surface—specifying its function and confining it to it. But after three decades during which local political capacity, the simple ability to manage one's own affairs through one's own institutions, melted away in the face of close-up and pervasive military control, that is not easy to do. The soldiers are dug in, and, in many places at least, removing them would remove as well whatever is left of a national presence and an enforceable order; and they have in any case, as East Timor demonstrated, very little willingness to accept restrictions.

So far as the state's integrity goes, the call to national unity in the name of a shared ideal seems to be a wasting asset. Whatever is going to hold the place together, if, in the face of population movements, regional imbalances, and ethnic suspicions, anything is, it is not going to be settled by an ingrained sense of common identity and historical mission, or by religious, "Islamic State" hegemony. It is going to be something a good deal more patchy, capricious, and decentered—archipelagic. In whatever direction Gus Dur looks with his one good eye there seems nothing to do but hang in there, try something, stay loose, hope for the best, and above all keep moving. Nothing if not mercurial, nimble and ingenious, and, blithely unaware, or unconcerned, that his position is impossible, he seems made for the moment, however long—it could be days or years—the moment lasts.

—*April 12, 2000*

On the Devastation of the Amazon

"This is the Brewer Explorer Survival knife," said Charlie, . . . "6 ¼-inch stainless steel blade, Rockwell Hardness 56–58; 2 ¾-inch saw extending from the handle towards the point; on the left here a 180-degree clinometer for calculating the height of mountains; on the right instructions for five ground-to-air signals. . . . [It] converts . . . into wire cutters. . . . It can also be made into a harpoon [and holds] six fish hooks, . . . nylon fishing line, two lead sinkers, one float, an exacto blade, two sewing needles, three matches, a flint stick and a suture needle with suture material attached. It's made by Marto of Toledo and imported into the US by Gutman at $150. But you and Simon can have one. It's good for skinning alligators. And when the Yanomami have had a go at you you can sew each other up round the arrow holes."
"The Yanomami?"
"Yeah. The most violent people on earth. Some anthropologists think they were the first people to reach South America from the North. They have very fair skins, occasionally green eyes. They are the largest untouched group of Indians left in the rainforest. The other Indians are terrified of them. My friend Napoleon Chagnon called his book on them *The Fierce People*—I'll give you a copy, and Jacques Lizot's too, *Tales of the Yanomami*. It's all perfectly understandable—they grow a few plantains, but basically they're hunter-gatherers and there's not much food in these forests. So when times are bad they kill the new-born girls; so there are never enough women to go round; so they fight over them. Within the tribe, in formalised duels, they hit each other over the head with ten-foot-long clubs. Outside the tribe they raid each other's

Originally published as "Life among the Anthros," *New York Review of Books* 48, no. 2 (8 February 2001). The book under discussion therein is as follows: Patrick Tierney, *Darkness in El Dorado: How Scientists and Journalists Devastated the Amazon*.

settlements for women and kill the enemy men with six-foot-long arrows tipped with curare. And on top of all that they've no concept of natural death, so if anyone dies from a fever it's the result of malign magic worked by an enemy shaman. Each death must be avenged."
I stood there stupidly, holding the enormous Brewer Explorer knife.
"And this still goes on?" I said, shaken.
"They are killing each other," said Charlie, "*right now.*"

—Redmond O'Hanlon[1]

Anthropologists have left an indelible imprint upon the Yanomami. In fact, the word *anthro* entered the Indians' vocabulary, and it is not a term of endearment. For the Indians, *anthro* has come to signify something like the opposite of its original Greek meaning, "man." The Yanomami consider an *anthro* to be a powerful non-human with deeply disturbed tendencies and wild eccentricities—an Olympian in a funk.

—Patrick Tierney[2]

Our land, our forest will only die off if the white man destroys it. Then the streams will vanish, the earth will become parched, the trees will dry up, and the rocks of the mountains will split with the heat. The xapiripë spirits who live on the mountains and play in the forest will run away. Their fathers, the shamans, will no longer be able to call them to protect us. The land-forest will become dry and empty. The shamans will no longer be able to deter the smoke-epidemics and the evil beings who make us fall sick. Thus, all will die.

—Davi Kopenawa Yanomami[3]

The Yanomami tribe in the [Amazonian] rainforest has always worried about losing its turf. But never has that battle involved a cyberspace incursion. The tribe is fighting a Florida woman who has claimed the name Yanomami.com and is offering to sell rights to it for $25,000. "The Yanomami name is not up for sale," wrote tribal leader Davi Kopenawa Yanomami in response. In an increasingly common practice known as "cybersquatting," the woman registered the World Wide Web address after hearing of an upcoming Hollywood movie on the tribe.

—*Newsday*[4]

I

We are entering, we are told, a weightless, frictionless, speed-of-light age in which we will all be but address nodes in an endless flow of information packets, scurrying message handlers continuously assaulted from all directions. So far as scholarly life is concerned, that is still more specter than reality; promises (or threats) of e-books and downloadable doctoral theses and flooded-over inboxes aside, communication still proceeds at a more or less human pace, in a more or less politic manner. However, to judge from the on-line blizzard of charge and countercharge that has attended the mere rumor of Patrick Tierney's blistering indictment of anthropological practice in the Venezuelan Amazon, *Darkness in El Dorado*, it may not do so very much longer. Such established academic customs as looking into books before reviewing them, editing drafts before publishing them, and couching even polemic in consecutive argument may well be on the way out—runes and relics of a less hurried time. In cyberspace, it is velocity that matters. Velocity and volume.

The first intelligence that Patrick Tierney's *j'accuse* broadside was on the way came in the form of a breathless, six-page, single-spaced e-mail sent to "the President, and the President-elect" of the American Anthropological Association, a couple of weeks before the book was scheduled to appear (and a couple of months before it actually managed to do so), by two well-known Amazonian specialists and human rights activists, Terence Turner, professor of anthropology at Cornell, and Leslie Sponsel, professor of anthropology at the University of Hawaii, Manoa.[5]

"We write," they said, "to inform you of an impending scandal that will affect the American Anthropological profession as a whole in the eyes of the public, and arouse intense indignation and calls for action among members of the Association." They had obtained galley copies of a book by "an investigative journalist" describing "the actions of anthropologists and associated scientific researchers . . . among the Yanomami of Venezuela over the past thirty-five years"—actions "which in [their] scale, ramifications, and sheer criminality and corruption [are] unparalleled in the history of Anthropology." As the AAA, due to assemble in sixty days for its annual meeting, "will be called on by the general media and its own membership to take collective stands on the issues [the book] raises, as well as appropriate redressive actions. . . . The sooner you [as presidents of the Association] know about the story that is about to break, the better prepared you can be to deal with it."

"The focus of the scandal" the book exposes, they continued, is the long-term project for the study of the Yanomami, sponsored by the Atomic Energy Commission as part of its post-Hiroshima effort to determine the effects of radiation on human subjects, and organized in the mid-Sixties "by James

Neel, the human geneticist, in which Napoleon Chagnon, Timothy Asch, and numerous other anthropologists took part." Tierney "presents convincing evidence" that Neel (who directed the radiation studies in Japan after the war) and Chagnon (probably the most prominent, and certainly the most controversial, student of the Yanomami) "greatly exacerbated, and probably started the epidemic of measles that killed 'hundreds, perhaps thousands'. . .of Yanomami" in 1968 by inoculating them with an outmoded and "counter-indicated" live-virus vaccine, after which they "refused to provide any medical assistance to the sick and dying Yanomami, on explicit orders from Neel," who, anxious to test his "extreme eugenic theories" in a "natural," and "untouched," human society, "insisted to his colleagues that they were only there to observe and record the epidemic, . . . not [to] provide medical help."

Further, Chagnon, together with Asch, an ethnographic filmmaker, who worked with him for about ten years before they fell out in bitterness and recrimination, is said to have staged artificial "wars" between villages for documentary purposes, mock fights which often turned into real battles, shedding real blood. Together with Neel, he colluded with "sinister Venezuelan politicians attempting to gain control of Yanomami lands for illegal gold mining concessions." And all by himself he allegedly cooked and recooked his data, much of it in fact as invented as his films, to support his "neo-Hobbesean," sociobiological view of Yanomami life as brutal, violent, and congenitally murderous:

> This nightmarish story—a real anthropological heart of darkness beyond the imagining of even a Josef [sic] Conrad (though not, perhaps, a Josef Mengele). . . . This book should shake anthropology to its very foundations. . . . [It] will be seen (rightly in our view) by the public, as well as most anthropologists, as putting the whole discipline on trial, [and] it should cause the field to understand how the corrupt and depraved protagonists could have spread their poison for so long while they were accorded great respect throughout the Western World and generations of undergraduates received their lies as the introductory substance of anthropology.

And if all that didn't concentrate the presidents' minds sufficiently: "As both an indication and a vector of its public impact, we have learned that *The New Yorker* magazine is planning to publish an extensive excerpt, timed to coincide with the publication of the book on or about October 1st."

Though Turner and Sponsel later claimed, quite implausibly, that their letter had been a confidential memorandum not meant for general circulation, posting it electronically rendered it immediately available to just about anyone within the range of just about anyone else's "forward" command, and the howl of protest, outrage, glee, and *Schadenfreude* was vast and virtually instantaneous.

It rocketed through the media behind screaming headlines: MACHO AN-THROPOLOGY (*Salon*), ANTHROPOLOGY ENTERS THE AGE OF CANNIBALISM (*The New York Times*), MAD DOG ANTHROPOLOGISTS (*The Nation*), THE WAGES OF ANTHROPOLOGICAL INCORRECTNESS (*The National Review*), IS ANTHROPOLOGY EVIL? (*Slate*), YANOMAMI: WHAT HAVE WE DONE TO THEM? (*Time*), "SCIENTIST" KILLED AMAZON INDIANS TO TEST RACE THEORY (*The Guardian*). The *Chronicle of Higher Education, Science, US News, USA Today*, UPI, AP, the *Los Angeles Times Magazine*, and Reuters had bylined, and on-lined, features on the matter, as did *Forbes*, "the capitalist tool," which extended its attentions beyond anthropology—"a mind-set aching for activist causes"—to sociology and psychology as well: "People become sociologists because they hate society, and they become psychologists because they hate themselves."

Beyond the media, a variety of interested institutions, commentators, and marching societies fired off barrages in one direction or another. The University of Michigan, where Neel had taught for nearly fifty years (he died in February 2000, aged eighty-four, full of just about every honor save, unaccountably, the Nobel Prize), went on line with a twenty-page "investigation," accusing Tierney of pursuing "an anti-science agenda." A team of "evolutionary psychologists" (that is, sociobiologists) from the University of California, Santa Barbara, from which Chagnon had recently retired, posted a seventy-page "preliminary" report, "The Big Lie," calling Tierney's allegations ignorant, malicious, laughable, and "deliberately fraudulent." Bruce Alberts, the president of the National Academy of Sciences, and a longtime friend of Neel's, weighed in with a statement attacking Tierney for doing "a grave disservice to a great scientist and to science itself."

Dr. Samuel Katz, codeveloper of the measles vaccine Neel had used, posted an open e-mail to be displayed "in any place or fashion where . . . it may be helpful in aborting the posthumous assassination of Jim Neel," saying that the vaccine was not "virulent," could not cause measles, and never had done so in millions of applications. (Terence Turner, who said he had now found the time to consult an expert of his own, as well as, perhaps, to catch his breath, withdrew the "greatly exacerbated and probably started the epidemic" part of the accusation, and apologized to Katz—"now that I have had a chance to research the matter myself, I am in complete agreement with you.") Asch's filmmaker colleagues rushed to deny that he had ever staged anything, in the Amazon or anywhere else. (He, too, had died—in 1994, of cancer—suggesting, toward the end, that his Yanomami films were misleading and should be withdrawn from circulation.)

With the publication of the "extended excerpt" in *The New Yorker*, a feverish attack upon it and upon the magazine for publishing it, posted on *Slate* by John Tooby, the lead author of the "Big Lie" report, and a sharp response to that by the editors of *The New Yorker*, also on *Slate*, the battle was fairly well joined.[6] It remained only for the American Anthropological Association to somehow express itself, and its response came, with wild unclarity and a good deal of ax-grinding, at its meeting in San Francisco in mid-November.

Two plenary sessions, both crowded with hundreds of anthropologists, journalists, visiting scholars, and, this being California, passing agitators, were held on successive evenings. The first consisted of a seven-member panel of experts—an epidemiologist, an immunologist, a specialist in medical ethics, a former student in Neel's lab now a "scientific investigator" in Brazil, the head of Venezuela's Bureau for Indigenous Indian Affairs, herself a Waru Indian, a designated defender of Chagnon (Chagnon himself, holed up in northern Michigan considering options, refused to attend what he called "a feeding frenzy in which I am the bait"), and, down at the end of the table, looking abstract and detached, or perhaps just bemused, through nearly three hours of non-stop attack, Patrick Tierney.

In turn, each of the other panelists, save the Indian woman, who remarked the absence of native voices in the discussion and called for Yanomami participation in any future inquiry, pronounced Tierney's accusations of a vaccine-induced epidemic false and slanderous and his "anti-science approach" threatening to medical assistance programs throughout the world, after which Tierney said mildly that he was against neither vaccination nor science, that he understood that he had written a "wrenching book" that many people would find difficult to come to terms with, and that he hoped that the Santa Barbara and Michigan people would give Chagnon's work as careful a going over as they had given his, and, sensing perhaps that he was a bit outnumbered, he more or less left it there. The next evening's session, at which some thirty people, including Turner and Sponsel (but not Tierney, who was off to the Berkeley-to-Boston interview circuit), spoke for five minutes each, was, since almost no one had read the book which had only that day finally been published, hardly more clarifying. In the end, the president and the president-elect did what such people usually do in such circumstances: they asked a past president to head up a commission to look into the question of whether an official committee of inquiry should be formed.[7]

II

Tierney's opus—three parts, eighteen chapters, 398 sources, 1,599 footnotes—which has to be the only work to have been nominated for a major literary prize (the National Book Award, nonfiction) while its author, having withdrawn the galleys from circulation, was still busily revising it to counter al-

ready published attacks, is, whatever else it is, full of production values. A series of loosely linked set pieces—"Savage Encounters," "Outbreak," "Atomic
Indians," "The Na-poleonic Wars," "Gardens of Hunger, Dogs of War," "To
Murder and to Multiply"—it tells its story, a few statistical excursions and medical discussions aside, largely through setting, character, and dramatic incident.

A Venezuelan political adventurer, environmentalist, and strip miner (and
the inventor of that "explorer survival knife") parachutes into the jungle to
separate two French anthropologists intent, for some reason, upon killing one
another. The mistress of the president of Venezuela, "dressed in white," wear-
ing "enormous boots and an immense white hat," helicopters about Indian
country, ferrying US journalists, travel agents, and other celebrities in search
of "virgin villages" and "authentic primitives." Chagnon, stripped to his draw-
ers, decorated with feathers, dancing and chanting, and drugged out of his
skull on local hallucinogens, breaks arrows over his head as he ritually "kills" a
terrified small boy. There are homosexual harems, goldfield massacres, captiv-
ity stories, soul-eating shamans, guerrilla invasions, four sorts of missionaries,
and the death agony of an Indian woman and her newborn infant impassively
filmed by a British television crew. And it is all driven forward by furious au-
thorial voice-overs—oracular, condemnatory, comprehensive, and unforgiving:

> In the end, the Yanomami concluded Chagnon was simply out to rip
> them off. He wanted complete control of the films and the blood and the
> budget, and he intended to give them only crumbs from his rich table.
> The man who had once incorporated the fearsome Vulture Spirits now
> landed his helicopter in the middle of [Indian villages] in the company
> of Venezuela's leading [gold miner].
>
> Sadly, [Neel] took both his beliefs and his experiments with him into
> the rain forest. [He] and his eugenic disciples imbued the impersonal
> nature of evolution with a personal animus: natural selection became
> selfish, murderous, cruel, and deceitful. Doctors trained by the AEC
> gave the Yanomami a radioactive tracer and a vaccine that was poten-
> tially fatal for immune-compromised people. Scientists kept on filming
> and collecting blood in the midst of epidemics. These brave men took a
> long walk on the dark side, but in the artificial brilliance of ground zero,
> they could see no shadows.
>
> The attempt [by Chagnon] to portray the Yanomami as archetypes of
> ferocity would be pathetic were it not for its political consequences—for
> the fabulous distortions this myth has perpetrated in biology, anthropol-
> ogy, and popular culture. . . . Just as [Margaret] Mead's beliefs about
> sexual freedom and child rearing worked their way into public-policy
> debates, Chagnon's ferocious Yanomami have become proof to some

social scientists that ruthless competition and sexual selection cannot be legislated away by idealistic do-gooders. The Yanomami are the Cold Warriors who never came in from the cold.

Hard charges demand hard evidence, or, failing that, at least an enormous mass of it. Tierney's approach to assembling such a mass, a project he says took eleven years, much of it on site, mapping itineraries, interviewing Indians, and reading mission-station reports, was to trace, relentlessly and with great ingenuity, the obscure and complicated doings of his main suspects, Neel and Chagnon, between 1966, when the former, project in hand, first arrived on the Orinoco, and 1995, when, at long last definitively *non grata* (he had been expelled at least twice before), the latter finally left it. The result is uneven, in many places vague or insubstantial, and in some, it is, as the critics have charged, simply unfair—ideologized second-guessing. But, as the instances accumulate and their implications come home, it all, in some strange way, begins to add up. Whatever caused the measles epidemic (and that issue, it should be said, plays a much less prominent part in the book than it does in the discussion of the book), a case gets made, however clumsily, that something was seriously amiss in the relation between these confident and determined *soi-disant* "scientists" with their cameras, their vials, their syringes, and their notebooks and the beset and puzzled, put-upon "natives" to whom they looked for facts to fill them with—something in their encounter was deeply, and mutually, misconceived.

"Why do [these *anthros*] want to study us so much?" one Indian who had watched them at work for thirty years and remembered running screaming into the forest when they first arrived, and rather wished that he had stayed there, asked plaintively: "[They] have a brain; Yanomami have a brain. [They] have two eyes; Yanomami have two eyes. [They] have five fingers; the Yanomami have five fingers. Why are they so interested in studying us?"

The problem was not just the thousands of blood and urine samples, the mysterious radioactive iodine tracers, or the ill-explained medicines and inoculations, which seemed more accompaniments of disease than cures for it. Nor was it just the visitors' practice of taking reproductive histories which required the revelation of personal names, a matter so deeply tabooed and emotionally disturbing to the Indians that it almost got Chagnon, ruthless in the matter, killed at one point. Nor was it the earnest tabulation of murders, murderers, and victims, the playing off of rival families and competing headmen for movie-making purposes, or the bribing of members of the tribe with steel axes and machetes, occasionally even shotguns—all profoundly destabilizing interventions in a wood and clay village culture. It was not even just the grandiose plan (fortunately aborted when the president of Venezuela was overthrown and his wondrous mistress fled the country) of Neel, Chagnon, and their gold-rush, tourist-hunting allies "to turn the Yanomami's homeland into the world's largest private reserve," a six-thousand-square-mile research station and "biosphere" administered by themselves. The problem was that the *anthros* (and the *médicos*), reductionist to the core, conceived the object of their study not as a people but as a population. The Yanomami, who indeed had the requisite sorts of brains, eyes, and fingers, were a control group in an inquiry centered elsewhere.

Neel, who actually had the sort of romantic conception of Indians that people who haven't had much to do with them beyond watching them perform commonly have—brave, manly, direct, colorful, and uncorrupted by civilized appetites—went to the Yanomami hypothesis in hand. As the closest thing to an "untouched," "unacculturated," "natural" human community still around, a last living representative of our ancestral condition, the fundamental forces driving human evolution should be, he thought, more readily discernible among them than they are among modern populations, where such dysgenic institutions as the decline in childhood mortality, medical treatments for the elderly, the defective, and the disabled, draft deferments for the privileged and the nonbelligerent, and the disappearance of polygamy mask and distort them, degrading the species. In particular, it should be possible to find "a clear association, at least for males, between 'ability' and reproductive performance, a result of the greater fertility of leaders or headmen."[8] It is this program, "the search for the leadership gene," with which Chagnon, then a graduate student in search of a thesis topic, decided to associate himself and his career. Neel wrote:

> For these studies, the indispensable cultural anthropologist became Napoleon Chagnon. Nap . . . sought me out in Ann Arbor . . . having heard of our developing program. By virtue of the contacts I had already made, I could facilitate his entry into the field; he, for his part, . . . could put together the village pedigrees so basic to our work. [We] went through the same indoctrination concerning the nuances of genetic . . . pedigrees. . . . Those familiar with Nap's writings concerning the Yanomama know how well the lessons took.[9]

All too well. It was the attempt to establish Neel's Darwinian conjecture (whether or not one wants to call it "eugenic" rather depends upon definitions) that masculinity, violence, domination, and the appropriation of women are selectively linked in tribal society through the differential fertility of headmen, and thus that warfare and inequality were driving forces in the separation of *Homo sapiens* from other primates, that got Chagnon, "the indispensable anthropologist," into all the trouble. He spent a quarter of a century, in the field and out, desperately trying to find evidence for Neel's conjecture, counting, measuring, photographing, and perhaps stimulating violence, at the expense of his own more nuanced, immediate, finely detailed, and above all personally observed sense of what the Yanomami—less "the fierce people" than the resilient ones—were all about. The ethnographer, the connoisseur of the human particular, the celebrant of the special, gradually and, it turned out, irrecoverably disappeared into Neel's, and later E.O. Wilson's, totalizing visions. He became, like his namesake, the victim of a hypothesis.

There is a certain pathos in all this. One can sympathize with Chagnon's predicament in trying to be at one and the same time a responsible anthropologist and what one of his enemies has called "Neel's Kelly girl." Or at least one could, had he not, as he went on, become more and more extreme in his views, increasingly rigid, belligerent, and self-celebrating, as critiques arose on all sides. All who questioned him, his work, or his social Darwinism—and they include by now almost all of his Amazonian colleagues—were excoriated as "Marxists," "liars," "cultural anthropologists from the academic Left," "ayatollahs," "politically correct bleeding hearts," "pacifists," "limp-wristed anthropologists afraid to take on the [Church]," and "anti-scientific, post-modern moralizers" advocating "noble savage" conceptions of primitive life. He fell out with many of his students, with Asch, finally even, apparently, with Neel. In the end, he has retreated, taking an early retirement at sixty-two, to his own private northern Michigan St. Helena, dreaming of reconquest, vengeance, and vindication:

> His house can't be seen from the road because of all the trees; it's an ideal retreat for someone who wants privacy. But Chagnon has turned a small study by the front door into a war room. Beneath a portrait of Bonaparte, the anthropologist has battled for weeks to rebut Tierney's allegations, going through old notes and organizing support among former students and sympathetic colleagues. E.O. Wilson calls every other day. Richard Dawkins [of the "selfish gene"] and Steven Pinker [of the "language instinct"] have backed him publicly. UC-Santa Barbara and the University of Michigan maintain websites . . .posting point-by-point refutations of Tierney's arguments. "I'm considering legal action," says Chagnon.[10]

III

During the German occupation of France, André Gide published, and was allowed to publish because he was Gide, a series of "*interviews imaginaires*" in the public press commenting, in an oblique, Aesopian way, on various aspects of literature, politics, and the cultural scene. In one, he takes up the question, then current, of the supposed responsibility of the "intellectuals" for the fall of France, and he ends it with a striking parable. A rowboat, moored at a river-bank, sits low in the water. Into it step in turn (as I remember it), a fat politi-cian, a large general draped in medals, an enormous madam, and a bloated capitalist, the boat sinking deeper and deeper, water to the gunwales, as they board. Finally, a clergyman, thin as a rail, steps in and the boat finally sinks. The others all point at him: "It is he who is the culprit! It is he who has caused the disaster!"

Given all that has happened to the Yanomami over the past half-century, encountering anthropologists, and critics of anthropologists, as difficult as both may have been at times to deal with, surely ranks as historical small change, a very small blip on a very large curve. They have been caught up, these twenty thousand Indians, in the middle of the largest and most rapa-cious gold rush in history. The forests that shaped and supported them have been assaulted by international timber interests, bringing famine and malnu-trition. They have been intensively missionized, they have been ruled by two vigorously Hispanicizing nation-states from which the best they could hope was pity and inattention, and they have become, or anyway are in the midst of becoming, that merest of mere locations, a tourist destination. And they have been plagued by a good deal more than measles which, however grave, are a one-time thing, while the malaria, tuberculosis, and other respiratory diseases they suffer from now are chronic, debilitating, only gradually fatal. Morbidity rates are estimated to be as high as 35 percent, death rates nearly 10 percent a year; birth rates, in some areas, are approaching zero.

In the space of hardly more than a generation, the people (or the popula-tion) over whom all these ethnographers, geneticists, sociobiologists, human rights activists, and "advocacy journalists" have been quarreling so furiously have moved from being "untouched" to being "imperiled," from "recently contacted" to "at the edge of destruction." Now that their value as a control group, a (supposedly) "natural," genetically "ancestral population"—"the last major primitive tribe . . . *anywhere on earth*,"[11] is diminished or disappeared and the experiments upon them have ceased and the experimenters departed, what sort of presence in our minds, what sort of whatness, are they now to have? What sort of place in the world does an "ex-primitive" have?

It is difficult to say; the precedents are hardly encouraging. Perhaps that enterprising lady in Florida is on to something. A movie would certainly seem possible (Sean Penn as Napoleon Chagnon? Jennifer Lopez as the Presidential Mistress?). The exchange of on-line accusations would seem destined to go on for a while, entertaining the principals if no one else, perhaps for years. Whatever happens to the Yanomami in what we used to call the real world— "acculturation," "minoritization," immiseration, migration to shantytowns, or what E.O. Wilson in an imprimatur to one of Chagnon's books blithely calls "a leisurely and decent accommodation between their world and ours"[12]— their place in cyberspace seems assured. Anyone still looking for them will be able to find them with a modem and a search engine. Yanomami.com.

Which Way to Mecca?   PART I

We are, in this country right now, engaged in the process of constructing, rather hurriedly, as though we had better quickly get on with it after years of neglect, a standard, public-square image of "Islam." Until very recently, we had hardly more than the suggestions of such an image—vagrant notions of stallions, harems, deserts, palaces, and chants. A Peter Arno drawing in *The New Yorker* sixty-five years ago more or less summed the matter up. A stetson-hatted tourist leans out of his roadster to ask a turbaned man prostrate in prayer by the side of the road: "Hey, Jack, which way to Mecca?"

The reason for the rush to change this casual mixture of ignorance and in-difference is clear enough: September 11, suicide bombers, Kuta Beach, Osama, Nairobi, the Cole—and now the Iraq war. What isn't clear, and will not be-come so for quite some time, is where it all is taking us, what our sense of this obscure and threatening Other that has appeared suddenly—and literally—on our domestic horizon is going ultimately to be. The familiar, almost intimate enemy we precipitously lost with the dissolution of the Soviet Union is being replaced in our minds by something far less well defined, much further re-moved from the political history of nineteenth- and twentieth-century Europe and America. Communism, with its roots in the Enlightenment and the French Revolution, at least had a Western pedigree. Marx and Lenin emerged from historical backgrounds all too recognizable, with ideological intentions derived, on the face of them, from some of our dearest social hopes. But "Islam," a creed of Arabs, Turks, Africans, Persians, Central Asians, Indians, Mongols, and Malays, has been rather off our cultural map. What are we Americans to think about an inflamed competitor of which most of us know hardly more than the name?

Part one of a two-part review and essay. Originally published in the *New York Review of Books* 50, no. 10 (12 June 2003). Books under discussion therein are as follows: Bernard Lewis, *What Went Wrong? The Clash between Islam and Modernity in the Middle East*; Bernard Lewis, *The Crisis of Islam: Holy War and Unholy Terror*; Thomas W. Simons, Jr., *Islam in a Globalizing World*; M. J. Akbar, *The Shade of Swords: Jihad and the Conflict between Islam and Christianity*; and Karen Armstrong, *Islam: A Short History*.

There has been an avalanche in the last two or three years of books and articles—by historians, by journalists, by political scientists, by students of comparative religion, by sociologists and anthropologists, and by variously inspired amateurs—designed to assist us in answering this question, to give us a crash course in, as the phrase goes, "understanding Islam." "Jihad," a term most Americans had encountered, if they had encountered it at all, in dime novels or at Saturday matinees, has become a prime subject of popular and scholarly discourse. Works designed for that elusive figure, the general reader, have begun to appear on something called, variously and confusingly, "reformism," "modernism," "radicalism," "extremism," or "fundamentalism"—sometimes, even, "Wahhabism"—in contemporary Islam. Handbook explications of Islamic law, of the teachings of the Koran, of the fast, the pilgrimage, or the meaning of the veil are suddenly on offer. So are introductions to Islamic schooling, science, ritual, and scholarship, and accounts of the Shiite clergy, the ecstatic brotherhoods, and that mysterious flying object, "Sufism."

Bernard Lewis, perhaps the leading Orientalist of the day, has, at the fine old age of eighty-six, become a best-selling author, a television celebrity, an urgent hawk, and a know-your-enemy adviser to the vice-president of the United States. An attempt to introduce a course on the Koran at the University of North Carolina has produced a state-and-church cause célèbre and an outburst of right-wing sectarian rage. A short, self-confident book by Karen Armstrong, an English ex-nun with an urge to instruct, has become perhaps our most widely read guide to "the religion of the Prophet." Even the Italian media-madam, Oriana Fallaci, rather off the radar screen since her famous sendup interview of Henry Kissinger a decade or so ago, has checked back in with a screaming attack on anything Muslim, "Afghans and Bosnians and Kurds included," as well as anybody in the West who might consider saying something less than abusive about "the culture of the bigots with the beard and the chador and the burkah."[1]

And that is only the beginning. An ex-Trotskyite, ex-beatnik, ex-obituary writer from San Francisco who converted to Sufism in Bosnia and became Washington bureau chief of the Jewish *Forward* issues a zealotic attack on Saudi zealotry and gets himself fired from the Voice of America. The son of a prominent anti-Soviet scholar active during the cold war carries "the West vs. the Rest" polemic forward with a "the Muslims are coming, the Muslims are coming" call to arms. A South Asian exile, publishing under an assumed name in the United States, popularizes the work of an obscure group of Arabists from London's School of Oriental Studies dedicated to the textual deconstruction of the Koran, the Traditions, the Prophet, and "the myth of Mecca," whole and entire. A former Supreme Court clerk to Justice David Souter, now a law professor, searches through Islamic examples of state and government looking for signs and portents of democratic potential. An ex-CIA staff officer, with thirty years of practice in the Middle East, urges us to win the hearts and minds of "Muslim intellectuals," a growing class, he says, of open and tolerant cosmopolitan thinkers.[2]

Thomas Simons, Clinton's last ambassador to Pakistan, a career diplomat retired to Stanford's Center for International Security and Cooperation, sets "political Islam" against the background of a sweeping historical macrophase: "IT [i.e., information technology]- led globalization." Vartan Gregorian, the head of the Carnegie Corporation and former president of Brown University, in search of "the best means to facilitate multilateral dialogues between Western and Muslim intellectuals, professionals . . . clerics . . . and theologians," produces a power-point executive summary of what Islam is about for his board of trustees, and gets the Brookings Institution to publish it, the Rockefeller and MacArthur foundations to support conferences to examine it. Paul Berman, a historian of the New Left, his subject remaindered, turns his attention to ferreting out the "deep," "sophisticated" philosophy behind Islamic extremism so as to formulate a comparably reflective, comparably militant counterposition.[3] Many arrows fired in many directions with varying force, varying effectiveness, and varying intent. What are we to make of it all? Which way to Mecca indeed?

The problem is made all the more difficult by the fact that these arrows are not being fired randomly into the empty air, but, as the above catalog suggests, onto a scene already crowded with ideological combatants. The American idea of Islam, various, irregular, and charged with foreboding, is being built up at a time when the American idea of America is itself the subject of no little doubt and dispute, and the country as a whole seems embarked on a disconsonant and quarrelsome course. The forms the "What is Islam?" argument takes—"What do they really believe?" "How do they really feel?" "What do they really intend?" "What can we do about them?"—owe as much to domestic divisions, to warring conceptions of our national interest and national purpose, what we believe and feel and intend, as they do to the matted, instable, rapidly changing thought world they seek to represent. The effort to "understand Islam," to locate it, describe it, and reduce it to intelligible summary, is caught up in the excitements of the present moment. It is a thing of responses and reactions—of warnings, reassurances, advices, attacks.

The literally scores of books, good, bad, indifferent, and peculiar, pouring right now from our public presses represent, therefore, more than the opportune exploitation of an emergent mass market or, what is perhaps the same thing, a strategic shift in the winds of intellectual fashion. They represent the opening stages of something quite new, and in some ways unprecedented, in our national experience: the construction, live and in real time, out there in the common culture where we can see it made, watch it happen, observe its makers, and track its progress, of an enduring image of an alien phenomenon, obscure and worrisome, working its way in toward the center of that experience. From that point of view, a making up of a collective mind about an imagined object, what needs first to be assessed is less the reliability, knowledgeability, or scholarly standing of the writers clamoring for our attention and assent. That varies enormously and is beyond summary judgment. What needs first to be assessed is: What sort of thing is it that these determined reality instructors would have us think?

II

In that spirit, one more concerned with assumptions than findings, it is possible to mark out four main approaches, which, although neither unmixed nor self-contained, more or less divide and bound the overall field of argument and interpretation. There is, first, the "civilization" approach, which opposes "the West" as a whole to "Islam" as a whole and compares their fates. Second, there are the attempts to pick apart the various streams of contemporary Muslim thought and practice and place them within a culturally familiar grid of ideological contrasts—to sort "good" Islam (and "Islamists") from "bad," "real" from "false," "authentic" from "hijacked," "tolerant" from "terrorist" in terms of recognized categories of political expression. Third, there are conciliative, or reconciliative, efforts seeking out "many are the roads but God is One" convergences between Islamic teachings and those of the other major religious traditions so as to lay a positive course for their co-evolution. And finally, there are place-, or people-, or nation-focused studies that conceive of "Islam" less as a cohesive mega-entity persisting through time, than as a collection of particular, in many ways disparate, "family-resemblance" traditions coming into more and more immediate and difficult contact with one another as the vast and entangling forces of all-over modernity advance.

The "civilization" conception of things was, and is, the approach generally characteristic of what is usually referred to, sometimes descriptively, sometimes tendentiously, as "Orientalism"—that is, the world-historical, textual-philological, originally European, university tradition of "'Mid-' or 'Near' Eastern (or, sometimes, 'Semitic') studies," a tradition based, from Renan forward, on an underlying thematic contrast between "Christendom" and "the Islamic World." "Christendom," as a term, has rather gone out of fashion since the middle of the last century when first Oswald Spengler and then, in a different way, Arnold Toynbee put a bit in the shade the fashion of characterizing whole civilizations and their evolutions on the basis of their supposed "spirits." But recently it has experienced something of a revival, especially in geopolitical circles, with such writers as the Harvard political scientist Samuel Huntington and his conception of an impending "clash of civilizations" along "the bloody borders"—the Balkans, Central Asia, Sudanic Africa, the southern Philippines—that divide the Islamic from the Christian (or anyway, post-Christian) worlds.[4]

The most prominent figure here, as well as the most controversial, is, again, Bernard Lewis. Lewis, who was educated in Islamic history at the University of London's School of Oriental and African Studies before the Second World War, served during that war in British intelligence, and moved to Princeton in 1974. He is the author of more than twenty books and hundreds of articles on Near Eastern and Islamic subjects: the formation of the Turkish Republic; race, color, and slavery in Islam; the history of the Arab-speaking peoples; the political language of Islam; the Muslim discovery of Europe; the Jews of Islam; and the *avant la lettre* twelfth-century terrorist cult called, after its members' supposed addiction to hashish, "the Assassins." Possessed of an assured and liquid style, casually erudite, sardonic, dismissive, and given to grand conclusions, he has, by dint of tireless writing, lecturing, traveling, consulting, and media-swinging, established a public, quasi-official role for himself as the go-to authority on all things Middle Eastern.

His two most recent books, *What Went Wrong?* and *The Crisis of Islam*, evolved out of popular articles in *The Atlantic Monthly* and *The New Yorker*, written before September 11 and now seen to be prescient. They are well on the way to becoming the standard accounts of the us-and-them, war-of-the-worlds, believers-and-infidels conception of the Muslim mind. "For newcomers to the subject," *Time* magazine has proclaimed, "Bernard Lewis is the man." For *US News & World Report* he is "the scholar of the hour." For *National Review*, "the father of us all. . .when it comes to Islamic studies."

Lewis's argument is simple enough. Muslims the world over are caught up in a confused and resentful mourning over the loss of a cultural primacy that was once theirs and has now been lost. They are enraged alike at the West, history, infidels, and "modernity," as well as at themselves for having allowed matters to come to such a pass. At the time when Christian Europe was mired in the Dark Ages, what knowledge it had even of its own roots was mediated through Arabic translations of Greek manuscripts. The Muslim world—Damascus, Baghdad, Grenada, Istanbul, Fustat, Isfahan—was, for about a thousand years, not just the preeminent civilization in the world, it was, walled and self-contained and sequestered China aside, the only civilization:

> For many centuries the world of Islam was in the forefront of human civilization and achievement. In the Muslims' own perception, Islam itself was indeed coterminous with civilization, and beyond its borders there were only barbarians and infidels. . . . The remoter lands of Europe

were seen in much the same light as the remoter lands of Africa—as an outer darkness of barbarism and unbelief from which there was nothing to learn and little even to be imported, except slaves and raw materials. For both the northern and the southern barbarians, their best hope was to be incorporated in the empire of the caliphs, and thus attain the benefits of religion and civilization.

What changed all this was the Renaissance, the Reformation, and the Industrial Revolution: the revival of Western learning and the decay of Arabic, Persian, Moorish, and Ottoman culture; the rationalization of Christian doctrine and the petrification of Islamic; the growing military and economic disparity between the technologically developed, "scientific" West and the traditional, backward, "handicraft" East. The opening of the sea routes to India and to the New World in the sixteenth century, the Ottoman halt before the gates of Vienna in the seventeenth, and the entry of Napoleon into Egypt at the end of the eighteenth were but so many stages in the long withdrawing roar of Islamic grandeur, the descent of the once great Muslim world of Avicenna and Ibn Khaldun, Saladin and Suleyman the Magnificent, into "a downward spiral of hate and spite, rage and self-pity, poverty and oppression, culminating . . . in alien domination" and the radical xenophobia that has gone with it.

In *What Went Wrong?* this seesaw version of Christian-Muslim history— when the one is up, the other is down—is related in casual, restrained, almost regretful tones, punctuated with sly asides and *dégagé* observations; and that is, surely, the main reason, apart from the fortune of its spot-on timing, for the book's extraordinary public reception. At a time when so much history writing has abandoned causal, storybook, "and then, and then . . ." narrative for postmodern nonlinearity, skepticism, relativism, flash, and indeterminacy, the classical grand *récit*, breathing the authority of received scholarship, measured tone, the long view, and plain fact, comes as something of a relief. At least someone knows.

But in *The Crisis of Islam*, written after September 11 (*What Went Wrong?* was written just before it; a brief postcript describing the attack as "the latest phase in a struggle that has been going on for more than fourteen centuries" was added upon publication), Lewis dramatically abandons this donnish and deliberate deep-view position for intense, and intensely contemporary, close-up polemic designed to arouse the West, and most especially the United States, to armed response. Mossadeq, Ba'athism, Suez, the Muslim Brotherhood, Wahhabism, the massacre at Hama, suicide bombers, Khomeini, the Taliban, the Islamic Salvation Front, Saddam, Osama—what was in the first work but implied and insinuated is here explicitly stated, *sans* nuance, *sans* reserve: Muslim rage at Muslim failure, "holy war and unholy terror," has become a threat, not just eventually and to Christendom, but here and now and to the world as a whole:

If the [Muslim fundamentalists] can persuade the world of Islam to accept their views and their leadership, then a long and bitter struggle lies ahead, and not only for America. Europe . . . is now home to a large and rapidly growing Muslim community, and many Europeans are beginning to see its presence as . . . a threat. Sooner or later, Al-Qa'ida and related groups will clash and the other groups will clash with the other neighbors of Islam—Russia, China, India—who may prove less squeamish than the Americans [have] in using their power against Muslims and their sanctities. If the fundamentalists are correct in their calculations and succeed in their war, then a dark future awaits the world. . . .

III

But the notion of Islam as a "civilization"—an autonomous, continuous, self-organizing thought world, border-guarded and set apart—is not confined to the Muslim/Christian, Orient/Occident way of looking at things. One can also see Islam, thus imagined, as a particular example of a general process, a distinct and special version of a developmental progression characteristic of human history overall. Or one can see it against the background of its involvements, also troubled, also longstanding, also worsening, with another "great religion," this one a large-scale, long-lived cultural formation neither Western, scriptural, monotheistic, nor (at least until recently) proselytizing. Or, and perhaps most familiarly, least self-consciously, one can see it as the persistence across the centuries of an original revelatory moment, a fixed prophetical message, restated and redescribed under the varying pressures of time and circumstance but, in the very nature of the case, unchanged and unchangeable.

Thomas W. Simons Jr., who was the US ambassador to Pakistan between 1996 and 1998, and before that (1990–1993) to Poland and deputy assistant secretary of state for the Soviet Union, Eastern Europe, and Yugoslavia, and before even that a Council on Foreign Relations Fellow at the Hoover Institution and a doctoral student at Harvard specializing in European history, is obviously the sort of figure who would be inclined to think big. In *Islam in a Globalizing World*, a short, sweeping, rather breathless book (there are almost more citations than there are sentences), Simons sees Islam, not just at present, but over the entire course of its thirteen-hundred-year career, as "the world's most powerful engine, agent, and vehicle of globalization, and . . . [its] most sharply contested battleground."

Since the fall of communism, and of the class-and-domination terminology that went with it, Simons says, the idea of globalization has emerged as a "common denominator in analyses of world affairs." Defined as "the impulse among humans to reach . . . beyond the families and kinship groups that historically have provided their first self-definition and best security; to multiply and strengthen their ties via interactions with other human beings; and to argue about why they should or should not do these things," globalization is a historical constant. How far it extends, how fast it moves, and how deeply it penetrates at any particular time or place varies with "the state of technology, social organization, and conceptualization." But rather like the dialectic, it is always there, driving and directing the pace of change.

It is not so difficult to fit so vague a phenomenon as "Islamic society" into so pliable a scheme. For "the first thousand years" of that society's existence (from Muhammad's death in 632 to the second Vienna siege in 1683), Muslims, like Christians, Hindus, and Chinese, "lived in agricultural economies from which rulers based in cities extracted and spent surpluses in ways that generally had religious sanction." "The astounding expansion" of "the small Muslim community the Prophet had established in the Arabian merchant cities of Mecca and Medina," its engulfment of Syria, Egypt, North Africa, Anatolia, Iraq, and Persia over the course of a few centuries, launched the most powerful and far-flung movement toward cultural, political, and economic integration the world had ever seen. The Umayyads, Abbasids, Buyids, Seljuqs, Timurids, Safavids, and Ottomans (they all pass by in a dizzying, "meanwhile in Afghanistan" procession) represent but so many turns "in history's wheel," so many stages in the foundation of a Nile-to-Oxus globalization—Hodgson's "Islamicate"—still very much in place.

The appearance of "globalization by blood and iron" after the eighteenth century, and the imperialism—Napoleon, Algeria, and the Great Game—it brought with it, "coarsened" matters somewhat and led to a "progressive simplification and brutalization of the [increasingly revivalistic] Islamic discourse." But it was not until the 1970s, when "globalization led and driven by coal, steel, and petroleum [gave] way to globalization led and driven by information technology"—"IT"—that the classic Islamic world began to come, dangerously and definitively, apart. The dispersion of religious authority, the weakening of the nation-state, the failure of "defensive modernization . . . strapped to the chariot-wheel of import substitution," and an emerging sense of elite betrayal all conduced to a new radicalism that was "the real starting point for the intricate, winding paths that led some thirty years later to the stupefying attacks on the World Trade Towers and the Pentagon." Well, perhaps—though recent events suggest that the shaping force of steel and petroleum may be far from spent, and who knows where any fatality starts.

There is, in any case, another, more easterly, less developmentalist position from which to look at the long and relentless expansion of the Islamicate, another enormous confusion of mythological tales, micro-states, and magical traditions into whose cultural space it has long since obtruded—i.e., "India."

In his exuberant, overwritten, rambling and contentious, but for all that sporadically incisive *The Shade of Swords*, M.J. Akbar, Muslim founder-editor of
the English-language Indian daily *The Asian Age*, former Congress MP, and a
nonstop commentator on all things political, describes how "the rise of Islam"
looks from Delhi.

It looks horrendous. (Akbar's jacket photo of a raging-turban mob of anti-
US demonstrators thronging the streets in Peshawar after September 11 con-
veys the view he takes of Islam, as do his chapter titles—"The Joys of Death,"
"Circle of Hell," "History as Anger.") And what is more, it looks—whether he
discusses Kashmir, the Taliban, Zia ul-Haq, or Ramzi Youssef—increasingly
menacing. The first hundred or so pages of Akbar's book is given over to an
offhand, Sunday-supplement account of the rise of Islam and its engagements
with Christianity—engagements that were virtually always hostile, always ignorant, always unperceiving. But it is in the final hundred pages or so, when
he turns to his own, South Asian, side of things ("Jihad in the East: A Crescent
over Delhi"), that he contributes something, if not more measured, at least
more shaded and directly felt.

Partition ("a history of anger and a literature of revenge divided India and
created Pakistan") was but the most dramatic stage in the long-term production on the subcontinent of a Crescent and Saffron Robe struggle, a jihad and
counter-jihad that would match, both for persistence and for violence, the
Cross and Crescent one to the west. Kashmir, Bangladesh, the destruction of
the Babri Mosque, the rise of Hindu radicalism, and the appearance of Osama
bin Laden, an export from the one battlefront to the other, in Kabul and Kan-
dahar: "The jihad is never over." "Defeat is only a setback in a holy war." "The
jihad goes on." And the stakes by now are nuclear.

In short, for Akbar, as for Lewis and for Simons, "Islamic civilization" is to
be seen more in the perspective of its reactions to what surrounds it, to what
confronts it and what it confronts—the West, the East, globalization—than it
is to the promptings, whatever they might be, of its spiritual character. It is its
encounters with others, rather than with itself, that have shaped it. In her
Islam: A Short History, Karen Armstrong, author of a number of earnest, tract-
like books on religious subjects—Buddhism, Genesis, medieval mystics, Judaism, fundamentalism, devotional poetry, "Christianity's creation of the sex
war in the West," and her own experiences as first an aspirant and then a
breakaway nun[5]—takes another tack and portrays the course of Muslim history as a temporal unfolding from a revelatory foundation, the carrying forth
of a settled faith into an unsettled world:

> The historical trials and tribulations of the Muslim community—politi-
> cal assassinations, civil wars, invasions, and the rise and fall of the ruling

dynasties—were not divorced from the interior religious quest, but were of the essence of the Islamic vision. A Muslim would meditate upon the current events of his time and upon past history as a Christian would contemplate an icon, using the creative imagination to discover the . . . divine kernel. An account of the external history of the Muslim people [is not] of mere secondary interest, since one of the chief characteristics of Islam has been its sacralization of history.

This approach to the matter has at least the advantage of being more or less the way the vast majority of believing Muslims look at things, and Armstrong writes with a crisp, catechistic authority that gives her book (like Lewis's, it is a national best seller) a ready appeal. The lack of concern with specifically religious conceptions and specifically spiritual motivations in most of the "understanding Islam" literature does produce something of a Hamlet without the Prince effect.

But, still, an account "through the eyes of faith" of the "external history" of Islam has difficulties of its own, for it involves accepting the Koranic account of things, and especially of the Prophet and the Prophecy, more or less at face value. Viewing the whole career of Islam in the world, all those assassinations, wars, invasions, and dynasties, as a temporal unfolding out of its "primitive," revelatory moment—Muhammad in Mecca and Medina, the transmission of the Koran, the battle at Badr—risks being seen, rather like viewing Christianity as an extension of the story "He was born, He was crucified, He was resurrected" told in the Gospels, as at once naive and apologetic, a just-so Sunday-school tale too simple to be credible, too coherent to convince, too deeply absorbed in its inner impulses to see very clearly what has, in the hard course of events, become of them.

Indeed, any attempt to conceive of "Islam" in sweeping, "civilizational" terms—Lewis's, Simons's, Akbar's, Armstrong's, or anyone else's—is in some danger of conjuring up cloudscapes mighty like a whale and concocting Joycean big words that make us all afraid. A descent into the swirl of particular incident, particular politics, particular voices, particular traditions, and particular arguments, a movement across the grain of difference and along the lines of dispute, is indeed disorienting and spoils the prospect of abiding order. But it may prove the surer path toward understanding "Islam"—that resonant name of so many things at once.

Which Way to Mecca?   PART II

I

Since the end of the cold war, when a lot more collapsed than walls and regimes, many of the large-scale concepts by means of which we had been accustomed to sorting out the world have begun to come apart. East and West, Communist and free world, liberal and totalitarian, Arab, Oriental, underdeveloped, third world, nonaligned, and now apparently even Europe have lost much of their edge and definition, and we are left to find our way through vast collections of strange and inconsonant particulars without much in the way of assistance from finely drawn, culturally ratified natural kinds.

After the bolt-from-the-blue attacks on the World Trade Center in 1993 and 2001 further disturbed our sense that we understood what was going on in the world and could handle it, "Islam," about which we had, in any case, only the most general of notions, began to undergo the same sort of decomposition for us. It, too, has rather fallen apart as a settled and integral object of knowledge about which it is possible to have a view and a theory. Introductions to Islam, and bottom-line evaluations of it as a religion, a culture, a society, a weltanschauung, or a civilization, continue to be written and continue to be consumed.[1] But they seem to be of declining force, relics of a time when things were, so we thought, more of a piece and better arranged.

More than any other single thing, it has been the rising tendency to ideologize faith in so much of the Muslim world that has made it increasingly hard to arrive at summary accounts of what is happening there. The movement

---

Part two of a two-part review and essay. Originally published in the *New York Review of Books* 50, no. 11 (3 July 2003). Books under discussion therein are as follows: Gilles Kepel, *Jihad: The Trail of Political Islam*; Daniel Pipes, *Militant Islam Reaches America*; Stephen Schwartz, *The Two Faces of Islam: The House of Sa'ud from Tradition to Terror*; Paul Berman, *Terror and Liberalism*; Graham E. Fuller, *The Future of Political Islam*; Noah Feldman, *After Jihad: America and the Struggle for Islamic Democracy*; Riaz Hassan, *Faithlines: Muslim Conceptions of Islam and Society*; and Muhammad Qasim Zaman, *The Ulama in Contemporary Islam: Custodians of Change*.

from religion to religious-mindedness, from Islam to Islamism, from a rather quietist, withdrawn, and scholastic immersion in the fine details of law and worship, the ordinary piety of everyday life, to an activist, reformist, increasingly determined struggle to capture secular power and turn it to spiritual ends, has transformed what once was, or seemed to be, a historical macroentity to be set beside Christianity, the West, science, or modernity, into a disorderly field of entangled differences about which it is difficult to say anything at all except that it seems at once various and volatile. "The militant Islamic movement," the French political scientist Gilles Kepel writes in his *Jihad: The Trail of Political Islam*,[2] perhaps the most detailed, and certainly the most comprehensive, examination of it that has thus far appeared, "[is] a phenomenon whose emergence was as spectacular as it was unforeseen":

> At a time when the decay of religion in the private sphere appeared to be an irreversible trend of modern life, the sudden expansion of political groups proclaiming the Islamic state, swearing by the Koran alone, calling for jihad, and drawing their activists from the world's great cities was an event that cast into doubt a host of previous certainties. Worldwide, the initial reaction was dismay. To leftist intellectuals, Islamist groups represented a religious variant of fascism. To middle-of-the-road liberals, they were no more than born-again medieval fanatics.
>
> But gradually, as Islamist numbers increased, the left discovered that Islamism had a popular base and, casting about for the mass support so critical to their ideology, Marxist thinkers of every stripe began to credit Islamist activists with socialist virtues, while, on the right, it began to dawn on people that Islamists were preaching moral order, obedience to God, and hostility to the "impious" materialists—that is, to the communists and the socialists. More and more people, both within the Middle East and without began to view Islamism as the authentic creed of modern Muslims, to see in it the outline of an Islamic civilization within the multicultural world of the coming twenty-first century.

Kepel sees this new Islamism as stemming from a "cultural revolution," from a collective change of mind inspired and given direction by the teachings of a handful of religious intellectuals, and driven forward by the foundering of secular, modernizing nationalism everywhere from Algiers and Tehran to Karachi and Jakarta. Scarcely a generation after many Muslim nations gained their independence from colonial rule, "the Islamic world entered a religious era that largely canceled out the nationalist period which preceded it." From the 1960s and 1970s and on into this century,

> . . . . petro-Islam [was built] on the ruins of Arab [and third-world] nationalism. . . . What had previously been viewed [by Western observers,

by secular intellectuals, by reforming elites] as a conservative, somewhat retrograde religion, whose social and political relevance was declining in the face of progress and modernization, suddenly became the focus of intense interest, hope, and dread.

Kepel traces the founding impulse, the originating, cultural-revolution phase of all this, to the writings and agitations of three men during the very years, the 1960s and 1970s, when state-led, nation-building development reached its highest peak, with Nasser, Boumedienne, Z.A. Bhutto, Sukarno, and the nonaligned, *tiers mondiste* rest. There was the incendiary Egyptian dogmatist Sayyid Qutb, whom Nasser finally hanged in 1966, arguing from his prison cell that the contemporary leaders of the Muslim world, including "the Pharaoh" who had put him there, were not in fact Muslims at all, but modernized pagans, faithless products of the "new ignorance" now sweeping the world.

There was as well the mercurial Pakistani publicist Mawlana Mawdudi, who died in 1979 after a half-century career as a religious politician alleging plots and counterplots and pressing for the creation of "an Islamic state"—a country governed directly by God via a literalist application of koranic law. And, most consequentially, there was Ruhollah Khomeini, the long-in-exile Shiite cleric concocting the crabbed and intricate theocratical conceptions that led to the Iranian revolution. Taken together, the ideas of these men inspired, between approximately the toppling of the Shah in 1979 and the triumph of the Taliban in 1996, a series of separate and independent, but yet somehow connected, local explosions—the Armed Islamic Movement in Algeria, the civil war in the Sudan, the Iran-Iraq war, Luxor, Kashmir, the storming of the Meccan mosque, the disintegration of Lebanon, the al-Aqsa intifada, as well as the eruptions in Chechnya, Bosnia, and the Moro Liberation Front. Many thousands died—in Iraq and the Sudan, perhaps a million each. It was not just the borders of Islam that turned out to be bloody.

Oddly, Kepel's own conclusion, after reviewing all this storm and disorder in fine detail, is that "political Islam," stalled in Algeria, factionalized in Sudan, defeated in Afghanistan, derailed in Malaysia, diluted in Iran, and put on the defensive everywhere by a world aroused against it after 9/11, is now in full decline:

> Violence . . . has proven to be a deathtrap for Islamists as a whole, precluding any capacity to mobilize the . . . constituencies they need to seize political power. . . . The Islamist movement will have much difficulty reversing its trail of decline as it confronts [the] twenty-first century.

Aside from the fact that things don't exactly look that way in Palestine, Aceh in Indonesia, Kashmir, or northern Nigeria (or, just yesterday, in Saudi

Arabia or Morocco), this would seem to be a conclusion in some danger of instant and definitive disconfirmation. Kepel may, in fact, be suffering from the written-just-before, published-just-after 9/11 syndrome I noted earlier[3] as afflicting a number of recent works on Islam and Islamism. The change in subtitle in the English edition, with its hurried, postscript efforts to sustain the neat, two-part structure of expansion and decline—a structure built too deeply into the original narrative to be revised very easily in the translated one—suggests as much.

In any case, those who have followed the interpretation of jihad and militant Islam "from tradition to terror," most of whom owe a great deal, acknowledged and unacknowledged, to Kepel and his intellectualist, war-of-ideas view of what has been going on, have not taken so relaxed a position. Indeed, they have beaten the drums of alarm with a rising sense of desperation. "Unnoticed by most Westerners," Daniel Pipes, the tireless neoconservative polemicist, has written in the latest of his long series of fire-bell-in-the-night outcries, *Militant Islam Reaches America*, "war has been unilaterally declared [by the Islamists] on Europe and the United States." "The war against [Islamic terrorism]," the one-time beat poet-become-Sufi-devotee Stephen Schwartz writes in his all-out onslaught on the Saudis and everything about them, *The Two Faces of Islam*, "is . . . a war to the death, as the second world war was a war to the death against fascism." "To read is to glide toward death," says the intense and hyperpolitical "new radical" Paul Berman, recruiting Sayyid Qutb to his attack upon Western complacency in the face of the Islamicist threat, *Terror and Liberalism*, "and gliding toward death means you have understood what you have read."

II

Taken together, and for all their differences, which are more of focus than they are of thought, Pipes, Schwartz, and Berman represent a particular, and particularly well-defined, approach to constructing "Islam" (and "Islamism") as a formed idea in the American mind: they regard it not as a product of events and processes foreign to Western history and culture, most especially modern Western history and culture, but as extensions of that history and that culture— old wine in only slightly new, awkwardly relabeled bottles. The apparently exotic is in fact the familiar with a different accent. The twenty-first century, so far anyway, is just a rerun of the twentieth with the names changed. It is quite clear what it is we are faced with in Iraq, Iran, Syria, Saudi Arabia, Pakistan, or the southern Philippines—or, for that matter, in Jersey City and along Atlantic Avenue in Brooklyn: "totalitarianism." All we need is the wit to recognize the fact and the courage to act upon it.

Pipes's version of this it-is-later-than-you-think approach to political Islam is the simplest of the three, the least burdened with complexities and reservations. His chapter titles give a clear-enough sense of both tone and temper, where he is coming from, where he is going: "Battling for the Soul of Islam," "Do Moderate Islamists Exist?," "The Western Mind of Militant Islam," "Echoes of the Cold War Debate," "'We Are Going to Conquer America,'" "'Who is the Enemy?'" All the way down, it is a Manichaean world, divided everywhere, as much among Muslims as among ourselves, between good and evil, perilously balanced:

> A battle is now taking place for the soul of Islam. On one side stand the moderates, those Muslims eager to accept Western ways, . . . ready to integrate in the world. On the other stand the Islamists—fearful, seeking strong rule, hoping to push the outside world away.

And so on and on. Moderate, secularist Turkey faces off against immoderate, sectarian Iran. (But the West is hardly helping the situation.) "Infected by the twentieth-century disease, Islamists make politics 'the heart of' their program." (But Western liberals dismiss their threats as mere rhetoric.) At a moment when "the European-derived extremes of the Communist left and fascist right are tired and on the whole ineffectual, militant Islam has proved itself to be the only truly vital totalitarian movement in the world today." (But a number of wrongheaded Western observers have declared it to be a dying creed.) It is perhaps not altogether surprising that when President Bush recently nominated Pipes, who runs an activist think tank in Philadelphia and writes columns for *The New York Post* and *The Jerusalem Post*, to be a director of the Congress-founded "US Institute of Peace," the Council on American-Islamic Relations, a D.C.-based action group, suggested he lacked detachment and called on the White House to withdraw his name.

Stephen Schwartz, who has also run into political difficulties in the capital, and stirred thereby a teacup-storm on the right, is a strange and outlandish figure.[4] He grew up in San Francisco as part of the City Lights literary crowd around Lawrence Ferlinghetti, whom his father had published; he became a so-far-left-he's-right Trotskyist-anarchist under the *nom de guerre* "Comrade Sandallo," worked for a while as an obituary writer and street reporter for *The San Francisco Chronicle*, shifted his affections and his energies to Reagan during the micro-war in Grenada, and ultimately made his way as a freelance journalist to Sarajevo in the 1990s, where he converted to Islam and joined a Naqshabandi Sufi order. He changed his name again, at least for some purposes, to Suleyman Abmad, and found the Medusa's head every conspiratorialist needs: "Wahabism."

Wahhabism (so called after an eighteenth-century legist, Muhammad bin 'Abd al-Wahhab, who wrote and preached in northwest Arabia, largely, it seems, to an empty desert) is the name generally given to the radically puritanical version of Islam dominant to the point of absolutism in present-day Saudi Arabia—the sort that stones adulterers, decapitates apostates, forbids female car-driving, and, apparently, breeds such people as Osama bin Laden. Rather little is known about Wahhab, whose scholarly output seems to have been both small and unoriginal. But he has become, since the petroleum rise of the House of Saud, which has taken him on as its spiritual totem, the exemplary figure just about everywhere of severe, ultra-orthodox, totalistic Islam—what Schwartz, whose rhetoric has survived his allegiances, calls "Islamofascism."[5]

His book consists in a monomaniacal tracing out, laborious and repetitive (the word "wahhabi" or "wahabbism" appears in almost every paragraph), of the thousands of ways, ingenious, insidious, and implacably relentless, in which the machinations of the House of Saud in the service of this mad creed reaches out to poison the souls of Muslims, turn them against one another, against us, against everybody. Mobilizing their petro-dollars to found religious schools all over the world, set up popular-front-type propaganda foundations, finance lobbying efforts, bribe the powerful, infiltrate legitimate organizations, recruit supporters, eliminate enemies, and most especially to finance jihad, terrorism, and the destruction of Israel, the Saudis work tirelessly to turn Islam, in its essence a peaceful, mystical, unifying force "preaching love and healing," into a world-dividing, world-destroying "two-faced" one.

There is, of course, more than a grain of truth in this, as there is in any comprehensive indictment of faction-ridden politics, and the Saudi factions, like the Ayatollahs, Hamas, Syria, and Mubarak are, surely, playing for keeps. But Schwartz's discussion (he has virtually nothing to say about the concrete details of intra-Islamic conflict and, except for the Koran, he does without source references) is a prime example of how to transform an arguable argument into an obsessional fantasy:

> With the collapse of the Soviet State, Wahhabism effectively replaced the Communist movement as the main sponsor of ideological aggression against the democratic West. . . . The ideological division of humanity into "two worlds" has been promulgated on different bases: Wahhabism applied a religious distinction, Communism a class standard, and Nazism a racial criterion. . . . Wahhabism, like the other totalitarian ideologies . . . compelled members of the new middle classes in the Saudi kingdom and the Gulf states to eagerly kill and die, rather than to procreate and live. . . . The conduct of the Saudis was devious. They assured the West of profound affection, while fomenting worldwide adventurism and seeking to bring every Sunni Muslim on the face of the earth under their control. . . . The Wahhabi-Saudi regime . . . embodies a program for the

ruthless conquest of power and a war of extermination. . . . [Its] face . . . is a great deal uglier than that of a general Islamism, or radical Arab nationalism, . . . or even of Soviet Communism, and its threat to the peace of the world is immensely greater.

Paul Berman's book *Terror and Liberalism*, which is a rambling, one-thing-and-another discourse on what he takes to be the general direction of liberal political thought since the 1930s, differs from those of Pipes and Schwartz only in being somewhat better written and coming, ostensibly, from "the left"—another of those seemingly natural categories that appear to have lost, along with its mirroring twin, a certain amount of force and definition.[6] Carrying forward political ideas developed on the non-Communist, "vital center" left in Europe and America just before and just after World War II—Camus, Orwell, Arendt, Koestler, Arthur Schlesinger Jr., Leon Blum, André Glucksmann—Berman sees Islamism as a continuation of anti-rational ideologies arising all over the Continent in the late nineteenth and early twentieth centuries, ideologies that led on to Italian, Spanish, and German fascism, as well as Russian Bolshevism. Drawing on Dostoevsky and Baudelaire, Luigi Galleani and Martin Heidegger, modern terrorism was born in the salons of Europe. The Muslim version is a mere derivative.

In extending this dark genealogy to the Near and Middle East, Berman relies mainly on a deep reading of Sayyid Qutb, whom he regards as a major, if malefic, thinker, a figure comparable, he says, to "the greatest of modern authors." In Qutb, born seven years before Camus, "his fellow North African," can be found, transformed into a koranic idiom and turned toward the regeneration of a fallen world, all the great themes of European irrationalism: the hatred for capitalist culture, the integralist view of society, the purificatory function of death, the conception of a moral vanguard, the call to direct action, the dream of a purified world. The terror war is neither new nor unprecedented: "It is the same battle that tore apart Europe during most of the twentieth century—the battle between liberalism and its totalitarian enemies."

Perhaps. It would be comforting to think so. Better, surely, a devil you know. But the thought arises, as it does with Pipes and Schwartz, that what is going on here is less an attempt to "understand Islam" than an effort to describe it in such a way that an approach to dealing with it, moral, necessary, clear, and proven, emerges of itself—one which, now that we are the only Supergrand and the Force is really with us, should prove quicker, less costly, and altogether more effective than it was the first time around. Berman writes:

The point [has] to be made clear to everyone around the world that, no, you cannot fight the United States; no, you will be clobbered; no, you won't survive; no, crowds of adoring people on the street will not chant your name—you will lose, and lose again, and lose still more.

III

So much for the warriors, cold and colder. Beyond this sort of aggressive judgmentalism—terror, jihad, "why do they hate us?"—there are also now appearing a number of more empirical and policy-oriented diagnostical works, less concerned with announcing what "Islam" and "Islamism" essentially are than with discerning what, conceivably, they might in time become, and how we ought, from our side of things, to react. Studies of the views and aspirations of contemporary Muslim intellectuals, of political processes and governmental institutions in existing Islamized states, of differences in social attitudes from one region or section of the Islamic world to the next, and of the changing roles of religious scholars and clerics, the schoolmen of Islam, in secular, everyday politics, all direct themselves toward describing a religion that is more an evolving collection of contrasts, an array of possible ways of living and believing, than it is a closed and permanently settled transcendental ideal.

Two just-published books in this general, what's-happening, where-are-things-going tradition, one by Graham E. Fuller, a retired vice-chairman of the National Intelligence Council of the CIA with twenty years of "experience" in the Middle East (he has "visited," he says, virtually every Muslim country in the world), and one by Noah Feldman, a thirty-two-year-old NYU law professor and former clerk to both David Souter on the Supreme Court and Harry Edwards on the D.C. Court of Appeals, address the question: "Is Islam capable of democratization?" And both come up, surprisingly, with positive responses.

In *The Future of Political Islam*, Fuller says he doubts his views reflect those of today's CIA, although they seem more than a little reminiscent of "the Company" during its cold war heyday when it was home to so many of Berman's Congress for Cultural Freedom, Quiet American-type, "hearts-and-minds" liberals. He places his hopes mainly on younger, educated, at least semi-secularized Muslim intellectuals—scholars, teachers, professionals, literary figures, journalists, civil servants, technicians—a rapidly growing class of independent thinkers who show both a useful dissatisfaction with received ideas and a refreshing hunger for new ones, which we ought to be in the business of providing. The real issue, he says, is not whether such people fit our received notions of liberal democrats or not; the real issue is what it is they really want. And what it is they really want, according to the summary accompanying Fuller's book, is a voice in their own political order, a voice they do not have under the present reign of monarchies, autocracies, claques, and theocracies:

> Islamists . . . represent the largest, and often the sole alternative to most entrenched authoritarian regimes today. They continue to flourish, grow, evolve, and diversify. [They are] violent and peaceful, radical and moderate, ideological and pragmatic, political and apolitical [and] they are not going away anytime soon. . . . They are the vehicle for numerous Muslim aspirations: a desire to restore Muslim dignity and voice in the world, to create a new Islamic identity, to remove present dictators, to achieve democracy and greater social justice, to restore a moral compass to Muslim society, to achieve greater power for the Muslim world, to reject foreign domination, and [to defend] the rights of oppressed Muslim minorities everywhere.

When they come to power via free elections, as they so very nearly did in Algeria in 1990-1991, and as they actually did in Turkey, first in 1996 and again in 2003, and, at least temporarily, in 1999 in Indonesia, such people will doubtless be "prickly and suspicious of the US—at least at the outset." Muslim populations, "long pent up and suppressed and silenced . . . will initially burst out of the pen like a Brahmin bull, and it might take some time for them to calm down and get over their accumulated anger." But, given patience, delicacy, and the ability to listen on our part, and "the abandonment by Washington of relentlessly harsh, peremptory, and unilateralist polices toward the Muslim world in the context of the War Against Terrorism," genuine progress toward democracy is possible. "Islamists have embarked on a notable odyssey"—the effort to mobilize their religion and culture in the service of modernization and social development. "We [must] hope [they] will persevere to work toward renewed understanding of Islam in the modern age,. . .find allies in the process, and move toward the changes and reforms so desperately needed."

If all this seems a bit Jimmy Carter-ish, Noah Feldman, who has just been commissioned by some part or other of the Bush administration to help the Iraqis write a new constitution (he worked earlier, while at Yale, helping the Eritreans write theirs), is even more optimistic. In *After Jihad: America and the Struggle for Islamic Democracy*, he traces the "democratic idea" through the sacred texts of Islam, the Koran, the Traditions, the "Law," looks for harbingers of civil society in existing political arrangements, and, all the glasses half-full, finds reason for hope virtually everywhere.

Picture, he says, "a state recognizably Islamic, populated by Muslims and committed to the political principles of democracy." How might such a state arise? It might, he thinks, grow out of the constitutional monarchies of Jordan and Morocco, which, under their new young kings, are already less autocratically governed. It might emerge in Turkey, where democracy is rooted and now needs only to overcome its hostility, inherited from Ataturk and maintained by the secularist army, to Muslim religious expression. It might even come about in a future Palestine, "where the very newness of the enterprise, the scrutiny and assistance of the world, and the political experience of self-realization" could produce "democracy inflected by Islam." It might, somehow, develop in autocracies like Egypt or Algeria, where the shell of democracy exists in the form of elections and parliaments "and needs to be filled by its spirit." Even Pakistan could be an Islamic democracy if its experiment with federalism pays dividends and "its latest military leader proves better than those who came before." The oil monarchies of the Gulf may "surprise the world" and make good on their promises to empower their already elected legislatures and become "mini-democracies to inspire Saudi Arabia."

At this point, the impulse, surely, is to cry "lotsa luck." But there exists, in fact, at least some evidence that such changes, however difficult and however slow they may be coming, are nonetheless far from simply out of the question. Two just-published empirical studies, both carried out by believing Muslims trained and working in modern institutions of learning and within modern scholarly traditions—attitude research in the one case, social history in the other—look at "really existing Islam," rather than some schematized and tendentious image of it. One, called *Faithlines: Muslim Conceptions of Islam and Society*, by Riaz Hassan, a young sociologist trained at the Punjab and Ohio State Universities and now teaching at Flinders University in Australia, rests on a large-scale survey of attitudes carried out in four quite different, widely separated countries—Egypt, Kazakhstan, Indonesia, and Pakistan. The other, called *The Ulama in Contemporary Islam: Custodians of Change*, by Muhammad Qasim Zaman, an intellectual historian who teaches in the humanities and religion departments at Brown, is a study of the activities over more than a century of a powerful clerically led social movement in India, Pakistan, and now, latterly, Afghanistan. Together they not only demonstrate that Fuller's new Muslim intellectuals exist; they show what the world they describe looks like to someone who inhabits it.

Hassan organized and directed teams of local and foreign interviewers, all of them Muslims, in his four countries (which account, as he points out, for about half the population of Muslim majority countries) and conducted 4,500 extensive schedule-interviews inquiring into everything from the subject's belief in miracles or the devil to his (or her—about a quarter of his respondents were women) attitudes toward gender roles, Christianity and Judaism, Darwinian evolution, the role koranic law should play in government, how women should dress in public, or whether they agree with such statements as "human nature is unchanging" (in Pakistan, 86 percent did, in Kazakhstan, 41 percent).

The details of the findings are endlessly fascinating (for example, that 98 percent of Indonesians have experienced "a sense of being afraid of Allah," but only 65 percent of Egyptians—and apparently hardly any Kazakhs; and that in Indonesia only 14 percent of men and 8 percent of women think higher education is more important for men than women, while in Pakistan the figures are 57 percent and 31 percent). But what is most striking about the results overall is how widely particular religious conceptions and attitudes vary among the four countries—from orthodox intensity in Pakistan, still suffering under its sense of being a minority with respect to the Hindus on the subcontinent, through popular street-preacher revivalism in Egypt's exploding, disheveled urban slums, to the complex syncretic pluralism—"many are the ways"—that has characterized multi-ethnic Indonesia for centuries and is now taking on semi-denominational form, and on to the relaxed tolerance amounting almost to indifferentism in Kazakhstan, just out from under the absolute secularist domination of the Soviet Union. Any notion of Islam as a bloc universe, everywhere the same in content and outlook, can hardly survive such findings. The sense that everywhere Islam is moving on, if in varying directions, and not just setting its face against "modernity," the West, and internal change, comes out very strongly.

Zaman's book is a different sort of work altogether, but presents a similar image. It is a detailed, carefully researched monographic study of the development of the Deobandi brotherhood, which, starting out in British India in the late nineteenth century as a Sufi-driven reformist reaction against colonial rule, moved on to become central in the intense "mosque-and-state" debates surrounding the formation of Pakistan, and finally provided much of the impetus and many of the leaders—that is, the *talib* students—for the Taliban insurgency in Afghanistan. Among other things, it demonstrates that the received image of Muslim clerics—ulamas, ayatollahs, mullahs, faqihs—as passive, unworldly reactionaries bound to an atemporal, socially withdrawn Islam is thoroughly misconceived. In many places, by now perhaps most, they are seen as members of vanguard groups in the renovation of traditional Islamic society and belief:

> Even as they strive to demarcate and defend their own religious sphere, the ulama . . . continue to enlarge their audiences, to shape debates of the meaning and place of Islam in public life, to lead activist movements in pursuit of their ideals. For them, there is no single way of defending their ideals or of making them practical or relevant in the world. There are different paths to adopt.

The US is, by now, it will have been noticed, a Middle Eastern power. What we will do as such, especially in the midst of Shiite factional struggles in

Baghdad, terror bombings in Riyadh and Casablanca, the continuing vitality of al-Qaeda, and all sorts of street conflicts throughout the region and beyond, remains to be seen. But certainly the conception of "Islam" being so desperately built up before our eyes by professors, politicians, journalists, polemicists, and others professionally concerned with making up our minds will be of great importance in determining what we do. Here, for once, the line between writing and the world is direct, explicit, substantial, and observable. And, we shall doubtless soon see, consequential.

On the State of the World

I

The recent tsunami in southern Asia, in which perhaps a quarter-million people of all ages and conditions were swept indifferently away by a blind cataclysm, has, at least for the moment—perhaps only for the moment—concentrated our minds. Fatality on such a scale, the destruction not only of individual lives but of whole populations of them, threatens the conviction that perhaps most reconciles many of us, insofar as anything this-worldly does, to our own mortality: that, though we ourselves may perish, the community into which we were born, and the sort of life it supports, will somehow live on. The suggestion that this may not be true, that calamity if great enough, or fecklessness if chronic enough, may put an end to the foundations of our collective existence, that beyond its separate members society itself is mortal, is hardly a new idea. Ancient history collects instances, science fiction constructs narratives; the myths of all nations parade warning examples. But the empirical study of how societies die, the comparative examination of cases and the systematic calculation of possibilities, has barely begun. There are not, as yet, any life expectancy tables for civilizations, and the autopsies, partial and archaeological, are inconclusive about the cause of death.

Jared Diamond is a biogeographer and evolutionary psychologist at UCLA, and the author of a sweeping, relentlessly environmentalist account of the reasons for the emergence of the modern West to political and economic predominance, which sold a million copies and won a Pulitzer Prize. Richard Posner is a judge on the US Court of Appeals for the Seventh Circuit who, between opinions, has published dozens of free-fire polemics on everything from aging and public intellectuals to the rational organization of sex and the

Originally published as "Very Bad News," *New York Review of Books* 52, no. 5 (24 March 2005). Books under discussion therein are as follows: Jared Diamond, *Collapse: How Societies Choose to Fail or Succeed* and Richard A. Posner, *Catastrophe: Risk and Response*.

economic analysis of law. They have, as one would expect, rather different approaches to the question of social fatality.[1] For Diamond, it is a gradual, cumulative affair, accelerating only toward the end when some hard-to-fix tipping point is mindlessly passed. There is a progressive misuse of the natural resources upon which the society is based to the point where collective life collapses into a self-consuming Hobbesean state of nature. For Posner, "catastrophe" is a distant, extrapolated culmination of present trends, an annihilating accident, implicit and unnoticed, waiting to happen—"a momentous tragic usually sudden event [producing] utter overthrow or ruin."

Whether societies waste away in ecological neglect or are destroyed by foreseeable disasters they have failed to prevent, for both writers vigilance and resolve are the price of survival. Awareness is all. However much they may differ in style and method (and they occupy the poles of the social sciences—dogged, fact-thick empiricism on the one side, model-and-calculate political arithmetic on the other), these are consciousness-raising books, tracts for the time. It is later than we think. Later even than we have thought to think.

II

Jared Diamond formulates the problem as he sees it in the simplest and most straightforward of terms: "Why," as his book jacket puts it, "do some societies, but not others, blunder into self-destruction?" "Why do some societies make disastrous decisions?" "What does it all mean to us today?" And he addresses it equally directly, with the most elemental, describe-and-classify sort of comparative method: the kind of approach he took in earlier works to chart the bird populations of highland New Guinea or trace the evolution of primate sexuality. Look at this, look at that; note the similarities, note the differences; find the thread, tell the story—a natural history of societal failure.

Accordingly, he sets out, in differing degrees and depth of detail and in no particular order of importance, a wide variety of particular cases, opportunistically chosen: archaic societies like Easter Island, the ancient Maya, and the Greenland Vikings, which long ago collapsed into self-produced ecological disaster; third-world emergent states like Rwanda, Haiti, and the Dominican Republic that, disorganized, mismanaged, backward, and overpopulated, are well along toward producing such an outcome for themselves; modern or modernizing civilizations, like China, Australia, and the United States, that appear at the moment to be dynamic and flourishing, but in whom the first premonitory signs of overreach, waste, decline, and ruin are beginning to appear. Then, from the evidence of these cases, he constructs a short and miscellaneous checklist of factors that together and separately "contribute" to a society's fate: the inherent fragility of its habitat, the stability of its climate, the friendliness or hostility of its neighbors and trading partners, and, most important of all, the conclusive and decisive determinate force, "the society's responses to its environmental problems." Within the bounds of chance and circumstance, peoples, like individuals, make their own destiny. Choosing well or badly among policies and possibilities, they determine themselves what ultimately becomes of them.

Take Easter Island, at once the most mysterious and the most dramatic ("no other site that I have visited made such a ghostly impression on me") of the once thriving and creative human communities that have simply died and disappeared, vanished whole and entire from the face of the earth. "The most remote habitable scrap of land in the world," 1,300 miles away from its nearest neighbor, sixty-six square miles in area, it was, for nearly eight hundred years, about 900 to 1700 AD, home to a population, at its peak (the estimates, being based on archaeological surveys and explorers' reports, vary widely), of anywhere from six to thirty thousand neolithic yam and taro growers.

Outliers of the great canoe-borne Polynesian civilization that spread across the southern Pacific from New Zealand to Hawaii during the first millennium of the Christian era and essentially cut off, once they had arrived and settled in, from anyone else in the world, they nevertheless managed somehow to carve hundreds of enormous stone statues, fifteen to seventy feet tall, between ten and 270 tons, and raise them to the top of great displaying platforms scattered across the whole island. Images, apparently, of ancestors, gods, or deified chiefs, these now lie toppled and broken, like so many gravestones, across a despoiled and ruined landscape—"the most extreme example of forest destruction in the Pacific . . . among the most extreme in the world . . . the whole forest gone . . . all of its tree species extinct."

Just how, and by what steps, this ingenious people descended, over seven or eight centuries, into generalized disorder and, when they had cut down the last of the forest and destroyed the whole of the island's animal life, into murder, suicide, starvation, and cannibalism is far from clear. There is only archaeological evidence—settlement sites, kitchen middens, hillside quarries, vast crematoria containing thousands of bodies and huge amounts of bone ash—to go by. Rivalry among competing chieftains (the statues get bigger and bigger over time), natural fluctuations in food resources, and epidemic disease probably all played a part, as did increasingly popular rebellion:

Easter Islanders' toppling of their ancestral moai reminds me of Russians and Romanians toppling the statues of Stalin and Ceauşescu. . . . The islanders must have been filled with pent-up anger at their leaders for a long time. . . . I wonder how many of the statues were thrown down one by one at intervals, by particular enemies of a statue's owner, . . . how many were instead destroyed in a quickly spreading paroxysm of anger and disillusionment, as took place at the end of communism.

In any case, the destruction was mindless, total, protracted, and self-inflicted, a lesson and a warning to the way we live now:

> Easter's isolation makes it the clearest example of a society that destroyed itself by overexploiting its own resources. . . . The parallels between [the island] and the whole modern world are chillingly obvious. Thanks to globalization, international trade, jet planes, and the Internet, all countries on earth today share resources and affect each other, just as did Easter's dozen clans. [The island] was as isolated in the Pacific Ocean as the earth is today in space. When the Easter Islanders got into difficulties, there was nowhere to which they could flee, nor to which they could turn for help; nor shall we modern Earthlings have recourse elsewhere if our troubles increase. . . . [The] collapse of Easter Island society [is] a metaphor, a worst-case scenario, for what may lie ahead of us in our own future.

Diamond describes his other fallen civilizations in similarly monitory tones: so many societal *memento mori*, death-head reminders to the live and prospering. The pre-Puebloan Indians of the American Southwest, the fabled Anasazi "ancient ones," built large apartment complexes, entrepôt towns, and intricate irrigation systems, but succumbed to small-scale climate shifts, land struggles, and overcrowding. The great Mayan cities of the Yucatán were strangled by declining crop yields, runaway deforestation, and a primitive transport system. And the Greenland Vikings, to whom he gives a hundred deliberate pages, disappeared, after four and a half centuries of hardscrabble persistence, in the face of narrowing habitats, disrupted trade connections, and a stubborn unwillingness to adopt Eskimo technologies. Everywhere and every time, when societies have perished they have done so through their own neglect and self-delusion. It was not their environments, however severe, that did them in; or anyway not their environments alone. It was their failure to rise to the challenges those environments posed.

With this moral in hand, Diamond then proceeds in a similarly fact-upon-fact, dogged-does-it manner to examine a miscellaneous collection of contemporary societies in adaptionist terms. The Rwanda genocide, generally attributed to "ancient hatred" tribal conflicts, is blamed instead on a Malthusian crisis: a headlong population increase that produced lethal intrafamilial tensions. Young men could not acquire farms, adult children could not leave home, farm size declined precipitously, gross inequalities engendered internecine jealousy. On the Caribbean island of Hispaniola, two scarred and impoverished third-world societies, Franco-African Haiti and Spanish-Indian Dominica, offer, side by side, a study in contrasts: the first "the poorest country in the New World, and one of the poorest in the world outside of Africa," ruined, resourceless, a development basket case; the second still bearing the marks of a caudillo state, with a dependent, top-down economy, politicized forestry, and an artificial construction boom complete with urban traffic jams.

Australia suffers from overgrazing, "land mining," and man-made desiccation, leading "those of us inclined to pessimism or even just to realistic sober thinking" to wonder whether the country is "doomed to a declining standard of living in a steadily deteriorating environment." China, a "lurching giant," big and fast-growing, and ecologically heedless, is ravaged by pollution, waste, and "the world's largest development projects"—dams, floodings, water diversions— "all expected to cause severe environmental problems . . . the disruption of major ecosystem[s] . . . [the] uprooting [of] millions of people."

In the United States, Los Angeles, where he lives, is choked with smog and traffic, its elite having retreated to gated communities; Montana, where he spends his summers, once among the top ten states in per-capita income, is now forty-ninth out of fifty, because of the decline of the extraction industries— logging, coal and copper mining, oil, and gas—which have left behind them a poisoned landscape and a second-home society of self-absorbed seasonal visitors, "half-retirees" from the megapolitan coasts. "Failure to anticipate," "failure to perceive," "rational bad behavior," "disastrous values," "unsuccessful solutions," "psychological denial," "groupthink" are present everywhere.

There are some signs of hope. Japan has managed its forests effectively, highland New Guinea has stabilized its garden economy, radical reform is beginning in Australia, environmentalist activism is growing in the United States. But in general, the prospects are bleak. The modern world is caught up in an "exponentially accelerating horse race" between bigger and bigger environmental problems and increasingly desperate attempts to deal with them. "Many readers of this book are young enough, and will live long enough, to see the outcome."

III

Richard Posner's conception of the sorry end awaiting us if we are insufficiently alert is as futuristic as Diamond's is haunted by history. Collision with an asteroid that could shatter the earth into a thousand pieces. Precipitate global warming that could, paradoxically, turn it into a giant snowball. A runaway particle experiment that could squeeze the planet down to an uninhabitable hyper-dense marble. Gene-spliced pandemic, nuclear-winter war, run-amok robots, self-assembling nanomachines, billionths of a meter across, gobbling up everything in their path until they have consumed all of life. A cloud of extinction events, bodeful and indeterminate, hovers on the world horizon or just over it. Unless we rethink how we order our lives and manage our technology, and perhaps even if we do, the worst may be yet to come.

The main problem, over and above their mind-bending dimensions, is that these various sorts of megacatastrophes seem to most people either so far off, so unlikely, or so thoroughly beyond what they have even vicariously experienced—psychologically off-scale, conceptually out-of-sight—as to be beyond the range of rational estimation or practical response. We are both emotionally disinclined and intellectually ill-equipped to think systematically about extreme events. Absorbed as we are in the dailiness of ordinary life, and enfolded by its brevity, the calculation of remote possibilities and the comparison of transcendent cataclysms look pointless; comic, even. That, Posner argues, must change, and change radically if we are to have a chance of averting, for ourselves and our descendants, a final annihilation:

> The dangers of catastrophe are growing. One reason is the rise of apocalyptic terrorism. Another . . . is the breakneck pace of scientific and technological advance. . . . The cost of dangerous technologies, such as those of nuclear and biological warfare, and the level of skill required to employ them are falling, which is placing more of the technologies within reach of small nations, terrorist gangs, and even individual psychopaths. Yet, great as it is, the challenge of managing the catastrophic risks is receiving less attention than is lavished on social issues of far less intrinsic significance, such as race relations, whether homosexual marriage should be permitted, the size of the federal deficit, drug addiction, and child pornography. Not that these are trivial issues. But they do not involve events of potential extinction or the modestly less cataclysmic variants of those events.

The first necessity is obviously to distinguish the threats. Where are we to begin? Are natural accidents like tsunamis, earthquakes, volcanic eruptions, glaciations, and asteroid collisions the most pressing danger? ("An asteroid that struck what is now Mexico 65 million years ago, though estimated to have been only 10 kilometers . . . in diameter when it entered the earth's atmosphere, is believed to have caused the extinction of the dinosaurs. . . . A similar collision is believed to have occurred 250 million years ago wiping out 90 percent of the species living then.") Or is it a germ-war pandemic, "the possibility that science, bypassing evolution, will enable monkeypox to be 'juiced up' through gene splicing into a far more lethal pathogen than smallpox ever was"? Or a laboratory accident? A shower of quarks in a particle accelerator self-reassembled into "a very compressed object called a strangelet [that] would keep growing until all matter was converted to strange matter"? A similarly generated "phase transition" that would "rip the fabric of space itself" and "[destroy] all the atoms in the entire universe"?

Genetically modified crops? Artificial life? Mechanical super-intelligence? Species loss? Greenhouse pollution? Cyberterrorism? Posner reviews them all in turn, in a hectic flurry of piled-up fact-bites, speculative calculations, passing quarrels, and offhand policy dicta—an orderless mixture of assertion, guess, remark, and opinion for which the term "farrago" would seem to have been invented. The result, perhaps unsurprisingly, is rather like a lawyer's brief. If one line of reasoning fails to carry, try another. If one expert demurs, find one who doesn't.

The threats identified, the costs of their impact, should they contrive to occur, must be somehow assessed, a formidable task when you are dealing with minuscule probabilities, anomalous events, and world-shaking consequences. Posner largely handles the problem of estimating danger via sheer postulation—weird and (one assumes, unintentionally) madcap burlesque. "Suppose the cost of extinction of the human race . . . can be very conservatively estimated at 600 trillion dollars [and there is] a 1 in 10 million annual probability of a strangelet disaster." "Suppose there is a 70 percent probability that in 2024 global warming will cause a social loss of $1 trillion." "Suppose that [a] $2 billion expenditure reduces the probability of [a bioterrorist attack] from .01 to .0001." That done, cost-benefit analysis, the assigning of numerical weights to policy proposals—emission taxes, sky-search programs, early-warning systems, accelerator inspections—can then be applied (at least theoretically: "people have trouble placing a money value on 'products' remote from what they are accustomed to find offered for sale") to determine what proportion of its resources society as a whole, and especially American society, "dollar-weighted . . . about one-fourth of the world," ought to devote to one or another of them: where this or that catastrophe should rank on our scale of worries.

On this basis, page after page of statistical assumption (most people "would rather have a reasonable assurance of living to 70 than a 50 percent probability of living to 50 and a 50 percent probability of living to 90") and speculative number crunching (". . . let me make a wild guess that the benefits [of Brookhaven's Relativistic Heavy Ion Collider] can be valued at $250 million per year"), Posner arrives at a series of sweeping conclusions, confident and emphatic, and not a little unnerving, concerning what it is that, "better safe than sorry," needs posthaste to be done.

An International Environmental Protection Agency to enforce treaty-determined environmental norms—a stronger and more binding Kyoto Protocol—should be created. (Conservatives' worry that international institutions put the United States at the mercy of other nations is misplaced: "as the world's most powerful nation, the United States tends to dominate international organizations, and, when it does not, it ignores them with impunity.") A worldwide police agency, "a greatly strengthened Interpol," is needed to deal with bioterrorism, "precisely because it is a police problem as well as a scientific and medical one." (Not just the investigation and apprehension of terrorists as such "but also of innocent scientists who by failing to observe security precautions may become [their] unwitting accomplices" demands a global system of official surveillance.) The policy of allowing foreign students open access to our universities ought to be reexamined. ("It is doubtful that all of those who [have] returned home [have], by virtue of their sojourn in the United States, become inoculated against rabid anti-Americanism.")

Scientists, whose "goal is knowledge, not safety . . . cannot be entrusted with the defense of the nation and the human race." ("The Large-aperture Synoptic Survey Telescope . . . would as we know be an ideal tool for identifying potentially hazardous near-earth objects. The principal advocates of the project, however, are interested not in near-earth objects, but in remote galaxies.") They need to be brought to a more responsible awareness of their social duty—perhaps by a science court manned by "scientifically literate lawyers," perhaps by a federally funded "Center for Catastrophic-Risk Assessment and Response." "Johnny-one-note civil libertarians uttering fallacious slogans," peddling "bromides about free speech," and obsessing over "coercive interrogation" may object that such measures break constitutional norms. But since September 11, "the marginal cost of civil liberties [has] increased dramatically." As the risk is great, so must be the response:

> In wartime we tolerate all sorts of curtailments of our normal liberties . . .
> conscription, censorship, disinformation, intrusive surveillance, or suspension of habeas corpus. A lawyer might say that this is because war is a legal status that authorizes such curtailments. But to a realist it is not war as such, but danger to the unusual degree associated with war, that justifies the curtailments. The headlong rush of science and technology has brought us to the point at which a handful of terrorists may be more dangerous than an enemy nation. . . . It has been a commonplace since Thomas Hobbes wrote *Leviathan* that trading independence for security can be a profitable swap. . . . Only the will is wanting.

IV

For all their differences—Diamond's pageant and panorama, Posner's hodge-podge and swirl, Diamond's materialism, Posner's utilitarianism, Diamond's earnest prophesying, Posner's belligerent policy mongering—both are engaged, at bottom, in the same sort of exercise: engineering a social mood. They are out to alter attitudes, redirect mind-sets, refocus worries; transform the currents of popular feeling. They ask, in somewhat different ways, the same question: "Is the modern way of life globally sustainable?" And they give, on the basis of somewhat different material, the same answer: "Not as it stands."

Looking around, one finds it hard to argue. There are enough calamities, actual and looming, natural and man-made, to give anyone pause, even if they still fall a bit short of Diamond's isolate and castaway Easter Island or Posner's world-devouring nano-machines. Kobe and Banda Aceh, Bhopal and Chernobyl, September 11 and Madrid, Rwanda and Darfur; AIDS, deforestation, overpopulation, urban sprawl, pollution, and the proliferation of industrial waste seem near out-of-hand; and it is, in fact, difficult to imagine a world in which the Chinese use of automobiles matches the American. Yet it is possible to wonder whether the situation will yield to alarm and entreaty, the cry havoc persuasion of large numbers of minds. Decline and fall melodramas and sci-fi scenarios may serve to italicize crisis, but it is not so clear what they do to engage it.

What is most striking about both Diamond's and Posner's views of human behavior is how sociologically thin and how lacking in psychological depth they are. Neither the one, who seems to regard societies as collective persons, minded super-beings intending, deciding, acting, choosing, nor the other, for whom there are only goal-seeking individuals, perceiving and calculating rational actors not always rational, has very much to say about the social and cultural contexts in which their disasters unfold. Either heedless and profligate populations "blunder" or "stumble" their way into self-destruction or strategizing utility maximizers fail to appreciate the true dimensions of the problems they face. What happens to them happens in locales and settings, not in culturally and politically configured life-worlds—singular situations, immediate occasions, particular circumstances.

But it is within such life-worlds, situations, occasions, circumstances, that calamity, when it occurs, takes intelligible shape, and it is that shape that determines both the response to it and the effects that it has. However "natural," "physical," or "material" they may be, and however unpredictable or unintended, collapse and catastrophe are, like coups and recessions, riots and religious movements, social events.

A cataclysmic flood in southern Asia projects world powers into the midst of the most local of local conflicts—Sumatran separatism, Sri Lankan civil war. An AIDS pandemic shakes the foundations of family life and alters power relationships across an entire subcontinent. The state's response, selective and defensive, to a nuclear accident in the Ukraine alters the whole language of rights and obligations in an emerging nation. An industrial accident in a US-owned plant in central India leaves behind it a quarter-century of litigation and legislation, claim and counterclaim, that shapes attitudes toward every-thing from the limits of corporate responsibility to the foundations of dis-tributive justice. The introduction of efficient methods of selective harvesting into the Indonesia rain forests by Japanese multinationals rearranges the rela-tionships between the forests' inhabitants, the urban-centered central govern-ment, and the broader world of global trade.

Monographic attention to such critical examples should take us further than either Diamond's chronicles or Posner's scenarios toward whatever un-derstanding and whatever control of the disruptions and disintegrations of modern life are actually available to us.[2]

PART III

The Idea of Order: Last Lectures

The Near East in the Far East

Lucette Valensi's extensive work on the social history of the Mediterranean has been, for all its variety of subject and focus, almost continuously concerned which the way in which cultural forms arising within one stream of history, one historic civilization, work out when projected into the interior of another: French and Algerian, Jewish and Muslim, Iberian and Moorish, Venetian and Ottoman. Ideas, sentiments and view of life, ways of being in the world, find some of their most striking, and most diagnostic, expressions far from their point of origin: in the way they color traditions quite other than their own, live with a particular vividness in a foreign place.

I should like to use this celebratory occasion to practice the difficult art Valensi has so carefully developed, and to cross over an even greater distance and an even broader difference: the Middle East and Southeast Asia. In particular, I wish to consider the role of Islam as a projection of, for want of a better term, "Arabic Culture or 'Civilization'" into the "'Culture' or 'Civilization' of Indonesia." This is, admittedly, a subject, at once very hard to focus, more than a bit touchy, and rather grand in scale. But, if only for those reasons, it provides a good "Valensian" subject: a familiar tradition inserted into an unfamiliar place.

Centrifugal Islam

Everyone is aware of the "international," "cosmopolitan," "transcultural" nature of Islam, and aware, too, that it has been thus virtually since its beginnings. A generation after the Prophet's death it had reached westward through

Originally published as "The Near East in the Far East: On Islam in Indonesia," *Occasional Papers*, Institute for Advanced Study, Princeton, no. 12 (December 2001). Lucette Valensi is the Director of Studies of the Institut d'Études de l'Islam et des Sociétés du Monde Musulman, which is a section of the École des Hautes Études en Sciences Sociales in Paris. She is author of, among other texts, *The Birth of the Despot: Venice and the Sublime Porte* (English translation 1993).

Egypt to Berber North Africa, eastward through Asia Minor toward Persia and India, after which it moved on to the Malay world in the one direction and to Black Africa on the other. But through all this cultural filtering—through Turkish mysticism, through Persian ecclesiasticism, through Mughal state formation—as intense and as various as any body of thought and belief has ever passed, the fact that its mid-eastern, Arabic character and image, however overlaid, reinterpreted, and further developed, has persisted tends to go unremarked. It is more sensed than specifically inquired into, more taken for granted than examined.

One reason why this aspect of the spread of Islam, and with it of certain aspects of "Arabic culture"—a term itself a bit in need of differentiation—has been passed over, if not precisely in silence, rather on tiptoe, is the ambivalence that inevitably accompanies such a process of cultural radiation over so vast and varied an area. Those on the receiving end of the project, anxious to maintain their own originalities and claim their own contributions, to be themselves rather than somebody else, are especially wary of analyses that trace some of their most prized beliefs and institutions to foreign sources. Just about everywhere that Islam has spread beyond its Arabian and Fertile Crescent homeland, the question has arisen as to what is "Islamic" and what is "Arabic" in the civilizational conglomerate, the broad and inclusive set of beliefs and practices, values, and customs that make up *al-ālam al islāmīya*. Sorting out these two dimensions, the one supposedly "religious," the other supposedly "cultural," may be at bottom an impossible task, or a useless one. But that has not prevented peoples from Morocco to Indonesia, Bangladesh to Nigeria, Turkey to Afghanistan, from trying to do it continuously, repeatedly, and without much in the way of a clear and stable resolution.

Religion in general has been one of the major mechanisms by means of which particular local cultures have projected themselves onto a larger world screen throughout the course of history. Christianity, especially under the imperialist, evangelizing impulse that gripped it after the Reformation, brought European views and values to various parts of Asia and Africa, as well as to the New World. Buddhism, the movable form of Indicism, carried aspects of South Asian sensibility over into Southeast Asia, China, and even into Japan. But Islam has been particularly effective in injecting the tone and temper of the Near East into distant contexts, as well as, what is even more important, in maintaining and reinforcing them once they were injected.

The focus on Mecca and Medina as the sacred center of Dar al-Islam and the growing importance, as communications improved over the centuries, of the hajj; the maintenance of classical Arabic in Arabic script as the sole, untranslatable language of doctrine, as well as of law, prayer, poetry, ornament, and history; the strongly literary, iconoclastic, antiritualizing rhetorical bent; the scriptualist revitalizations of the first half of the last century—all these rigorist, not to say purist, institutions and movements have served to keep the traditions of Arabic culture, and a good deal of its feel as well, alive within even the most seemingly uncongenial contexts: African ceremonialism, South Asian hierarchism, Southeast Asian syncretism.

I once described Islam as a religion designed for export.[1] But what it has exported is not just a creed and a world view. At least in part, the ground out of which that creed and that world view grew has been exported along with it. Even more than Christianity, with its movable partitions and its adjustable scriptures, certainly more than Buddhism, without much in the way of either primordial center or fixed scripture, Islam has carried its native coloring with it. To become Muslim has not, to be sure, meant to become Arabized. But it has meant to enter into a complex and continuing, seriously ambivalent, relation to Arabic culture.

My own interest in this issue stems mainly from my own long term field studies in two culturally quite contrastive, both to one another and to that of the Near East, non-Arabian Islamic societies. I have worked in and on Indonesia and in and on Morocco, the frontier outliers of the ummat, the Wild West and the Mysterious East, for about a half century now, playing them off, one against the other.[2] They make, for such purposes, a useful, unusually accommodating pair. They even manage to change regimes more or less in synch. The death of King Hassan II after thirty-seven years of rule and the fall of President Suharto, hardly less a monarch, after thirty-three, came within months of each other a couple years ago, followed in both cases by weak and hesitant reformist regimes, plagued by a rising tide of Islamist dissension and disaffection, and deepening internal confusion. Here, however, I will for the sake of brevity and clarity, examine, or rather reexamine, only the Indonesian case. The Moroccan one is in some ways even more elusive and harder to get a grip on, while seeming on the surface much the simpler of the two. But as it would take another book to deal with the two comparatively and tease out the similarities within their differences, the contrasts which connect them, I will make my more general points in connection with Indonesia, leaving to another occasion the extension of such of that as might apply to Morocco.

Niche Formation

The most distinctive aspect of the historical career of Islam in Indonesia is that, more than anywhere else, even more than in India, it inserted itself, and rather late (mostly after the fourteenth century, and most decisively only after the seventeenth and eighteenth) into an ethnically, linguistically, geographically, and religiously complex and differentiated society. There was no "virgin ground" to "civilize" here, as there was, more or less, in compact and tribalized Morocco. There was a vast, archipelagic "country" (six thousand or so islands, flung out across two million square kilometers along the equator), which was already highly developed, if very unevenly, economically, politically, and culturally.

The brute fact that strikes any observer of Indonesia, however casual and at whatever period in its history, is its extraordinary diversity, so great that it makes, and has long made, identity definition—"Who are we? Malays? Muslims? Javanese? Asians?—a central, and continually evolving concern. A few simple dates and numbers will get this across. There are fifteen reasonably sizeable and up to five hundred small, reasonably distinct groups, speaking upwards of three hundred languages. The country has been colonized, for a shorter or longer time, in part or in whole, by the Portuguese, the Spanish, the Dutch, the English, and the Japanese—and, some would say, more recently and less formally, by the Americans. Commercial influences from India, from South Arabia, and most especially from China, the famous "oriental trade," have led to significant immigrant settlements over the whole course of its history.[3]

For more than a millennium, beginning about the fifth century of present era, Hindu- Buddhist civilizations (the two "religions" were barely separable then), migrant from eastern India, dominated Java, Bali, and certain regions of Sumatra, Kalimantan, and Sulawesi, leading to the construction of large, aggressive, very densely populated agrarian states focused around axis mundi symbolic capitals, mass ritual, spiritual hierarchy, and "divine" kings.[4] From about 1400, these kingdoms were challenged by powerful polyglot, polyethnic, poly-racial Muslim principalities on Java and Sumatra, particularly along the northern coasts, spread there by a large scale, international, long distance trade fluorescence, running from Aden and the Red Sea eastward across the Indian Ocean and the Malabar Coast, on through the Makassar Straits and the Java Sea to the Spice Islands edging the Pacific on the east. And as first the Portuguese and then the Dutch slowly gained hegemony after the seventeenth century, the country was progressively, if quite unevenly Islamized, until today it is, at least nominally (a qualification, as we shall see, of very great importance), about 85% Muslim, 7% Protestant, 3% Catholic, 2% Hindu, 1% Buddhist, and 2% "other"—mostly local, so-called "animists" or "pagans."

There is a great deal more to say about this formation of a highly cosmopolitan, multistranded, somewhat haphazard culture in what was then called, with appropriate plurality, the East Indies: about the unevenness of its distribution, about the relative weights of its various elements, and about the political and economic framework, authoritarian, imperialist, and intensely laboristic, within which it took place. But the essential point is that Islam as a religious and cultural impulse, an imported turn of mind, had to contend with a wide array of formidable competitors, within the play of which it had, as both late-coming and in general unarmed, somehow to position itself. Neither "conquest" (though there was violence enough involved) nor "colonization" (though there was some foreign settlement, mostly fugitive, here and there) are the appropriate terms for what happened in the Indies. "Niche-formation"—seeking out openings in a crowded landscape, occupying them, and then expanding them—is rather more descriptive of the advance of Islam, and with it of Near-Eastern thought forms, in most parts of Indonesia, from its very first intrusions until today.

I will not attempt to trace out this process of niche-formation and development here in concrete detail, both because it would take too long and because it would involve a cascade of names, places, events, and personalities, some of which (Salifiyyah, the Acehnese War, Hatta, Masjumi) might be generally recognizable, others of which (Hamza Fansuri, Demak, The Paderi Rebellion, Sarekat Islam) probably would not. What I want to do is outline its general shape: the institutions mediating it, the phases it has passed through, and most especially the role that Islam, with its Arabic aura and atmosphere, its echo of distant landscapes and distant tongues, has come to occupy in the ideological swirl of modern, independent Indonesia. Thus a genealogy rather more than a history: an ordering of inheritances, a sorting of traditions, an identity legend.

In these terms, I shall discuss, in turn and all too briefly, what seem to me to be three fairly readily discernable, though overlapping and intersecting, stages in this tale, not of events and personalities but of the construction of a place for Islam (and, concurrently, for the background hum of Arabic culture) in a conglomerate, Euro-Asian, or Asio-European, civilization exterior to it: (1) niche establishment, (2) niche expansion, and (3) niche consolidation. Taken together, they give a picture of what is usually called, somewhat negligently, as though it were some sort of ideological takeover by a fixed and seamless eternal vision, "the Islamization of Indonesia," that is rather different than those given both by canonical discussions of the matter and by revisionist accounts—by orthodox stories driven by doctrinal considerations, and by neo-orthodox stories driven by political considerations. We find, instead of a growing hegemony, a growing differentiation: the development not of a common consciousness, but of a deeply, and quite possibly permanently, divided one.

Mosque, Market, and School

To begin with niche establishment, the securing of a foothold, a beachhead, a base, an enclave, the main mediating institutions aside from the Prophecy as such, were the mosque, the market, and the school: in Indonesian, the *masjid*, the *pasar*, and the *pesantren*. Together, they formed an indissoluble triad, religious, economic, and social at once, around which, in this place or the other, at that time or the other, a recognizably Muslim community, an *ummah*, could crystallize.

The close association, the symbiosis even, of trade, traders, and the spread of Islam has been often remarked, as has the accompaniment of them by the so-called "Islamic college" (Arabic, *madrasah*), in part a sect, in part a school, in part a theatre of clerical authority. From the foundation of the Prophecy at the crossroads of trade routes in the Hejaz (at least reputedly—I recognize there is dispute about the matter), through the establishment of the great cosmopolitan emporium centered on Fustat, Basra, Quyrawan, and Sijilmasa in the "Arab Middle Ages" of the tenth and eleventh centuries, to the fluorescence of the "eastern trade" through Gujarat, Malabar, Malacca, and the Spice Islands in the fifteenth and sixteenth, the persistence of this relation between the trader, the scholar, and the Friday assembly as the animating nucleus of a portable Islam is clear and unmistakable. So far as Indonesia is concerned, the growth and proliferation of the intensely cosmopolitan port kings, sometimes called "Bazaar States," I alluded to a moment ago—Arabs, Turks, Persians, Chinese, Gujarati, Tamils, Javanese, Bugis, Malays, after awhile Portuguese and Hollanders, all tumbled in together, peddling cloth, spices, jewelry, slaves, cosmetics, and foodstuffs in a sliding-price marketplace—provided precisely the sort of fluid, decentralized, intensely competitive far-eastern environment in which this near-eastern form could project itself, defend itself, and, in time, expand.[5]

In itself, this establishment of a Muslim quarter (called, usually, a *kauman*, Malay from Arabic, *qawm* for "nation," "people," "ethnos") grouped around a mosque and instructed by itinerant charismatics, was hardly a matter of Arab incursion and settlement. Only a handful of Arab traders, Hadraumatis from what is now southern Yemen mostly, proceeded very far along the Alexandria, Aden, Cambay, and Makassar sea-highway before the beginning of the nineteenth century, though a fair number did so afterwards. Crowded with Persians, Turks, Indians, and, increasingly Malays and Javanese—all Muslims, if rather different sorts of Muslims—the *kauman*, within which a commercial pidgin called "bazaar Malay" became the language of communication as Arabic was the language of prayer, was as culturally pluralistic as the society that surrounded it. It was less set off from that society than a component of it: a community among communities.

The next stage, "niche expansion," consisted of, first, the increasing relative importance of the Muslim element within the bazaar states to the point where rulers who had been called "rajah," or some such name, without changing their general cultural dress and outlook very drastically, and their mode of operation hardly at all, came to be called "sultan," or some such; and then, second, and much more critically, the movement, slow, hesitant, and very uneven, of the mosque-market-school complex into the agrarian heartlands of the larger islands, Java, Sumatra, Kalimantan, and Sulawesi. The formation of a distinctive commercial culture—mobile, Malay-speaking, at least superficially Muslim—around "Asia's Mediterranean," the Java Sea, led to an extended, intense, and curiously indecisive struggle between it and the interior principalities—large, immobile, feudal, and Indic—a struggle further complicated by the increasing prominence of first the Portuguese and then the Dutch in the coastal emporium. Again, it is not possible to trace the progress of this from-the edges-inward transformation of Indonesian society and culture here: it is both too complex and too incompletely understood. Suffice it to say that from the sixteenth through the eighteenth century, and on into the nineteenth, the sort of encapsulated Islam characteristic of the bazaar-state *kaumans* worked its way into most parts of the archipelago at the same time as it was being transformed into a systematically exploited and bureaucratically governed European colony.[6]

The Pesantren Complex

The fact, and it is a fact, that Islam proceeded across Indonesia under the umbrella of Dutch hegemony, that it was, however accidentally, the historical beneficiary of an imposed, self-distancing imperial government bent on engrossment and export, has been somewhat obscured in recent discussions, when it hasn't been actively concealed. In great part, this is a result of the postcolonial desire, understandable enough in itself, to portray the colonial period as one in which the distinction between the intrusive and the indigenous was culturally clear and spiritually absolute; that insofar as the two were connected it was in terms of otherness and opposition, as separate, dissociated worlds, only antagonistically, and unequally, interacting. This is simply not true. The nineteenth and early twentieth centuries in Indonesia saw the construction of a Euro-Asian (or, again, Asio-European) society with a form, an outline, and a content of its own, a society whose main difference from what preceded it, and, indeed, from what followed it, was the configuration of its variousness. And it was within that society, the unfolding "Indies," sprawled and irregular but increasingly interconnected, that Indonesian Islam found its fixed, expandable niche.

The Dutch transformation of a string of tribes and islands flung out along the equator into a hierarchy of provinces and departments, and the attendant reduction, one after the other, of all the indigenous states and polities from one end of the archipelago to the other, provided an ordered, intelligible landscape, blocked out regions and culture areas—official "peoples"—across which the mosque-market-school complex could more easily move, navigate, and settle. It established itself as the primary mediator of Islamic fidelity and the Near Eastern connection, one after the other, in virtually all of the densely populated irrigated rice-growing regions, the settings within which the Indic agrarian states and statelets had arisen before them: central and eastern Java, west and northeast Sumatra, southeast Kalimantan, southern Sulawesi.[7]

The standard pattern, replicated again and again throughout the archipelago in more or less invariant form, was the foundation of what came to be known as a *pesantren*, literally a place for peripatetic Islamic students, or *santri*, traveling about in search of *'ilm*, religious knowledge or illumination. But a *pesantren* was more than an educational institution, a clerical academy concerned with the formal propagation of doctrine. A typical *pesantren* consisted (and consists: the country is still dotted with them, and they continue to provide the greater part of the institutional substructure of Indonesian Islamism) of a small, marked off, usually rural estate, located at the edge of a village or in the open field between villages: an Arcadian complex of: (1) a mosque, simple or elaborate, composite in style; (2) a home, usually spacious, for the religious leader (the *'alim*, or *kiyayi*, or *ustād*), who is in most case a *haji*, a returned Meccan pilgrim; and (3) anywhere from one or two to a dozen or more open veranda dormitories called *pondok* (from Arabic *funduq*, "inn," "hospice," "caravansary") in which the students, anywhere from a half dozen to several hundred, virtually all of them at this period male, lived. There were also often various workshops, fields, and so on attached to the *pesantren*, dedicated to it as a religious foundation—a *waqf*.

The students ranged from mere children of eight or nine to mature or even elderly men, though the great majority were adolescents or young adults. They cooked their own food, washed their own clothes, worked in the fields and workshops, traveled about the area as tailors, tinkers, mendicants, and market peddlers. Some stayed a month, some stayed for years. They were free to move from one *pesantren* to the next in order to study with other teachers and earn certificates (*ijāzah*) in particular branches of religious learning, though the ties with their original teacher, continuously renewed with gifts and visits at the *'ayād*, the Muslim high holidays, were considered almost supernaturally unbreakable. The teaching took place in the mosque. As, at least until recently, few of the *santris* knew much Arabic, it consisted of the *'alim* (who may not always have known that much either) reading from the Quran, a *hadith* collection, or some *fiqh* text or other; or, in some instances, where Sufi orders—Shattari, Qadari, Naqshbandi—had penetrated, from *ṭarīqah* devotional manuals. The *'alim* offered vernacular explications and commentaries as he went, which the *santris*, echo-chanting the text, noted in its margins, and memorized, after which the *'alim* signed the *ijīzāh* appropriate to that text for those students whom he deemed to have mastered it.[8]

In such a manner, step by step, over the course of three centuries, the partially sighted leading the largely blind, a *pesantren* network was established through the whole of the western part of the archipelago and, more sporadically, in the eastern, following along and constructing the local networks of cyclic, "solar system" markets that intensifying mercantile intrusion induced just about everywhere. The individual *pesantren* differed widely in size and importance; they waxed and waned, arose and disappeared, with the renown and fortunes, never that secure, of their *'alim*. But as the number of pilgrims, and of richer traders and landowners who could afford to be pilgrims, grew ever greater, especially after the beginning of the nineteenth century when the Dutch had made the sea lanes secure (Snouck Hurgronje reports hundreds of "Javans," the largest foreign contingent there, studying in Mecca in the 1880s, often for years at a time), the number of *pesantren*, and the number of *santri*, also grew until today there are an estimated forty thousand such schools with perhaps eight million or so students.[9] What started out as Muslim *kauman*-type niches in the multicultural bazaar states spread, on the backs of trade, discipleship, and restricted literacy, through the whole of the multicultural archipelago. Today, "santri" has become the general term, just about everywhere in the islands, for an observant Muslim, a strict, as opposed to a casual, a nominal, or, as the current idiom has it, a "statistical" adherent of Islam.

But however extensive this net, it remained, and remains, a niche, however large and internally developed, within the broader, motley and miscellaneous Indonesian society. By those same 1880s, when the Meccan connection was up and running, cosmopolitanizing a clerical elite, just about every major religious, or religio-cultural, tradition was to be found somewhere in the islands. The Dutch presence, in itself quite secular, facilitated the addition of Christianity, Protestant primarily, but as time passed Roman Catholic as well, to the mix. Important Christian enclaves were founded in east-central Sumatra, where German Lutherans were active, north Celebes, where Dutch Calvinists were, and various competing micro-denominations, of the sort the Netherlands was so fertile in producing, settled into one or another parts of the Lesser Sundas, the Moluccas, and New Guinea declared open by the colonial government to missionization. Like Islam, Christianity in Indonesia was a matter of marked out moral communities, some of them sizeable. But unlike Islam, the communities were separate and discontinuous, neither commercially, nor organizationally, nor culturally interconnected.

Beyond these, there was the Chinese minority, also grown large, and to a degree prosperous, under Dutch domination, set apart, mostly in towns and cities in a Sinic, dialect-divided world. There was a whole series of small, but often quite elaborate, Malayo-Polynesian tribal traditions, up-country particularisms unabsorbed into broader unities. And, most important, there was a large, unorganized mass of nominal, "statistical" Muslims—rather more, I would guess, though this can only be a guess, than half of the whole—eclectic in outlook, relaxed in creed, and syncretistic in practice, whose relation to the *pesantren* tradition and the Arabic aura it projected was at best nervous and mistrustful, at worst nervous and hostile. By the opening of the last century, the trans-local collective identities, the contrastively phrased religious and cultural *familles d'esprit*, that would confront one another in the illusory, and as it turned out fragile, uniformities of nationalism were already in place.

Nationalism, Reformism, and the Question of Identity

It is not possible to trace the development of the other constituents of the Indonesian assemblage . . . or collage . . . or miscellany . . . here, nor to describe their individual force and content with any specificity. I have attempted elsewhere something of this sort, just for Java, where I distinguished three such constituents: (1) the syncretic folk tradition of the peasantry, usually called *abangan*; (2) the Arabo-Indonesian (or Indo-Arabian) *santri* tradition I have been here discussing; and (3) a more self-consciously Indic, quasi-theosophical, illuminationist one, sometimes called Javanist, sometimes *priyayi*, after the Dutch-educated native civil servants who were, and whose successors are, its main exponents.[10] Others have essayed similar enterprises, with similar, or at least comparable, demarcations elsewhere. But most of the sorting out and specifying work, the identification of subnational but superlocal identity frames, which are, to my mind, the fundamental elements of whatever cohesion—in the nature of the case never much more than partial and never much less than tense—Indonesia displays, remains to be done, and I would not want to deny that there is broad room for argument on such matters. What is clear, nonetheless, is that, however such frames are defined and characterized, in this place or that, or whatever the overall inventory of them may turn out to be, they came into more and more direct and intimate conflict, one with the next, with the rise of nationalism and, most especially with the institution of the fragile and composite Republic, unitary only in name, that the clashes and insurrections of the end-of-the-war forties forced rather suddenly into being.

Insofar as religion is concerned, the entire history of the national struggle, which gets seriously underway in the nineteen-tens and twenties (there were, of course, foreshadows and adumbrations—protests, jacqueries, millennial enthusiasms—well before that), was an effort not so much to separate the identity frames, spiritual families, cultural positionings, or whatever, clearly out one from the other, to sort them into fixed, walled-off compartments. They were far too mixed and shape-shifting, and rather too interested in one another, for that. It represented an attempt either to institute some sort of moving balance among them according to their relative strengths and conflicting demands, also moving, or more radically, and as it turned out disastrously, to establish the clear and certain dominance of one or another of them over all of the others. Nationalism disturbed, and in the event destroyed, the external and arbitrary, essentially racial division of rights, powers, and opportunities under which the East Indies functioned by bringing the "who are we?" question into intense, unavoidable, and unavoidably political, focus. If there was to be an Indonesian people—*one* Indonesian people, as the barricades slogan, "One Country, One Language, One People," had it—then the religio-cultural pluralism inherited from the previous three centuries of accelerating change and differentiation had to be confronted. Its terms had to be reset, its boundaries redefined, its weights recalibrated. And that did not prove as easy to do as it was to desire.[11]

Nor was the task made any easier by the fact that at the same time as nationalism (secular, egalitarian, and radically unitary in its aims and institutions) took hold in the archipelago, religious reformism was setting in with similar determination in the Arabic-speaking Near East, a development that began soon afterward, via the usual connections (the *hajj*, study at Al-Azahr, the increasingly important religious press, and so on) to have an abrupt and tearing impact on the Indonesian *santri* community. The writings and teachings of Jamal al-Din al-Afghani, Muhammad Abduh, Rashid Rida, and others in the so-called *salafiyah* movement just before and just after the turn of the nineteenth century, a bookish and to some degree internally contradictory movement which, in Ira Lapidus's words, "combined the reformist principles— return to the Quran and the sayings of the Prophet, the right of independent judgment in religious matters, abandonment of a stifling conformity to outmoded tradition, and opposition to cultic Sufi practices—with a modernist responsiveness to the political and cultural pressures of Europe," induced a pervasive and deep-going tension, rising at times to open conflict, into *santri* Islam.[12] I have described this development at some length, not only for Indonesia, but for Morocco, where it was at least as consequential and tradition-disruptive, under the rubric of "scripturalism," (a term I still prefer to the usual alternatives: "fundamentalist," "reformist," "modernist") elsewhere, and I will not repeat that discussion here.[13] Suffice to say that, running alongside and in complex relation to the rise of nationalist agitation, intensified urbanization, and the steady erosion of the Dutch hold on things, the scripturalist incursion, something new out of the Middle East, divided the Indonesian *ummah*, as it divided that of the Arab heartland, into reformist and traditionist, or perhaps more accurately, integralist and pluralist, camps.

Simplifying (again!) a story that will not really simplify, as urbanization increased contact with Europeans and with European ideas intensified, and commercial life migrated more and more emphatically town-wards, a part of the community migrated with it to establish a scripturalist presence—a new Arabism in a new niche. The organizational vehicle of this re-statement and re-institutionalization of things emphatically Muslim, was a large, and as it soon became, nationwide social welfare organization called Muhammadiyah. Founded by urban merchants, mullahs, and mosque officials in the former Indic capital, Yogyakarta, in 1912, and claiming, by century's end, more than twenty-five million members, it set up clinics, orphanages, youth groups, women's organizations, relief depots, and most critically, graded, professionally taught Western-style schools offering systematic, Indonesian-language instruction in secular subjects side by side with, also rather more systematized, less cultic Islamic ones.[14] And in response, both to it and to the increasing power of the nationalist movement as such, a number of *pesantren 'ulema* in the east and central Javanese countryside (including, most notably, the grandfather of the recent, and recently displaced, President of the country) set up a counter organization called Nahadatul Ulama—"The Renaissance of the Religious Teachers." Dedicated to the preservation and extension of the *pesantren* way of life, and to the traditionalistic, and by now quite Indonesianized, conception of Islamic piety that flourished there, it too spread and grew extremely rapidly to become, at upwards of thirty million members, what is said to be the largest Muslim organization in the world.[15]

The following decades, the nineteen forties, fifties, and sixties (the years of the Japanese Occupation; of the Revolution; of the Sukarno-Hatta balanced-ticket Republic; of the formation of impassioned, belief-driven national parties; of the first general election pitting these parties against one another as radical, "if we win it's our country" alternatives; of the institution, when the elections only reinforced hostilities; of "guided," that is manipulated, "democracy," trying to smooth it all over with rhetoric and symbolics; of the descent into popular massacre, a hundred thousand? five hundred thousand? three-quarters of a million? people killed or exiled, when it wouldn't smooth; of the emergence of the Suharto autocracy from the rubble, calming things for the moment by fastening a military clamp on them) have been often and for the most part well-chronicled, and so have the ups and downs throughout it all of the *santri* community. Suffice it to say that the immediately post-colonial years saw both the headlong politicization and ideologization of all the constituents of the *assemblage*, and a series of failed attempts, bloody and spectacular, to contain them within some sort of larger consolidative order. (The Cold War further complicated the picture, projecting Communism into the mix, as did, from the other side of the ledger, another disturbance out of the heartland, the appearance on the local scene of the totalistic sort of Islamism associated with Wahabbism and the Muslim Brotherhood: Sayyid Qutb, Hasan al- Banna', Hasan al-Turabi, and so on). By 1998, when Suharto, his manipulative eclecticism, corrupt a bit here, oppress a bit there, smile benignly, exhausted in its turn, fell, the very permanency of the country, its continued integrity, seemed at risk; the "who are we?" question near to beyond answering.

Permanent Pluralism?

An anthropologist who works on a particular country for a half-century, the span of both its career as an aspiring state and his own as an aspiring scholar, leads an awkward life. He has continually to revise his perception of his "object of study," which is, anyway, not an "object"in the first place, but a massive, turbulent subjectivity caught up in a no less turbulent encompassing world. But he has, also and at the same time, to maintain a vision of that object steady and crystalline enough to say something general and intelligible about it, something not entirely trapped within the immediacies of the present moment. Changing your views in public is embarrassing enough, especially when those views have been forcefully stated. Reasserting them, unchastened and unchanged, after ruin, upheaval, and all sorts of accident have intervened, is even more so. But this is the predicament in which longtime observers of Indonesia, all we would-be Myrdals or Crèvecoeurs, Tocquevilles or Bryces, anxious to sum up other people's lives and prospects, now find ourselves caught.

The change, the ruin, the upheaval, and the accident, is particularly visible at the moment, after the so-called "Asian crisis" of 1998 (a sixteen percent drop in GDP, twenty million unemployed) and the nervous relaunching of party-based electoral government; and the scholarly ethos, not only of the anthropology profession, but of the whole of the human sciences right now, directs us toward an intense, at times it seems a nearly exclusive concern with it. Like journalists, we seem powerfully attracted to the idea that we are responsible for writing the first draft of history, or for concocting a plausible account of tomorrow's weather out of the evidence of today's precipitation. These are, in themselves, reasonable endeavors (though we get rained on a lot), hardly avoidable, occasionally useful. But, at the same time, Indonesia has by now been around long enough, not just as a culture and a colony but as an autonomous state and would-be nation, for us to begin to essay some views as to what some of the abiding characteristics of this "object" might be, to provide a sketch at least, to change the metaphor to something I am more comfortable with, and that fits rather better with our Arabist concerns, of the figure in the carpet.

The figure I think I see, or glimpse, or imagine, and which I have been trying, rather breathlessly, to sketch here, is one of a foundational diversity—hundreds of landscapes, languages, peoples, regimes, faiths, economies, forms of life, ways of being in the world—only made more diverse, and more ineluctable, as time has passed and modernity, at least tentatively, appeared. Such a conception runs counter, I realize, to the highly integralist views of Indonesia, nationalist and sectarian, cultural and religious, political and psychological, that have come by now to be conventional wisdom, both inside the country and outside it. The country, and I think it genuinely a country—a bounded field of love and contention, a habitat, a homeland, a *heimat*, a *patria*, a place to remember and to long for—is built on difference, and on the sufferance of difference. All attempts to disguise that fact, or to deny it—radical nationalism, radical Islamism, radical leftism, most recently, radical developmentalism, perhaps next, radical localism—are, and consistently have been, non-starters, recipes for cataclysm, short and long term.

It is as a difference among differences, a particularity among other such particularities, that I have sought, both here and generally, to portray Islam in Indonesia. Seeing it as a weaving of (some aspects of) "Arabic Culture" into a carpet already dense with foreign forms and figurations, is of course not the only way to see it. For some, indeed, and particularly lately, as a certain neo-scholastic, sometimes called "substantialist" revisionism, an effort to create a social theology, has set in both among some Western educated *santris* and some anxious-to-help foreign scholars, this way of looking at things is regarded, when it isn't considered anti-Islamic altogether, to be oblivious to the increasing prominence of "genuine" Muslim commitment in Indonesian life since the mid-sixties and early seventies, its steady progress toward political, social, and spiritual hegemony. Perhaps this is so, but I am not persuaded that such a progress is underway or, that if it is underway, that it is progress. Any attempt to proceed on the basis that it is, that religious wholeness, and with it cultural wholeness, is finally within reach, that "the Islamization of Indonesia" is finally at hand, will end no better than all the other efforts to fasten a settled personality upon the country. It does not have such a personality, it does not need one, and, in my view anyway, it is not, at least not soon, perhaps not ever, going to get one. It is not just locally, accidentally, and temporarily pluralist. It is, to commit a philosophical solecism and a political truth, pervasively, essentially, and permanently so.

If this is true, then reflections about the future based on the past, about what direction things might henceforth move, given how they have done so heretofore and where they now seem to stand, take a surprising turn. The most striking aspect of the present scene in Indonesia, as anyone who reads the newspapers, or even the headlines, will know (IS INDONESIA BREAKING DOWN? . . . BALKANIZATION OF INDONESIA MAY BE FAR FROM HYPOTHESIS . . . ONE COUNTRY OR MANY?), is the accelerating spread of scission and separatism, the upsurge of micro-violence and capsule war. Aceh, Ambon, West Kalimantan, Irian, the Moluccas. Not all of this is religiously inspired, of course, but none of it is free of echoes and resonances of the niche-building history I have been describing. The niche/*familles d'esprit*/ *assemblage* way of putting a society together, and a polity to govern it, may be, now that iron-hand modes of rule—colonial, demagogic, military—have, for the moment anyway, been set aside as unworkable and worse, nearing something of a testing point: Can a nation thus conceived long endure? Is it even a nation? Need it be? Only—as sightless seers, eyeless in Gaza, always say when they would to escape from a discourse they know how to launch but not how to get out of—only time will tell. What is clear, even to seers, however, is that the present moment in Indonesian history, and the history of Islam and the Arabic register within Indonesian history, is a particularly decisive one, one on which rather more depends than immediate result and short run direction.

There have been such moments before, of course. Eighteen-thirty, when colonialism congealed, was one. Nineteen-forty-five, when the Revolution began, was another. But there has been none more critical in the determination of the very viability of so various, ill-coordinated, and multiplex an actor (it has been compared at times both to a headless centipede and to an elephant with beri-beri) in the modern world of unit states, hierarchic power-blocs, and hegemonic ambitions.

What is clear, insofar as anything is clear, is that some of the shapes of our common future, which grows more common by the day, will find their first expression in Indonesia, and other centipede and elephant countries—Nigeria, Southern Africa, the South Asian subcontinent, Brazil—over the rest of this just-born century. Finding a political, social, and cultural form within which so internally diverse a country can function and sustain a workable identity, will be neither quick nor easy, neither merely linear nor free of violence and other disorders. It took three hundred unquiet years (if one starts one's counting with Westphalia and finishes it at the Risorgimento) to evolve and implant the sovereign, and enfolded, nation-state in Europe, an achievement promptly followed by two world wars. And to construct a successor, if one is to be found, better adapted to the realities of a fluid, uncentered, thoroughly mixed up, improvisational world—what I have elsewhere called "the world in pieces"— will hardly be quicker, easier, or less troubled.[16]

Whatever new sort of something new comes out of Indonesia in the years and decades ahead, and I am persuaded that something will, pretty or unpretty, it is virtually certain that the *santri* tradition, and with it the long-distance resonances of Arabic culture, will be centrally involved. The ascent to the presidency of the Republic of that quicksilver grandson of the founder of Nahdatul Ulama, Abdurrahman Wahid, however brief it turned out to be, places that tradition (he was born and grew up in his grandfather's and father's east Javanese *pesantren*, studied in Cairo and Baghdad) at the very center of Indonesian political life for virtually the first time.[17] Whether and how long it stays there remains to be seen, besieged as it is from all sides, religious and secular alike. But its force, and the force of the *santri* tradition in all of its varying forms and directions, will surely be deeply implicated in whatever emerges: nationalist reaction, national dissolution, or (dare we hope?) a new form of architecture, a change of heart.

And so far as Arabic culture is concerned, it may well be that its nature, its power, its possibilities, and its limitation will be as clearly exposed in the distant environs to which it has migrated, largely in the casements of Islam, as it is in Arabia, Egypt, and The Fertile Crescent. The study of culture, too, needs to be dispersed and deparochialized, set free of origins, totality, and the will to purity. Looking obliquely at the edges of things, where they come together with other things, can tell you as much about them, often, as can looking at them directly, intently, and straight on.

An Inconstant Profession

Introduction

I have arrived, it seems, at that point in my life and my career when what people most want to hear from me is not some new fact or idea, but how I got to this point in my life and my career. This is a bit discouraging, not just because of its *momento mori* overtones (when you are seventy-five, everything has *memento mori* overtones), but because, having spent the whole of my adult life trying to push things forward in the human sciences, I am now being asked to consider what that has entailed—why I think my direction can be called forward, and what, if that direction is to be sustained, the next necessary thing might be. As a result, I have engaged in the past few years in at least two more or less organized attempts to describe the general curve of my life as a working anthropologist, and this essay will be the third, and, I trust, the last. Talking about one's self and one's experiences in a homiletical manner—"go thou and do likewise"—is a bit much the first time around. Recycled, it loses charm altogether.

The first of these essays in apologetical retrospection, originally given as a Harvard-Jerusalem lecture in 1990, became the chapter entitled "Disciplines" in my book *After the Fact* (1995). There I concentrated mostly on matters of research and scholarship, most especially on my long-term fieldwork in Indonesia and Morocco—a story of projects leading to outcomes leading to other projects leading to other outcomes. The second, originally given as an American Council of Learned Societies "Life of Learning" lecture in 1999, became the first chapter, entitled "Passage and Accident," of my most recent book, *Available Light* (2000). There I presented a more personal, semi-introspective account of both my life and my career; a sort of sociointellectual autobiography and self-accounting. This time—this last time—I want to do something else: namely, to trace the development of anthropology as a field of study over

Originally published as "An Inconstant Profession: The Anthropological Life in Interesting Times," *Annual Review of Anthropology* 31 (2002):1–19.

the more than half-century, 1950–2002, I have been involved in it, and to trace, too, the relationships between that development and the broader movements of contemporary history. Though this also, of necessity, produces something of a "the things I have been through and the things I have done" sort of narrative, I am, for the most part, not concerned with either my work or my persona. I am concerned with what has happened around me, both in the profession in which I have been, however loosely and at times uncomfortably, enclosed, and in what we are pleased to call "the wider world," in which that profession has been, however marginally and insecurely, enclosed. That world is with us late and soon: There is very little in anthropology that is genuinely autonomous; pretensions to the contrary, however dressed in the borrowed clothes of "science," are self-serving. We are, like everybody else, creatures of our time, relics of our engagements.

Admittedly, this is a little vast for a short essay, and I am obliged to pass over some very large matters very quickly, ignoring detail and suppressing nuance and qualification. But my intent is not to present a proper history, an inclusive summary, or a systematic analysis. It is, instead,

1. To outline the succession of phases, periods, eras, generations, or whatever, both generally and in anthropology as such, as I have lived through it, and them, in the last half of the last century, and,
2. To trace the interplay between (for the most part, American and European) cultural, political, social, and intellectual life overall and anthropology as a special and specialized profession, a trade, a craft a *métier*.

Whether such broad-stroke, impressionistic, the-view-from-here sketching will yield much in the way of insight into how things are, and have been, heading in our field remains to be seen. But, absent a crystal ball, I know of no other way.

So far as phases, periods, eras, and the like are concerned, I shall, for my own convenience, mark out four of them. None of them is internally homogeneous, none of them is sharply bounded; but they can serve as useful place-markers in a lurching, tangled, digressive history. The first, roughly between 1946 and 1960—all dates are movable—was a period of after-the-war exuberance, when a wave of optimism, ambition, and a sense of improving purpose swept through the human sciences. The second, about 1960 to about the mid-1970s, was dominated, on the one hand, by the divisions of the universalized cold war, and, on the other, by the romances and disappointments of Third-Worldism. From 1975 or so to, shall we say, in honor of the fall of The Wall, 1989, there was, first, a proliferation of new, or anyway newfangled, approaches to social and cultural analysis, various sorts of theoretical and methodological "turns," *Kehre, tournures d'esprit*; and then, on the heels of these, the rise of radically critical and dispersive "post-" movements, brought on by increasing uncertainty, self-doubt, and self-examination, both within anthropology and in Western culture generally. Finally, from the 1990s until now, interest has begun to shift toward ethnic conflict, violence, world-disorder, globalization, transnationalism, human rights, and the like, although where that is going, especially after September 11, is far from clear. These, again, are not the only cuts that could be made, nor even the best. They are but the reflections, diffuse and refracted, in my own mind of the way of the world and the ways of anthropology within the way of the world.

Postwar Exuberance

During the Second World War, American anthropologists were, like American sociologists, historians, psychologists, and political scientists, drawn, almost to the man or woman, into government service. After it ended, in what was, in the United States anyway, not that long a time, three or four years, they returned, immediately, again almost to the man or woman, to academia with their conception of themselves and their profession radically altered. What had been an obscure, isolate, even reclusive, lone-wolf sort of discipline, concerned mainly with tribal ethnography, racial and linguistic classification, cultural evolution, and prehistory, changed in the course of a decade into the very model of a modern, policy-conscious, corporate social science. Having experienced working (mostly in connection with propaganda, psychological warfare, or intelligence efforts) in large, intellectually diverse groups, problem-focused collections of thrown-together specialists, most of whom they had previously known little about and had less to do with, anthropologists came back to their universities in a distinctly experimental frame of mind. Multi- (or inter-, or cross-) disciplinary work, team projects, and concern with the immediate problems of the contemporary world were combined with boldness, inventiveness, and a sense, based mainly on the sudden availability of large-scale material support both from the government and from the new mega-foundations, that things were, finally and certainly, on the move. It was a heady time.

I encountered all this at what may have been its point of highest concentration, greatest reach, and wildest confusion: Harvard in the 1950s. An extraordinary collection of persons and personalities had gathered there, and at the nearby Massachusetts Institute of Technology, launching programs in all directions. There was the Department of Social Relations, which—chaired by the systematic sociologist Talcott Parsons, and animated, rather diffusely, by his rather diffuse "General Theory of Social Action"—combined sociology, anthropology, clinical psychology, and social psychology into an at least terminologically integrated whole. There was the Russian Research Center, headed by the cultural anthropologist Clyde Kluckhohn; the Psychological Clinic, headed by the psychoanalyst Henry Murray; the Laboratory of Social Relations, headed by the social statistician Samuel Stouffer. John and Beatrice Whiting, in from Yale, assembled a team and began exploiting the newly created Human Relations Area Files for comparative correlation studies of socialization. And at MIT, there was the Center for International Studies dedicated to stimulating modernization, democratization, and takeoff in the new states of Asia and Africa and the stranded ones of Eastern Europe and Latin America. Just about everything that was in any way in the air in the social or, as they soon came to be called as the pressures toward unification intensified, the behavioural sciences—from group dynamics, learning theory, and experimental psychology to structural linguistics, attitude measurement, content analysis, and cybernetics—was represented by one or another Institute, one or another Center, one or another Project, one or another entrepreneur. Only Marxism was missing, and a number of the students happily provided that.

For me, as a would-be anthropologist—one who had never had an anthropology course and had no particular aim in mind except to render himself somehow employable—the figure I had most to come to terms with in this swarm of talkative authorities was Clyde Kluckhohn. A driven, imperious, rather haunted man, with an enormous range of interests, a continuously restless mind, and an impassioned, somewhat sectarian sense of vocation, he had read Classics at Oxford as a Rhodes Scholar. He had studied the Navajo and other peoples in the American Southwest since having been sent there as a teenager for his health, and he knew his way around the corridors of power, both in Washington (where he had worked as consultant to the Secretary of War and directed morale surveys for the Office of War Information) and, an even greater achievement (considering he had been born obscure in Iowa) at Harvard. The author of what was then the most widely read, and best written, statement of what anthropology was all about, *Mirror for Man* (1949), a past president of the American Anthropological Association, a fierce controversialist, a player of favorites, and a master money-raiser, Kluckhohn was rather a presence.

Of the various collective enterprises (thinking back, I count at least eight, and there were probably more) that Kluckhohn was at that moment either directing, planning, or otherwise animating, I myself became involved, in turn, in three, which, taken together, not only launched my career but also fixed its direction.

The first, and smallest, was the compendium of definitions of culture Kluckhohn was preparing in collaboration with Alfred Kroeber, then in his late seventies and concluding a sovereign career in detached retirement. I was given what, with the aid of other, more senior, graduate students, they had assembled and what they had written in the way of commentary, and I was asked to review it and offer suggestions. I had some suggestions, most of them expository, a few of which were attended to; but the most fateful result of the experience for me was that I was inducted into the thought-ways of the particular form of anthropology then called, rather awkwardly, pattern theory or configurationalism. In this dispensation, stemming from work before and during the war by the comparative linguist Edward Sapir at Yale and the cultural holist Ruth Benedict at Columbia, it was the interrelation of elements, the gestalt they formed, not their particular, atomistic character, as in previous diffusion and culture area studies, that was taken to be the heart of the matter. A phoneme, a practice, a role, an attitude, a habit, a trait, an idea, a custom was, as the slogan had it, "a point in pattern"; it was systems we were after, forms, structures, shapes, contexts—the social geometry of sense.

A large number of expressions of this approach to things current in anthropology appeared at that time. Perhaps the most visible and influential, though as it turned out not so long-lived, was the so-called culture and personality movement, in the service of which Kluckhohn, Murray, and a junior member of the Social Relations Department, David Schneider, put together a more or less definitive reader. Strongly influenced by psychoanalytical ideas and by projective testing methods, it sought to relate the processes of individual psychological development to the cultural institutions of various societies. Abram Kardiner and Ralph Linton at Columbia, Cora DuBois, first at Berkeley then at Harvard, Erik Erikson, also first at Berkeley and then at Harvard, and Kluckhohn himself in his Navajo work were perhaps the most prominent figures in the movement, and Margaret Mead was its battle-fit, out-front tribune; but it was very widespread. Closely allied to culture and personality there were the so-called national character or culture-at-a-distance studies, such as Benedict's on Japan, and Mead's, Rhoda Métraux's and Geoffrey Gorer's on Europe and America, and, of course, those of the Russian Research Center, where sociologists, psychologists, political scientists, and anthropologists attempted to assemble a collective portrait of "the new Soviet man" out of the analysis of communist writings and refugee life-histories.

My interest in all this was limited by what seemed to me its somewhat mechanical, destiny-in-the-nursery quality and the vastness of its explanatory ambitions. So I drifted instead toward another of Kluckhohn's large-scale, long-term, multi-discipline, multi-inquirer, systematical enterprises in the interpretation of cultures, the so-called Comparative Study of Values or Ramah (later Rimrock) Project. This project, methodical and well financed, was dedicated to describing the value systems (world-views, mental attitudes, moral styles) of five geographically adjacent but culturally discrete, small communities in northwestern New Mexico—Navajo, Zuni, Spanish American, Mormon, and Anglo (or Texan). Over a period that finally stretched to twenty years or so, dozens of researchers from a wide variety of crossbred specialties—moral philosophers, regional historians, rural sociologists, American Indianists, child psychologists—were dispatched to one or another of these sites to describe one or another aspect of the life being lived there. Their fieldnotes, hundreds upon hundreds of pages of them, were then typed up on cards and filed in the Human Relation Area Files manner at the Peabody Museum of Anthropology, where they could be commonly consulted and a long string of special studies, and finally a collective volume, written. As for me, I did not go to the Southwest but worked for some months in the files, then already vast and varied, on a subject set by Kluckhohn—the differential responses of the five groups to problems set to them all by the common conditions of their existence as small, rural, more or less encapsulated communities: drought, death, and alcohol. Mormon technological rationalism, Zuni rain dancing, Spanish-American dramatic fatalism in the face of drought, Navajo fear of ghosts, Mormon eschatological schemes, Anglo grief-avoidance in the face of death, Zuni sobriety, Mormon Puritanism, and Navajo spree drinking in the face of alcohol—all were outlined, rather schematically, and attributed, rather speculatively, to their differing value systems. But whatever the limitations of the report I produced (and it wasn't all that bad as a first pass at things), the experience turned out to be both a sort of dry-run for the kind of field research—comparative, collaborative, and addressed to questions of meaning and significance—that I would spend the rest of my life pursuing; and a transition to the next phase or period of the immersion of anthropology in the movement of the times: the age of modernization, nation-building, and the all-enveloping Cold War.

Modernization and the Cold War

The Center for International Studies at the Massachusetts Institute of Technology, which I mentioned earlier as part of the cluster of social science holding-companies emerging in post-war Cambridge, was set up in 1952 as a combination intelligence gathering and policy planning organization dedicated to providing political and economic advice both to the rapidly expanding U.S. foreign aid program and to those it was ostensibly aiding—the "developing," "under-developed," or, for the less sanguine, "backward" countries of Asia, Africa, and Latin America. At first, the Center, something of an anomaly in an engineering school not much given at that time to social studies of any sort, was hardly more than a secretary, a suite of offices, a name, a large amount of money, and a national agenda. In an effort simply to get it up and running, Kluckhohn, who, still moving in mysterious ways, had again been somehow involved in its formation, proposed that a team of doctoral candidates from Harvard social science departments be formed and sent to Indonesia under its auspices to carry out field research in cooperation with students from that country's new, European-style universities. Five anthropologists, including myself and my then wife, Hildred, also a Social Relations student; a sociologist who was a historian of China; a social psychologist; and a clinical psychologist were given a year of intensive work in the Indonesian language and sent off for two years to the rice fields of eastern Java (not all of them got there, but that's another story) to carry out, ensemble, parallel, interconnected, and, so it was hoped, cumulative researches: the Ramah Project model updated, concentrated, and projected abroad.

The ups and downs of this enterprise, which itself came to be called "The Modjokuto Project" and the degree to which it achieved the ends proposed to it have been retailed elsewhere. For the present "March of Time" sort of story, its significance lies in the fact that it was, if not the first, surely one of the earliest of what soon turned into a flood of efforts by anthropologists, or teams of them, to adapt themselves and their tribes-and-islands discipline to the study of large-scale societies with written histories, established governments, and composite cultures–nations, states, civilizations. In the years immediately following, the number of such country-focused projects multiplied (as did, of course, as a result of decolonization, the number of countries), and a sort of super-discipline called area studies, eclectic, synoptical, reformative, and policy-conscious, came into being to support them.

When the Modjokuto team left for Southeast Asia, the Center, as I mentioned, did not yet really exist as a going concern, so its connection with the work we did there—essentially historical and ethnographic, a refitted community study—was nominal at best. By the time we returned to Cambridge, three years further on, however, it had become a large, bureaucratized organization with dozens of specialized researchers, most of them economists, demographers, agronomists, or political scientists, engaged in development planning of one sort or another or serving as in-country policy consultants to particular governments, including that of Indonesia. The work of our team seemed, both to the Center staff and to ourselves, to be rather to the side of the Center's mission, inconsonant with its "applied" emphasis and too concerned with what the program-minded types took to be parochial matters. We drifted away into writing our separate theses on religion, kinship, village life, market selling, and other irrelevancies, and beginning, finally, our academic careers. I, however, was rather more interested in developmental questions, and in state formation, than my colleagues, and I wished to return as soon as possible to Indonesia to take them up. So, after gaining my doctorate, I rejoined the Center and became more directly involved in its work and with the master idea that governed it: modernization.

This idea, or theory, ubiquitous in Third World studies during the 1960s and early 1970s, and, of course, not all that dead yet, stemmed from a variety of sources. Most particularly, it grew out of the writings of the German sociologist Max Weber and his American followers (of whom, Talcott Parsons was perhaps the most prominent, and certainly the most insistent) on the rise of capitalism in the West. Weber's conception of the history of the West since the Renaissance and the Refomation was that it consisted of a relentless process of economic, political, and cultural rationalization, the instrumental adjustment of ends and means, and he saw everything from bureaucracy, science, individualism, and double-entry bookkeeping to the industrial organization of labor and the disciplined management of inner life as expressions of such a process. The systematic ordering of the entirety of human existence in rational terms, its imprisonment in an "iron cage" of rule and method, was what, in its essence, modernity was. In particular, his famous, in some quarters infamous, Protestant Ethic thesis—that the harsh, predestinarian beliefs of Calvinism and related inner-worldly ascetic doctrines of the sixteenth and seventeenth centuries provided the moral legitimation and driving force for the tireless pursuit of profit and bourgeois capitalism—spurred a whole host of studies designed to support and extend it, to find signs and portents of such progress-producing value systems in that most residual of residual categories, the nonmodern, nonrational, noncapitalist non-West.

As for me, my original thesis proposal, put temporarily aside to address myself to describing Javanese religion more generally for the purposes of the common project, was to pursue the possibility that reformist (or modernist) Islam might play a role in Indonesia similar to that which Weber's Calvinism supposedly played in the West. So, after writing a short book at the Center on the history of Javanese agriculture, which ascribed its failure to rationalize along the capital-intensive, labor-saving lines experienced earlier in the West and, in a somewhat different way, in Japan, to the colonial policies of the Dutch, I headed back to Indonesia hoping to address the Weberian thesis in a more direct and systematic, hypothesis-testing way. I would, I thought, spend four or five months each in a strongly Islamic region in Sumatra, a strongly Calvinist region in Sulawesi, and a Hindu region in Bali and try to ferret out the effects, if any, of different varieties of religious belief on the modernization of economic behavior.

But a funny thing happened on the way to the field. The cold war, previously fought out (the rather special case of Korea perhaps excepted) in the client and satellite states of Europe, shifted its center of gravity to the Third World, and most especially to Southeast Asia. All this—the Malaya emergency, the Vietnam war, the Khmer Rouge, the Huk rebellion, the Indonesian massacres—is much visited, much disputed, history, and I will not rehearse it again here. Suffice it to say this development altered the whole scene of action for those of us trying to carry out field studies in such suddenly world-critical places. The induction of the obsessions and machinations of the East-West confrontation into entrenched, long-standing divisions in religious, ethnic, and cultural life—another, less foreseen, form of modernization—brought local, hand-to-hand politics to a furious boil just about everywhere it occurred, and it occurred just about everywhere.

From the end of the 1950s to the beginning of the 1970s, the charismatical, hero-leaders of the new states—Nehru, Nkrumah, Nasser, Ben Bella, U Nu, Ayub Khan, Azikwe, Bandanaraike, Sihanouk, Ho, Magsaysay, Sukarno—bedevilled within and without by these pressures toward ideological polarization, struggled to position their countries in the ever-narrowing, unfilled space between the powers: neutral, nonaligned, newly emerging, "*tiers monde.*" Indonesia, which soon found itself with both the largest Communist Party outside the Sino-Soviet bloc and an American-trained and -financed army, was in the very forefront of this effort, especially after Sukarno organized the Bandung Conference of 29 Asian and African nations, or would-be nations, in that west Javanese city in 1955. Nehru, Chou, Nasser, and Sukarno himself all addressed the Conference, which led on to the formal creation of the nonaligned movement. All this, and the general unfolding of things, made of Indonesia perhaps the most critical battleground after Vietnam in the Asian cold war. And in the mid-1960s it collapsed under the weight: failed coup, near civil-war, political breakdown, economic ruin, and mass killings. Sukarno, his regime, and the dreams of Bandung, never more than dreams, or self-intoxications, were consumed, and the grimmer, less romantic age of the kleptocrats, Suharto, Marcos, Mobutu, Amin, and Assad emerged. Whatever was happening in the Third World, it did not seem to be the progressive advance of rationality, however defined. Some sort of course correction in our procedures, our assumptions, and our styles of work, in our very conception of what it was we were trying to do, seemed, as they say, indicated.

An Explosion of Paradigms

By the time I got back to the United States toward the beginning of the 1960s (my neat little three-way project spoiled by the outbreak of anti-Sukarno rebellions in Sumatra and Sulawesi, I had spent most of the year in Bali), the destabilizing effects of the deepening of the great power confrontation in Southeast Asia were beginning to be felt with some force there as well. The profession itself was torn apart by charges and countercharges concerning the activities, or supposed activities, of anthropologists working in Vietnam. There was civil rights and "The Letter from Birmingham Jail," civil liberties and the Chicago Seven. The universities—Berkeley, Harvard, Columbia, Cornell, Kent State, Chicago—erupted, dividing faculty, inflaming students, and alienating the general public. Academic research on "underdeveloped" countries in general, and on "modernization" in particular, was put under something of a cloud as a species of neoimperialism, when it wasn't being condemned as liberal do-goodism. Questions multiplied rapidly about anthropology's colonial past, its orientalist biases, and the very possibility of disinterestedness or objective knowledge in the human sciences, or indeed whether they should be called sciences in the first place. If the discipline was not to retreat into its traditional isolation, detached from the immediacies of contemporary life—and there were those who recommended that, as well as some who wished to turn it into a social movement—new paradigms, to borrow Thomas Kuhn's famous term, first introduced around this time were called for. And soon, and in spades, they came.

For the next fifteen years or so, proposals for new directions in anthropological theory and method appeared almost by the month, one more clamorous than the next. Some, like French structuralism, had been around for a while but took on greater appeal as Claude Lévi-Strauss, its proprietor-founder, moved on from kinship studies to distributional analyses of symbolic forms—myths, rituals, categorical systems—and promised us a general account of the foundations of thought. Others, like "sociobiology," "cognitive anthropology," "the ethnography of speaking," or "cultural materialism," were stimulated, sometimes overstimulated, by advances in biology, information theory, semiotics, or ecology. There was neo-Marxism, neo-evolutionism, neo-functionalism, and neo-Durkheimianism. Pierre Bourdieu gave us "practice theory," Victor Turner "the anthropology of experience," Louis Dumont "the social anthropology of civilizations," Renajit Guha, "subaltern studies." Edmund Leach talked of "culture and communication," Jack Goody of "the written and the oral," Rodney Needham of "language and experience," David Schneider of "kinship as a cultural system," Marshall Sahlins of "structure and conjuncture." As for me, I contributed to the merriment with "interpretive anthropology," an extension, broadened and redirected by developments in literature, philosophy, and the analysis of language, of my concern with the systems of meaning—beliefs, values, world views, forms of feeling, styles of thought—in terms of which particular peoples construct their existence and live out their particular lives. New or reconditioned social movements, feminism, anti-imperialism, indigenous rights, and gay liberation, added to the mix, as did new departures in neighboring fields—the *Annales* movement in history, the "new historicism" in literature, science studies in sociology, hermeneutics and phenomenology in philosophy, and that elusive and equivocal movement, known, elusively and equivocally, as "post-structuralism." There were more than enough perspectives to go around.

What was lacking was any means of ordering them within a broadly accepted disciplinary frame or rationale, an encompassing paradigm. The sense that the field was breaking up into smaller and smaller, incommensurable fragments, that a primordial oneness was being lost in a swarm of fads and fashions, grew, producing cries, angry, desperate, or merely puzzled, for some sort of reunification. Types or varieties of anthropology, separately conceived and organized, appeared, one on top of the next: medical anthropology, psychological anthropology, feminist anthropology, economic anthropology, symbolic anthropology, visual anthropology; the anthropology of work, of education, of law, of consciousness; ethnohistory, ethnophilosophy, ethnolinguistics, ethnomusicology. What had been, when I stumbled into it in the early 1950s, a group of a few hundred, argumentative but similarly minded ethnologists, as they tended then to call themselves, most of whom knew one another personally, became by the late 1970s a vast crowd of scholars whose sole commonality often seemed to be that they had passed through one or another doctoral program labelled anthropology (there are more than a hundred in the United States alone, and perhaps that many more around the world).

Much of this was expectable and unavoidable, a reflex of the growth of the field and the advance of technical specialization, as well as, once again, the workings of the World Spirit as it made its way toward the conclusion of things. But change nonetheless produced both an intensification of polemical combat and, in some quarters anyway, angst and malaise. Not only did there appear a series of trumped-up "wars" between imaginary combatants over artificial issues (materialist vs. idealists, universalists vs. relativists, scientists vs. humanists, realists vs. subjectivists), but a generalized and oddly self-lacerating scepticism about the anthropological enterprise as such—about representing The Other or, worse yet, purporting to speak for him—settled in, hardened, and began to spread.

In time, as the impulses that drove the optimism of the 1950s and the turbulence of the 1960s died away into the routines and immobilities of Reagan's America, this doubt, disillusion, and autocritique gathered itself together under the broad and indefinite, rather suddenly popular banner of postmodernism. Defined against modernism in reproof and repudiation—"goodbye to all that"—postmodernism was, and is, more a mood and an attitude than a connected theory: a rhetorical tag applied to a deepening sense of moral and epistemological crisis, the supposed exhaustion, or, worse, corruption of the received modes of judgment and knowledge. Issues of ethnographic representation, authority, political positioning, and ethical justification all came in for a thorough going-over; the anthropologist's very "right to write" got put into question. "Why have ethnographic accounts recently lost so much of their authority?"— the jacket copy of James Clifford's and George Marcus' *Writing Culture* collection (1986), something of a bellwether in all of this, cried:

> Why were they ever believable? Who has the right to challenge an 'objective' cultural description? . . . Are not all ethnographies rhetorical performances determined by the need to tell an effective story? Can the claims of ideology and desire ever be fully reconciled with the needs of theory and observation?

Most of the work in this manner (not all of it so flat-out or so excited as this, nor so densely populated with rhetorical questions) tended to center around one or the other of two concerns: either the construction of anthropological texts, that is, ethnographical writing, or the moral status of anthropological work, that is, ethnographical practice. The first led off into essentially literary matters: authorship, genre, style, narrative, metaphor, representation, discourse, fiction, figuration, persuasion; the second, into essentially political matters: the social foundations of anthropological authority, the modes of power inscribed in its practices, its ideological assumptions, its complicity with colonialism, racism, exploitation, and exoticism, its dependency on the master narratives of Western self-understanding. These interlinked critiques of anthropology, the one inward-looking and brooding, the other outward-looking and recriminatory, may not have produced the "fully dialectical ethnography acting powerfully in the postmodern world system," to quote that *Writing Culture* blast again, nor did they exactly go unresisted. But they did induce a certain self-awareness, and a certain candor also, into a discipline not without need of them.

However that may be, I spent these years of assertion and denial, promise and counterpromise, first at the University of Chicago, from 1960 to 1970, then at the Institute for Advanced Study in Princeton, from 1970 on, mostly trying to keep my balance, to remember who I was, and to go on doing whatever it was I had, before everything came loose, set out to do.

At Chicago, I was once again involved in, and this time ultimately as its director, an interdisciplinary program focused on the prospects of the by now quite stalled and shredded—Biafra, Bangladesh, Southern Yemen—third world: the Committee for the Comparative Study of New Nations. This committee, which remained in being for more than a decade, was not concerned as such with policy questions nor with constructing a general theory of development, nor indeed with goal-directed team research of any sort. It consisted of a dozen or so faculty members at the university—sociologists, political scientists, economists, and anthropologists—working on or in one or another of the decolonized new states, plus a half-dozen or so postdoctoral research fellows, mostly from elsewhere, similarly engaged. Its main collective activity was a long weekly seminar at which one of the members led a discussion of his or her work, which in turn formed the basis for a smaller core group of, if not precisely collaborators, for we all worked independently, similarly minded, experienced field workers directed toward a related set of issues in what was then called, rather hopefully, considering the general state of things, nation building. Unable, for the moment, to return to Indonesia, by then fully in the grip of pervasive rage, I organized a team of doctoral students from the anthropology department, of which I was also a member, to study a town comparable in size, complexity, and general representativeness to Modjokuto, but at the far other, Maghrebian, end of the Islamic world: Morocco.

The Chicago department of anthropology, presided over at that time by an unusually open and supportive group of elders (Fred Eggan, Sol Tax, Norman MacQuown, and Robert Braidwood; Robert Redfield having only just died), provided an unusually congenial setting for this sort of free-style, thousand-flowers approach to things anthropological. Lloyd Fallers, Victor Turner, David Schneider, McKim Marriott, Robert Adams, Manning Nash, Melford Spiro, Robert LeVine, Nur Yalman, Julian Pitt-Rivers, Paul Friedrich, and Milton Singer were all there crying up, as I was also, one or another line of cultural analysis, and the interaction among us was intense, productive, and surprisingly, given the range of temperaments involved, generally amicable. But when, in the late 1960s, the Director of the Institute for Advanced Study in Princeton, the economist Carl Kaysen, invited me to come there and start up a new school in the Social Sciences to complement the schools in Mathematics, Natural Science, and Historical Studies in existence since Einstein, Weil, von Neumann, Panofsky, and other worthies had put the place in motion in the late 1930s and early 1940s, I, after a couple of years backing and filling, accepted. However exposed and full of hazard it might be, especially in a time of such division within the academy and the dubiousness of the very idea of "the social sciences" in the eyes of many humanists and "real scientists," the prospect of being given a blank and unmarked page upon which to write was, for someone by now addicted to good fortune, simply too attractive to resist.

Conclusion

It is always very difficult to determine just when it was that "now" began. Virginia Woolf thought it was "on or about December 1, 1910," for W. H. Auden it was "September 1, 1939," for many of us who worried our way through the

balance of terror, it was 1989 and the Fall of the Wall. And now, having survived all that, there is September 11, 2001.

My years, thirty-one and counting, at the Institute for Advanced Study
have proved, after some initial difficulties with the resident mandarins, soon
disposed of (the difficulties, not the mandarins), to be an excellent vantage
from which to watch the present come into being in the social sciences. Setting up a new enterprise in the field from a standing start—the whole field
from economics, politics, philosophy, and law, to sociology, psychology, history, and anthropology, with a few scholars from literature, art, and religion
thrown in for leavening—demanded much closer attention to what was going
on in these areas, not only in the United States but abroad as well. And with
more than five hundred scholars from more than thirty countries spending a
year as visiting fellows at one time or another (nearly a fifth of them anthropologists of various kinds, origins, ages, and degrees of celebrity), one had the
extraordinary experience of seeing "now" arrive, live and in color.

All that is well and good, but as the present immediate is, in the nature of
the case, entirely in motion, confused and unsettled, it does not yield so readily to sorting out as does, at least apparently, the perfected, distanced past. It
is easier to recognize the new as new than to say exactly what it is that is new
about it, and to try to discern which way it is in general moving is but to be
reminded again of Hegel's Dictum: the future can be an object of hope or of
anxiety, of expectation or of misgiving, but it cannot be an object of knowledge. I confine myself, then, in finishing up this picaresque tale of questing
adventure, to just a few brief and evasive remarks about how things anthropological seem to have been going in the last decade or so.

At the world-history level I have been invoking throughout as active background, the major developments are, of course, the end of the cold war, the
dissolution of the bipolar international system, and the emergence of a system,
if it can be called a system, which comes more and more each day to look like
a strangely paradoxical combination of global interdependence (capital flow,
multinationals, trade zones, the Net) and ethnic, religious and other intensely
parochial provincialisms (The Balkans, Sri Lanka, Ruanda-Burundi, Chechnya,
Northern Ireland, the Basque country). Whether this "Jihad vs. McWorld," is
genuinely a paradox, or, as I tend to think, a single, deeply interconnected
phenomenon, it has clearly begun to affect the anthropological agenda in ways
that September 11 can only accelerate.

Studies of ethnic discord, of transnational identities, of collective violence,
of migration, refugees, and intrusive minorities, of nationalism, of separatism,
of citizenship, civic and cultural, and of the operation of supra-national quasi-
governmental institutions (e.g., the World Bank, the International Monetary
Fund, UN bodies, etc.)—studies which were not thought to be part of anthro-

pology's purview even a few short years ago—are now appearing on all sides. There are works, and very good ones, on the advertising business in Sri Lanka, on television in India, on legal conceptions in Islam, on the world trade in sushi, on the political implications of witchcraft beliefs in the new South Africa. Insofar as I myself have been directly involved in all this, it has been in connection with the paradox, real or otherwise, of the simultaneous increase in cosmopolitanism and parochialism I just mentioned; with what I called in some lectures I gave in Vienna a few years ago "The World in Pieces," calling for an anthropological rethinking of our master political conceptions, nation, state, country, society, people.

Things are thus not, or at least in my view they are not, coming progressively together as the discipline moves raggedly on. And this, too, reflects the direction, if it can be called a direction, in which the wider world is moving: toward fragmentation, dispersion, pluralism, disassembly, -multi, multi-, multi-. Anthropologists are going to have to work under conditions even less orderly, shapely, and predictable, and even less susceptible of moral and ideological reduction and political quick fixes, than those I have worked under, which I hope I have shown were irregular enough. A born fox (there is a gene for it, along with restlessness, elusiveness, and a passionate dislike of hedgehogs), this seems to me the natural habitat of the cultural . . . social . . . symbolic . . . interpretive anthropologist. Interesting times, an inconstant profession: I envy those about to inherit them.

What Is a State If It Is Not a Sovereign?

What Sidney Mintz and I have in common, besides a certain gift for hanging around and a useful lack of gravity, is the experience of a deep-going disciplinary transformation, a professional change of mind, which, to have a name for it, I will call "anthropology's journey into history." Way back in the Boasian Paleolithic, the fact-gathering, trait-hunting horizon in which we both were formed and which, however transfigured and covered over, marks us still, and irrevocably, anthropology was largely tribe-and-island-focused, concerned with out-of-the-way peoples in out-of-the-way places or with the silent relics of deep time. Here and there, there was some concern with the modern and the developed—Hortense Powdermaker did Hollywood, Lloyd Warner Newburyport—but mainly to demonstrate that what served for the remote parochial served as well for the near-to-hand. It was only after World War II, when the relations between Euro-America and what came to be called the Third World changed, and changed dramatically, that deep-going revisions in what we thought we ought to be doing and how we thought we ought to be doing it began to appear.

Sidney encountered this reconstruction of aim, method, and self-definition at Columbia via Julian Steward, I at Harvard via Clyde Kluckhohn, both of them Americanists, both of them dissatisfied with ethnographic particularism, both of them given to large endeavors. The People of Puerto Rico Project and the Modjokuto Project, the one organized in the late forties (Steward et al. 1956), the other in the early fifties were, if not the first, certainly among the first team studies of differentiated societies enclosed in multiplex civilizations—semi-literate, semi-citied, semi-industrial, with peasants and plantations, clerics and curers, capitals and provinces, classes and masses, complicated places.

Well, as always: in for a penny, in for a pound. What started out as a mere adjustment of established procedures to novel problems—a more self-conscious

Originally published as a Sidney Mintz Lecture entitled "What Is a State If It Is Not a Sovereign: Reflections on Politics in Complicated Places," *Cultural Anthropology* 45, no. 5 (December 2004): 577–93.

ethnography for more self-conscious societies—turned out to project us and the profession generally into the midst of some of the profounder convulsions of the second half of the twentieth century. Decolonization, nation building, the cold war, *tiers-mondisme*, globalization, the new world disorder—anthropologists found themselves no longer lurking, isolated and barely noticed, along the farther edges of world history. They were caught up and set adrift in its central currents, with, as a matter of fact, rather little to guide them beyond a commitment to seeing things up-close and personally—locally and in fine detail.

How well we have managed there, floundering about in the swirl of things, is not for me to say. Incidental participants in great transformations—which is what I think this has been and what Sidney and I have been—are, like Pierre at Borodino, not necessarily the best observers of what overall is happening, why it is happening, and what it portends. But we are, as he was, at least useful as witnesses to the *in medias res* experience of it all, and, for my own part (I will stop ventriloquizing Sidney from here on in), I can only say that it has been, this happenstance journey into contemporary history, more than a little discomposing. Right after the war, when those team projects to Java and the Caribbean were launched, when "area studies"—South and Southeast Asia, Sub-Saharan Africa, the Near and Middle East—appeared and comparativism boomed, and when the "new (or 'developing,' or 'emerging') nations" became a recognized field of study, we thought ourselves engaged with a massive forward surge—Third World nationalism, decolonization, democratization, economic takeoff, modernization, the large, impatient dreams of Bandung. But, all too quickly, things turned sour and disappointing: ethnic upheavals, failed states, kleptocracy, stagnation, sacrificial terror, and madding crowds; Amin and Mobuto, Marcos and Suharto, Khomeini and Saddam; Ruanda-Burundi, the mosque at Ayodhya, the killing fields of (my *terrain*) eastern Java. The confidence and the optimism, to say nothing of the moral certainty, with which we moved into those complicated places—in my case, mainly Indonesia and Morocco—now seem more than a bit premature.

What seems rather clearer now, at least to me, than it did then is that social change will not be hurried and it will not be tamed, and that so far as state formation (my focus here) is concerned, whatever has already happened in supposedly better-organized places is less prologue than chapters in a different sort of story not to be reenacted. Whatever directions what is called (in my view, miscalled) "nation building" may take in Africa, the Middle East, Asia, or Latin America, a mere retracing without the wanderings, the divisions, the breakdowns, and the bloodshed of earlier cases—England, France, or Germany, Russia, the United States, or Japan—is not in the cards, nor is the end in compact and comprehensive political identities, hypostatized peoples. History not only does not repeat itself, it does not purge itself, normalize itself, or straighten its course either. The three centuries of struggle and upheaval that it took for Europe to get from the late medieval checkerboard of Westphalia to the marching nationalities of World War II will almost certainly be more than matched both for surprise and originality and for frustration by the course of things in—what should we call them now? the emerging forces? the postcolonials? the awkward adolescents? the developing world?—in the decades and tens of decades ahead. Neither the process nor its stages will be more than faintly, at times parodically reminiscent (think of "The United Arab Republic," "Guided Democracy," "The Central African Empire," or "The Burmese Road to Socialism").

At the very least, this suggests that serious rethinking is called for on the part of those of us—not only anthropologists but political scientists, historians, economists, sociologists, psychologists, journalists—self-appointed or professionally charged with determining what in fact is going on in these complicated places, where it is that things seem to be tending, and how, in the event, it may all come out. In particular, it suggests that the assemblage of large ideas, casually inherited from Western philosophy and political theory, upon which we have tended to rely for initial positioning and analytical guidance is due for reexamination and reconsideration, critique, and overhaul.

I tried to launch, for myself anyway, such a reexamination in a series of lectures I gave, nearly a decade ago now, at the Institut für die Wissenschaften vom Menschen in Vienna, now published as "The World in Pieces" in my *Available Light* (2000). There, after noting the dissolution of world-encompassing, world-dividing political blocs following the fall of the Wall, the collapse of the Soviet Union, and the end of the cold war in late eighties and early nineties, I tried (p. 221) to take a new look at some of

> the great integrative, totalizing concepts we have so long been accustomed to using in organizing our ideas about world politics, and particularly about similarity and difference among peoples, societies, states, and cultures: concepts like [all these terms in the heaviest of shudder quotes] "tradition," "identity," "religion," "ideology," "values," "nation," indeed even "culture," "society," "state," or "people" themselves. . . . Some general notions, new or reconditioned, must be constructed if we are to penetrate the dazzle of the new heterogeneity and say something useful about its forms and future.

Of these large, directive ideas I attended there mainly to two: that of "[a] nation," considered as, to quote the *OED*, "an extensive aggregate of persons, so closely associated with each other by common descent, language, or history, as to form a distinct race or people, usually organized as a separate political state and occupying a definite territory," and that of "[a] culture," considered as a bounded, coherent, more or less continuous structure of common sentiments and understandings—a form of life, a way, as we might say now, of being in the world. In an essay called "What Is a Country If It Is Not a Nation?" and in another called "What Is a Culture If It Is Not a Consensus?" I tried to show how poorly almost all of the "new states" and a fair number of the old as well, including our own, fit such characterizations, how increasingly difficult it is these days to find culturally solidary entities functioning as organized and autonomous (the techno-word is "sovereign") political communities: Norway, maybe, but there are Pakistanis there now; Samoa, I suppose, if you occlude the Euronesians. What I didn't do, though I originally intended to, was to go on to examine that other master category of the modern understanding so closely linked to these as to be virtually interfused with them—namely, "[the] state."

"The state," particularly the postcolonial state—Kinshasa, Abuja, Rabat, New Delhi, Islamabad, Yangon, Jakarta, Manila (some of them seem, indeed, hardly to reach beyond their sprawling capitals, and their names have a habit of changing)—has recently, of course, been the subject of a great deal of rather uncertain discussion as the enormous variety of its forms and expressions, the multiplicity of the regimes it houses, and the politics it supports have become apparent. There is talk of "failed states," "rogue states," "super-states," "quasi-states," "contest states," and "micro-states," of "tribes with flags," "imagined communities," and "regimes of unreality." China is a civilization trying to be a state, Saudi Arabia is a family business disguised as a state, Israel is a faith inscribed in a state—and who knows what Moldova is? But by far the bulk of the discussion, confused and anxious and inconclusive, has been directed toward the future of the predominant political form of the nineteenth- and twentieth-century West, "the nation-state." Is it going away? Changing form? Restrengthening? Indispensable? Due for a comeback? What can it mean in countries with dozens of languages, religions, races, localities, ethnicities, custom communities? Subcontinents like India? Archipelagos like Indonesia? "Mere geographical expressions" (as one of its first premiers once called it) like Nigeria?

The standard characterization of a "state" as (in Max Weber's formulation) a vested authority possessing a monopoly of legitimate violence in a territory and that of a "nation" as (in Ernest Renan's) the spiritual fusion of a collection of particulate *ethnē* into a *grande solidarité*, a common and transcending *conscience morale*, seem increasingly difficult of application to such tangled conglomerations as these, where not only is legitimacy dispersed and contested but an enormous catalogue of hybridized and shape-shifting parochialist groups—ethnic, religious, linguistic, racial, regional, ideo-primordial—rub up against one another in almost continuous friction and "the narcissism of small differences" (to use again Freud's overused phrase) seems the major driving force of political struggle. Compacted sovereignty, centered and inclusive, is hard to locate and rather looks like remaining so.

In slightly more than 40 years, Nigeria, which is said to have 400–500 "minorities" (and no true "majority"), a number of them running across its geographically indistinct, made-in-Britain borders, has gone from being a competitive confederation of three ethnically and religiously marked regional substates to being an invertebrate republic of first 12, then 19, then 30, and now 36 federal states via a secessionist civil war, an oscillation between parliamentary, military, and presidential regimes, the removal of its capital from its largest city in the southeast of the country to a jerry-built federal district constructed in the dead and backwoods middle, the establishment of nine official languages (including English), and the institution of Islamic law in about a third of the country, a country which is headed, at the moment, by a born-again Christian.

India started out in 1947, after the vast communal convulsion that was Partition, with a secularist central government under the cosmopolitan and intensely Anglicized Fabian socialist Jawaharlal Nehru and a countrywide Congress Party of local bosses trying to hold the vital center against a vast catalogue of regional, religious, linguistic, and caste-based provincialisms in the 25 states, 6 union territories, and 476 districts of what someone, perhaps it was J. K. Galbraith, has called "the world's greatest functioning anarchy." Since then, it has advanced—if that is the word—via the assassination of Indira Gandhi by Sikh militants after her intrusion into the Golden Temple, that of Rajiv Gandhi by Tamil ones after his intervention in the Sri Lankan communal war, and the long, lumbering collapse of the Congress into jobbery and faction (now, perhaps, beginning to be reversed) to the rise of a contrived and synthetic but locally accented political Hinduism, the resurgence of vernacular, ethnocratic regionalism, and the intensification of purist and populist—Bombay-to-Mumbai—anticosmopolitanism.

And Indonesia, my field of operations for about a half-century, has experienced, during its period of independence (also about a half-century), Sukarno's diffuse and declamatory nationalism, built for the most part out of a Jacobin reading of Javanese history, a regional civil war structured along cold war lines, a vast popular bloodletting along religio-political lines, General Suharto's militarized and even more Javanist version of Sukarno's determined integralism, and then, as parliamentary politics returned, the final, bloody failure of the attempt to annex Eastern Timor and a wave of regional, religious, and ethnic clashes throughout the so-called Outer Islands—Islamism in Aceh, sectarian killing in Kalimantan, the Celebes, and Ambon, and racially based separatist agitation in Western New Guinea. "Un plébiscite de tous les jours"—to quote Renan's famous outburst again—in which "tous [les] dissonances de détaille disparaisse dans l'ensemble" seems quite out of reach.

That historians, political scientists, philosophers, and sociologists focused on the modern West should experience difficulty in imagining a workable and comprehensive, let alone an effective, state that is not the expression of a proper nation—sovereign, single, and self-aware—is perhaps not entirely surprising, given that, for at least the past hundred years, since the dissolution of the old empires into their component peoples, that is the sort of thing they have had, for the most part, to deal with—France, Germany, Italy, Spain, Greece, Sweden, Ireland, Hungary, Poland, Portugal, Turkey, Egypt. But it is distinctly surprising that anthropologists, who have mostly involved themselves with less sorted-out polities in less shaped-up places, should be similarly bewitched.

With our ingrained obsession with detail and difference, with the-raw-and-the-cooked and matter-out-of-place, one might expect that we would seek to discover in the irregularities and divisions that we find on the ground the variousness of the forms that really existent statehood can and does nowadays take. But most of the work we have carried out since beginning our journey into history—normatively driven work on "development," "modernization," or "nation building" (all these things, again, in shudder quotes), on "hegemony," "modular nationalism," "*Herrschaft*," "*capital étatique*," "dependency," or "post-coloniality"—has been directed toward searching through the scramble and commotion that the new states present for the faint, premonitory signs of a movement toward (or a falling away from) a more recognizable and regular, standardized shape: the homogeneous color on the disjunctive map, the well-formed self in the well-pictured self-rule.

For this to change (and, as we shall see, it is finally beginning a bit to do so), there must be, it seems to me, a shift away from looking at the state first and foremost as a leviathan machine, a set-apart sphere of command and decision, to looking at it against the background of the sort of society in which it is embedded—the confusion that surrounds it, the confusion it confronts, the confusion it causes, the confusion it responds to. Less Hobbes, more Machiavelli; less the imposition of sovereign monopoly, more the cultivation of the higher expediency; less the exercise of abstract will, more the pursuit of visible advantage.

To make all this a bit less cryptic and rhetorically expressed, let me turn briefly to the two cases that, as I have mentioned, I know at first hand and out of whose oblique and partial comparability, the general samenesses connecting their specific differences, I have made, over the years, a small but rewarding ethnographical living: the Republic of Indonesia and the Kingdom of Morocco.

The one is a massive (212 million people now, 78 million when first I got there), splayed out (6,000 inhabited islands scattered across 5 million square kilometers of open sea), and tangled conglomeration: 15 significant ethnic groups, hundreds of small ones; 300, 400, or 500 languages, some of them unrecorded; Muslims, Catholics, Protestants, Hindus, "animists"; a Chinese commercial minority, a Papuan racial one, indigenized Arabs, in-migrant Indians. The other, a bit more than a tenth the size (30 million people, up from 12 million upon my arrival; 400,000 square kilometers), is a compact, readily traversed, unusually uncompartmentalized place—wall-to-wall Muslim, now that the Jews are gone; essentially Arabophone, now that the Berbers are bilingual; domestically ordered into indefinite, shifting, and catch-as-catch-can local alliances. Set in quite different sorts of regional neighborhoods (broken and particulate Southeast Asia, fluid and continuous North Africa), precipitate from different sorts of colonial experience (Dutch, mercantile, and long; French, technocratic, and short) and faced with different sorts of interior threats (peripheral secession and central delegitimization), they differ also, not surprisingly, in their political styles—the way statehood is conceived, authority is deployed, and dissension is counteracted.

To begin with Indonesia, let me give an outline account—sweeping, simplistic, and openly tendentious—of how things there have come to their present pass: one in which the continuing existence of the country as a political unit, an imperative government in an encompassing state, has increasingly come into serious question. The first five decades of self-rule (the new state was instituted at the end of 1949) have seen one after another impassioned and determined ideological thrust—Nationalist, Communist, Praetorian, Islamist—attempting to fasten a unique and definite identity upon the country, each of which has failed, none of which (except perhaps, in its original form, the Communist) has gone away, and all of which have brought on an even stronger sense of difference and disunion. Whatever the effort to construct a proper, spiritually pulled-together nation-state may have come to elsewhere, here it has been, to this point anyway, an elusive, spasmodic, disruptive project.

The Indonesian independence movement essentially got going, in general imitation of Mazzinian models, in the twenties and thirties of the last century. Under the theatrical leadership of Sukarno, a speaking subaltern if there ever was one (though he had studied engineering for a while in the Indies, he was a conspirator, agitator, and all-purpose subversive virtually from birth), it was a radically unitistic movement in a radically pluralistic situation—a characterization (or a fact) that applies, as I say, to the whole course of the republic's political history. During the nineteen-fifties and early sixties, this attempt to provide a conceptual foundation for an integral nationhood (which involved an odd and eclectic, hodgepodge combination of Indo-Javanese symbolism,

European civism, and a Maoist sort of peasant populism) increasingly faltered under the combined pressures of factional conflict, the induced hostilities of the cold war, and the uneven impact of economic change across the different regions of the archipelago.

In 1958, after the first general election demonstrated how incorrigibly divided the country really was (Nationalists, Islamists, and Communists split the vote more or less evenly), open rebellion, driven by vague ideas of devolution and federalism, broke out in Sumatra and Sulawesi. Sukarno put it down with the assistance of the army (or part of it: it was itself divided) and suspended parliamentary government in favor of a Javanese form of *Gleichschaltung* that he called, with his characteristic inventiveness, "NASAKOM" (Nationalism, Religion, Communism). By 1965 Java, the most populous and most developed of the islands (60% of the country's population, 40% of its gross domestic product, 7% of its area) was so intensely beset by culturally inflected partisan conflict that, after a palace-guard coup misfired in Jakarta, it was caught up in an enormous hand-to-hand bloodbath. Hundreds of thousands (some say a million) died, mostly in a three-month series of convulsive one-night massacres; thousands more were exiled or incarcerated, and a compact and authoritarian government, General Suharto's so-called New Order, took power in Jakarta. But, though Suharto turned away from Sukarno's hapless populism toward disciplinary rigorism and big push development, he continued and even intensified the sort of synthetic and symbolic, culturally eclectic coordination Sukarno had put in place. And when he, in turn, finally fell after 35 years of impassive, astringent rule, ethnic, regional, and religious violence— some of it now explicitly separatist in nature, a lot of it anti-Javanese, and much of it murderous—flared up again over a large part of the country.

The example of this renewed disaccordance that is best known to the world at large is, of course, the brutal liberation of East Timor. The Timor case was more a matter of a failed annexation than a proper separation. (It was a former mini-colony of the Portuguese that the Indonesian army, more or less on its own, had invaded after the fall of Salazar, held under martial law for a quarter of a century, and then lost control of in the confusion and disarray following Suharto's sudden departure.) But it nonetheless raised the general question of the substantial foundations of the Indonesian state, of its reach, its prerogatives, and its cultural complexion, all over again. At both ends of the archipelago— in Aceh in northern Sumatra, a center of Islamist discontent since colonial times and a reluctant adherent to the Java-centric republic in the first place, and in West New Guinea, called Irian, a Melanesian outlier whose political incorporation into the republic was indefinite, late, arbitrary, and contested— explicitly separatist rebellions broke out and were countered and punished by the military but only half-contained.

In between, in Kalimantan, Sulawesi, the Moluccas, and the Lesser Sundas, a sequence of local explosions, rather like the 1965 massacres in their terrible brevity, erupted, smoldered, and then erupted again, fueled by the return of competitive, who gets what, when, where, and how politics. And, with Yugoslavia dissolving in the daily press and Sri Lanka seemingly coming apart at the seams, the excited headlines began to appear at home and abroad: "PARADISE LOST IN ERUPTION OF HATRED," "THE BALKANIZATION OF INDONESIA MAY BE FAR FROM HYPOTHESIS," "INDONESIA'S YEAR OF LIVING CHAOTICALLY," "AMBON [where a Muslim-Christian pocket war broke out] MAY BE FATAL FOR INDONESIA," "IS INDONESIA BREAKING DOWN?"[1] Even its newly elected president, a modernist Muslim with a Javanese accent, predicted that the country would fall apart if he was deposed.

He was, and it didn't. (Sukarno's daughter, as impassive a figure as he was flamboyant but just as impervious and just as Javanese, succeeded him and is preparing to run for a second term.) But just how and why it didn't and hasn't—why even in the face of this sort of dispersed, low-intensity civil war it lumbers compositely on, an elephant, as the Indonesians themselves say, with beriberi—is very far from clear and only, now that the nation state illusion is finally coming into question, just starting to be researched. Perhaps its very complexity, the intricate crosscutting of its discrepant components, makes it difficult to find clear lines of difference along which to separate its parts, the natural joints at which to dismember it. Perhaps the practiced capacity of local groups to work out and make work practical arrangements, good enough and fair enough, holds things, more or less and for the moment, together. The military attentions of Jakarta, ruthless and unpredictable, the diffuse and fading afterglow of the anticolonial struggle and the revolution, and the mere inertia of the established familiar as well as the imaginative deal making of a grasping elite all doubtless play a part. What is clear is that, whatever it is that keeps things together and going, to date anyway, it is not "un plébiscite de tous les jours."

In Morocco—to turn to it now, again in a schematic and peremptory, implicitly comparative manner—neither the dispersion of nationhood nor the collision of subsocieties is the problem. The country is centered enough (all too centered, some would say), and what cultural cleavages there are are, relatively speaking (relatively speaking, especially to Indonesia), marginal, dormant, diffuse, or fading. The problem is that the place is defined neither by its edges, which as a matter of fact are both faint and porous and at points contested, nor by its cultural specificity, which hardly sets it off from the other new-state countries around it (Mauritania, Algeria, and the rest of the Arab West Maghreb), nor yet again by a massive and integralist, Morocco-for-the-

Moroccans, nationalist movement, which never really developed here beyond its embryonic stages. It is defined by the presence at its center and apex of a peculiar, and peculiarly ambiguous, institution, at once archaic, traditional, perseverant, and thoroughly remodeled: the Alawite monarchy.

The peculiarity of the monarchy ("Alawi" is the name of the dynasty that inhabits it) is not just that it exists but that, through the grand upheavals and transformations—modernization, political mobilization, decolonization, collective self-assertion, administrative rationalization, popular government—that have marked the so-called Third World Revolution in Asia, Africa, and, in a rather different way, Latin America, it persists. There are monarchies elsewhere in the Third World, if we can still call it that. (Someone has recently suggested "the two-thirds world.") But they are either the products of late-colonial manipulations, as in Jordan, Saudi Arabia, and the Gulf, or ceremonial hangovers of a reclusive past like Thailand, Bhutan, and Tonga. The Moroccan monarchy, however, is neither a pretense nor a relic. It is both formally sovereign and practically powerful, the first (at least most of the time) among unequals in a complex and ever-shifting field of personalized, situational, *sotto voce* power. Just about every book that has been written on the political life of *al-mamlakah al-maghrebia* (as the country, updated from a Protectorate, now officially calls itself)—*The Commander of the Faithful* (Waterbury 1970), *Le Fellah Marocain: Defenseur du Trône* (Leveau 1976), *Master and Disciple* (Hammoudi 1997), *Sacred Performances* (Combs-Schilling 1989)—has focused on this singular office and the hardly less singular personalities who have, since the coming of independence in 1956, filled it. And they have all asked essentially the same question: What is it that sustains it and its occupants in a world of elections, parliaments, ideologies, corporations, newspapers, and political parties? What is a Medici prince doing in a century like this?

The Moroccan monarchy, in one form or another, is, of course, a very old institution. Tribalistic versions of it run back to well before the great Berber dynasties invaded Andalusia in the eleventh century, and the Alawites, as such, appeared out of the dried rivers and oases of the pre-Sahara, claiming direct descent from the Prophet, in the middle of the seventeenth century—contemporaries of the Sun King, to whose daughter one of them proposed, unsuccessfully, to marry his son. But in another, much more pertinent sense it is a very young, brand-new one, emerging suddenly and surprisingly, more or less accidentally, at the center of an ad hoc, thrown-together government in the final, confusing days of the crumbling Protectorate. Unlike the nationalist movement that arose in the Dutch East Indies after two-and-a-half centuries of stock-company rule, nationalism in colonial Morocco (a regime that lasted, it should be remembered, only about three or four decades, and some of that as an everyone-comes-to-Rick's Vichy false front) was less a popular upsurge than a cloud of local *notables*—Sufi sheikhs, religious scholars, bazaaris, judges, soldiers, trade unionists, schoolteachers, mountain lords, desert anchorites, and tribal chieftains—desperately maneuvering for place in an abruptly volatilized, thoroughly disarranged political situation. Here there was no Sukarno inventing the masses, exciting them, and then driving them forward. The man who tried hardest to become one, the reform Islamist Allal al-Fassi, lacked both the luck and the brazenness, to say nothing of the appeal, to propel himself to power, and his main rivals, the secular intellectuals, were much too *rive gauche* to get their act together or to render it plausible to the fellah in the street.

As unrest rose and things grew perilous, the French panicked and exiled the royal family to Corsica and Madagascar *pour encourager les autres.* Then, when, in the shadow of the Algerian war, things got completely out of hand a couple of years later, they panicked again and brought them back, hoping for legitimacy. In so doing they transformed the king, Muhammad V, from a subservient, rather callow cardboard figure, indistinct, middle-aged, and virtually forgotten, into a national and—for the moment at least—a nationalist hero. Projected into the center of the cloud of competing somebodies, he brought the throne back less as a transcending, Grand Turk authority, which it had never in any case been, than as a consequent player, a largest-bear-in-the-garden *intrigant.* What he had recovered, or what had been recovered for him, was less an office than a license to practice. And when, four years later, he died, suddenly and prematurely, after a nasal operation thought to be minor, the mass outpouring of grief that ensued completed the process of a popular restoration, and his much more determined and battle-ready son, Hassan II, by then the army chief of staff, succeeded to a fully reinvented, refurbished, and resanctified kingship. He had only—only!—to set it into motion, to make it (and himself) real.

The vehemence with which he pursued this aim and the success he had in it is perhaps the one thing about him, his career, and his person that is generally known. In the sixties he crushed, one after another, a whole series of rural uprisings in the north, the east, and the south of the country, the traditional regions of tribal (and thaumaturgical) dissidence. In the seventies his dramatic, hairbreadth escapes from two attempts on his life, one in the air piloting a jet coming back from France, when he feigned death in the cockpit, and one at an Arabian nights seaside picnic crowded with foreign dignitaries, a number of whom died while he survived hiding beneath a handy piece of cardboard and talking his would-be assassins out of their intentions, made headlines everywhere. The drastic and unforgiving vengeance—lightless incarcerations in desert citadels—that he inflicted on his intimate enemies and the friends and relations of his intimate enemies during the grim, so-called years of lead which followed; his 1975 "Green March," nearly a half-million people dispatched on foot into the abandoned Spanish Sahara to claim it for his realm; and the quick and dirty suppression of large urban riots in 1965, 1981, and 1990 simply added to the effect. By the time he died in 1999, after 38 years of movement, maneuver, evasion, bluster, obduracy, and striking back, the materials of his kingship were fairly well in place.

But it was (and, now that his son, Muhammad VI, a much less emphatic personality, has succeeded him, calling himself, rather hopefully, "the people's king," it still is) an axis, a focal point, or a numinous presence around which an endless and intricate countrywide jockeying for domain and position takes place, not an overweening concentration of organized power. For all the flash and the off-hand violence and for all the celebrity of royal display, the kingship is as much a defensive (and a mediatory) institution, struggling to maintain its place and its quite relative and situationally dependent ascendancy in a vast field of large, small, and medium-sized machinators, provocateurs, adventurers, upstarts, and faction leaders—sheikhs, caids, chorfa, ulama, party bosses, ministrales, landlords, pashas, proprietors, café intellectuals, the famous miracle-working marabtin, sufi lodgemasters, qadis, and to Paris-and-back (or America-and-back) semiexiles—as it is a superlative force. Himself a semisacred figure, a *baraka*-charged descendant of the Prophet, enacting fidelity and defending faith, he has at the same time been, and has been forced to be, an intensely secular, intensely competitive, cut-and-thrust politician—a legislator, party chief, policy maker, *éminence grise*, and lightning rod, a player among players in a multiparty parliamentary system complete with ministries, pressure groups, local machines, and only somewhat manipulable elections. As a polity, "the Kingdom of Morocco" is a dispersed, pluralized, harsh, and haphazard clash of views and interests that, in its lack of definite form and consistent direction, looks more like a political Brownian motion than like the steady application of a Leviathan will.

This breathless and bravura comparison of two long-in-formation, complex, and troubled polities is not intended to be a remotely sufficient account of their workings or their evolution. For that, or something approaching it, one needs to read, for Indonesia, the works of such scholars as, *inter alia*, George Kahin (1952), Herbert Feith (1962), Benedict Anderson (1972), William Liddle (1970), James Siegel (1986), and Donald Emmerson (1974); for Morocco, those of, also *inter alia*, John Waterbury (1970), Rémy Leveau (1976), Abdullah Hammoudi (1997), Edmund Burke (1976), Dale Eickelman (1976), and Lawrence Rosen (1984), from whom I have derived, without either their knowledge or their consent and certainly without their agreement, my little vignettes and large summations. In invoking whole histories and sensibilities in so off-hand and reduced a manner, I am not attempting to set them in the tight and abstract categories of the social sciences, to fix them upon a typological wheel or place them in a *table raisonné*. Even less do I seek to discern their futures, which are quite out of sight. What I am attempting to do is to use them, or my figurations of them, to make an exact and wholly general point: namely, that they *are* figurations. What is a state if it is not a sovereign? The institutional projection of an ongoing politics, a display, a delineation, a precipitate, a materialization.

The state in Indonesia and Morocco, as in Nigeria and India (or, for that matter, in Canada, Colombia, Belgium, Georgia, or the United States) is less the shadowing forth of a quasi-natural peoplehood, the summarized will and spirit of a *pluribus unum* nation, neither of which seems more than wishfully or residually to exist, than a rather hurriedly concocted social device designed to give form enough and point to a clatter of crossing desires, contending assumptions, and disparate identities. The Indonesians live in a jagged, discontinuous, peoples-and-islands country gathered up for them by accident and the Dutch, in which the close-in immixture of cultural groupings—intimate, intricate, and charged with wariness and apprehension—is a primary fact of political life and its translocal, transethnic ordering. The Moroccans live in a country cut out of a more-or-less continuous and connected desert-edge landscape by late and incidental French and Spanish incursions, in which the putting together and taking apart of personal connections and private loyalties, the forming and unforming of ad hoc, handshake alliances, mount up toward a hardly more settled, more stabilized, or more exactly located center.

When these new men and women, these new Indonesians or Moroccans (to echo Crèvecoeur on the postrevolutionary American farmer) look beyond their immediate horizons of family, place, and community, which, by now, they do almost constantly, what they see is not a broad sweep of national feeling flowing inward toward and outward away from Jakarta or Rabat, gathering up everyone in its path into a general and consuming identity, an overriding and exclusive final loyalty. What they see in those central and consequential places is what they see close at hand: the working out of a particular and distinctive sort of politics in a particular and distinctive sort of world; how things happen around here, what sorts of things they are, and what sorts of ways are available to deal with them, harness them, or defend oneself against them.

This appears with particular clarity when one looks at what suddenly, over the past few years, has emerged as an acute and immediate, in some sense state-threatening phenomenon: irregular violence in the name of religion—Islamic terrorism. Both countries have, in fact, a history of Islamist dissent and sedition. I have mentioned the repeated religiously inspired uprisings in northern Sumatra, starting as early as the nineteenth century, and during the first, uncertain years of the republic's existence its very legitimacy was openly and violently challenged by an armed rebellion under the banner of Darul Islam (The House of Islam). (One of the first American anthropologists to work in the new state [I followed him by only a few months], Raymond Kennedy of Yale, apparently died at its hands in West Java.) In Morocco, matters have been a bit less dramatic, consisting of the periodic appearance of Muslim cliques and coteries, especially in the universities, and the periodic jailing or house arrest of their leaders, although after the rise of the Islamic Salvation Front in neighboring Algeria in the 1990s sent that country into a spiral of killing and counterkilling, concern with "the Islamist threat" spread rapidly in Morocco as well. In any case, with the 2002 bombing in Bali, which killed 202 people, and the 2003 one in Casablanca, which killed 41, jihadist Islam came, specifically and definitively, to both countries.

I cannot, obviously, go into the details, fine and unfine, of all that here. (Most of them are yet to emerge. Death sentences and prison terms have been given out in both places, but developed responses by either state, if they are to come, are not yet evident. And, of course, everything is further complicated by the alarums and excursions of U.S. foreign policy.) But that the distinct and characteristic political styles that I have just so sketchily outlined will inform and animate both the expression of Islamic furor and the response to it of the governmental apparatuses—Indonesia's vacillating presidency, Morocco's brushed-up monarchy—is already clear.

In Indonesia, the incursion, for the most part from elsewhere, of radical, totalistic Islam has fallen quite readily into the groups-and-countergroups pattern of the country I have been describing—has been taken up into the intense fear of separatism that is endemic to it. In Aceh, what began as and to a fair extent remains a hit-and-run insurrection by a small group of Islamist extremists, as much anti-Jakarta and anti-Javanese as they are puritanical and ultra-orthodox in their aims, has been turned into what has all too accurately been called "Indonesia's Chechnya" by the persistent perception of it by the central government and especially by the army as a country-dismembering separatist threat to be met with uncompromising hegemonical force—11,000 dead in 27 years of on-again, off-again quagmire repression. At the other end of the archipelago, in the "spice island" Moluccas, where the impact of Christianity under the aegis of Dutch missionization was particularly marked, a series of confrontations between self-proclaimed jihadists, many of them immigrant from other islands round and about (including, perhaps, the southern Philippines), and long-rooted, in-place Christians have also led to organized riots, hundreds of deaths, and again indiscriminate and largely unavailing army intervention. But, again, the pattern is general. Throughout the country confrontations between intrusive groups and those previously settled in this place or that— what Indonesians call *pendatang* (newcomers) and *asli* (originals)—have led not just to sectarian eruptions but to ethnic, cultural, tribal, ideological, and economic ones as well. (Petroleum deposits, being place-bound, are not—as Nigeria also demonstrates—altogether conducive to national unity.) If, as I believe, neither the separation of Indonesia into more workable and homogeneous parts nor the integration of it under the aegis of a pervasive, difference-drowning identity is, save perhaps here and there, on the cards, the country will have to develop effective ways of containing and stabilizing such multiplex and multiform differences—something it has hardly as yet begun to do.

And in Morocco, that master-and-disciple state, the situation is similar in its different way. The interplay and management of semisecret personal alliances and oppositions that characterize the larger part of political life there are all too readily penetrable by the Al Qaida-type small-cell, network terrorism that has come to be associated with Islamist subversion in the Middle East and North Africa. If it prospers, as it has in Algeria and is beginning to in Saudi Arabia, it will form a direct challenge to the religiously based, *amir al-muminin* "commander-of-the-faithful" legitimacy of the monarchy, the linchpin, so far as there is one, of the whole system. The ability to construct, sustain, disrupt, and reconstruct effective chains of personal loyalty is the key to order here, not an overall sense of national purpose and collective solidarity, which, so far as it exists, is a reflex of political life not its cause and foundation.

The general point, whatever the truth or lack of it in my surely debatable contrasts and characterizations, is that, in these complicated places anyway, the compact and sovereign nation-state animated by a distinct and singular populace—civic France or monadic Japan, Catholic Portugal or Buddhist Thailand—is neither present nor anywhere near to coming into being. What, its hour come round at last, is coming into being? Discerning that, not wishing-in the future or indicting the past, is, I would suggest, our urgent and instant task as scholar—professors of what happens.

If nothing else, I hope that I have by now persuaded you that the "journey into history" I described at the outset of this discussion as engulfing the anthropological careers of both Mintz and myself in the nineteen-fifties is fully under way. (Indeed, it has since engulfed those of the overwhelming majority of our contemporaries as well. The notes-and-queries bush ethnologist, ferreting out marriage rules and tabulating kinship terms, is almost as anomalous now as we were then.) The issue is no longer whether to undertake it or even where (anywhere they will let us in and someone will talk to us). It is what we are supposed to do, now that we are fair and certainly thus embarked. What is anthropology's contribution as a special science (not the vague and imperious "study of man," which I, at least, am ready to leave to the scholiasts and the textbook writers), a particular direction of thought and argument, of method and intent, in a research enterprise—political development in forming states—

crowded these days with skilled and well-armed, all too confident social scientists (I use the term loosely, which is the only way to use it): historians, economists, political scientists, sociologists, philologists, health workers, development agents, pundits, lawyers, psychologists, philosophers, *littérateurs*?

What I have been implicitly suggesting here and will now claim explicitly is that social anthropologists, even we Old Boasians, are peculiarly well-adapted, preadapted actually, to such research, to the study of politics in complicated places. And, now that Islam is the second religion of both France and Britain, 20 million Indians live outside of India, and immigration accounts for two thirds of America's (and all of California's) annual population increase, that means just about everywhere. Save perhaps for Iceland, which seems to have kept its gene pool fairly well intact, all the countries of the world and all the states that are, well or badly, designed to govern them and to give them a collective presence in the world are as intricate as German verbs, as irregular as Arabic plurals, and as various as American idioms. They are made, that is, for the comparative, morphological, ethnographic eye.

That eye looks less for iron law and repetitive cause than for significant form and revelatory detail, less for the conclusions toward which everything tends or the ideal which everything imitates than for the specificities that everything takes. The anthropological concern with difference, often misunderstood as a preference for it and an aversion to theory, is hardly more than the recognition, hard-earned in hundreds upon hundreds of detailed and extended field investigations, that difference is what makes the world go round, especially the political world. Heterogeneity is the norm, conflict the ordering force, and, despite ideological romances, left and right, religious and secular, of consensus, unity, and impending harmony, they seem likely to remain so for a good deal longer than the foreseeable future.

Consider, as an only somewhat dramatic example of how things stand these days, here, there, and everywhere, Neal Acherson's (2003:37) recent description of that Caucasian originality, Nagorny Karabakh:

"Nagorny" means "mountainous" in Russian, and "Karabakh" means roughly "black garden" in Turkish. Up to 1988, Nagorny Karabakh could be described as a hilly territory with a largely Armenian population, assigned to the Soviet republic of Azerbaijan; it was an enclave separated on its western side from the Soviet republic of Armenia by a belt of Azerbaijanian-settled territory. The Armenians are traditional Christian and speak Armenian; the Azeris are traditional Muslim and speak a language close to Turkish. Large Armenian minorities lived in Azerbaijan, especially in its capital Baku on the Caspian shore, while large Azeri minorities lived in Armenia. Even the population of Nagorny Karabakh was mixed. The town of Stepanakert was mainly Armenian; the old hill-top city of Shusha was mainly Azeri.

The interplay here (to have a kinder word for the migrations and murderings that have actually happened) of political arrangements—that is, states and substates, new states and old states (Armenia, Azerbaijan, Russia, the Soviet Union, now supplemented by the intrusions of Western and Near Eastern powers prospecting for oil)—and a wild assembly of languages, religions, histories, myths, lies, and psychologies, is, as I say, only relatively speaking extreme. The Balkan dilemma, how to govern a conglomerate, divided population, is now quite general. Nagorny Karabakh or Morocco or Indonesia is what "the field," our testing ordeal and measuring destination, for the most part looks like now.

There are, indeed, signs that we are beginning at last to recognize this and to abandon the, to my mind, rather shrill and overintellectualized villain-and-victim moralism that has marked so much of our recent work in this area for a more realistic and pragmatic approach—one dedicated to developing lines of research and frames of analysis that can both represent Nagorny Karabakh situations and uncover the directions in which they might conceivably be induced to move. Work on notions of "cultural citizenship" by Renato Rosaldo (2003) and his Southeast Asianist colleagues, on "states of imagination," by Thomas Blom Hansen and his Indianist ones (Blom Hansen and Stepputat 2001), or on the political charge of witchcraft fears in the new South Africa, by Adam Ashford (2000), are perhaps genuine straws in a real wind, as are Andrew Apter's (1992) on Yoruba rites of centrality and power, Michael Meeker's (2002) on the Ottoman shaping of Republican Turkey, and, if I may say so, my own on the theater state in Bali and Java.

The journey into history that Sidney's and my generation undertook under the impetus and guidance of that preceding us now continues, in its own way and with its own resources, in those that follow us. One of the few advantages of an unexpected longevity, as I am sure he will agree, whatever else he thinks of all of this, is the high good fortune of watching it happen.

References

Abrams, Philip. 1988 (1977). Notes on the difficulty of studying the state. *Journal of Historical Sociology* 19(1):58–89. [dmg]

Acherson, Neal. 2003. In a black garden. *New York Review of Books*, November 20, pp. 37–40.

Anderson, Benedict. 1972. *Java in a time of revolution: Occupation and resistance, 1944–46*. Ithaca: Cornell University Press.

Apter, Andrew. 1992. *Black critics and kings: The hermeneutics of power in Yoruba society.* Chicago: University of Chicago Press.

Ashford, Adam. 2000. *Madumbo: A man bewitched.* Chicago: University of Chicago Press.

Blom Hansen, Thomas, and Finn Stepputat. Editors. 2001. *States of imagination: Ethnographic explorations of the postcolonial state.* Durham: Duke University Press.

Burke, Edmund, III. 1976. *Prelude to protectorate in Morocco: Precolonial protest and resistance, 1860–1912.* Chicago: University of Chicago Press.

Chatterjee, Partha. 1993. *The nation and its fragments: Colonial and postcolonial histories.* Princeton: Princeton University Press. [the]

Comaroff, Jean, and John Comaroff. 1992. *Ethnography and the historical imagination.* Boulder: Westview Press. [the]

Combs-Schilling, M. E. 1989. *Sacred performances: Islam, sexuality, and sacrifice.* New York: Columbia University Press.

Connor, Walker. 1978. A nation is a nation, is a state, is an ethnic group, is a? *Ethnic and Racial Studies* 1:378–400. [the]

Corrigan, Phillip, and Derek Sayer. 1985. *The great arch: English state formation as cultural revolution.* London: Basil Blackwell. [dmg]

Eickelman, Dale. 1976. *Moroccan Islam: Tradition and society in a pilgrimage center.* Austin: University of Texas Press.

Eidson, John R. 1996. *Homo symbolans agonisticus*: Geertz's "agonistic" vision and its implications for historical anthropology. *Focaal: Tijdschrift voor Antropologie* 26/26: 109–23. [jre]

Emmerson, Donald. 1974. *Indonesia's elite: Political culture and cultural politics.* Ithaca: Cornell University Press.

Feith, Herbert. 1962. *The decline of constitutional democracy in Indonesia.* Ithaca: Cornell University Press.

Geertz, Clifford. 2000. *Available light: Anthropological reflections on philosophical topics.* Princeton: Princeton University Press.

Hammoudi, Abdelleh. 1997. *Master and disciple: The cultural foundations of Moroccan authoritarianism.* Chicago: University of Chicago Press.

Kahin, George. 1952. *Nationalism and revolution in Indonesia.* Ithaca: Cornell University Press.

Leveau, Rémy. 1976. *Le fellah marocain: Defenseur du trône.* Paris: Presses de la Fondation Nationale des Sciences Politiques.

Liddle, R. William. 1970. *Ethnicity, party, and national integration: An Indonesian case study.* New Haven: Yale University Press.

Lomnitz, Claudio. 1992. *Exits from the labyrinth: Culture and ideology in the Mexican national space.* Berkeley: University of California Press. [cl]

———. 2001. *Deep Mexico: An anthropology of nationalism.* Minneapolis: University of Minnesota Press. [cl]

Meeker, Michael E. 2002. *A nation of empire: The Ottoman legacy of Turkish modernity.* Berkeley: University of California Press.

Reyna, Stephen P. 1998. Right and might: Of approximate truths and moral judgements. *Identities* 4 (3–4):431–65. [jre]

Rosaldo, Renato. Editor. 2003. *Culture and citizenship in Island Southeast Asia: Nation and belonging in the hinterlands.* Berkeley: University of California Press.

Roseberry, William. 1989. *Anthropologies and histories: Essays in culture, history, and political economy.* New Brunswick: Rutgers University Press. [dmg]

Rosen, Lawrence. 1984. *Bargaining for reality: The construction of social relations in a Muslim community.* Chicago: University of Chicago Press.

Scott, James C. 1998. *Seeing like a state: How certain schemes to improve the human condition have failed.* New Haven: Yale University Press. [the]

Schulte Nordholt, Henk. 1996. *The spell of power: A history of Balinese politics 1650–1940.* Leiden: KITLV Press. [hs]

Siegel, James T. 1986. *Solo in the New Order: Language and hierarchy in an Indonesian city.* Princeton: Princeton University Press.

Steward, Julian, et al. 1956. *People of Puerto Rico.* Urbana: University of Illinois Press.

Waterbury, John. 1970. *The commander of the faithful: The Moroccan political elite, a study in segmented politics.* London: Weidenfeld and Nicolson.

White, Benjamin. 1983. Agricultural involution and its critics: Twenty years after. *Bulletin of Concerned Asian Scholars* 15(2): 18–31. [hs]

Shifting Aims, Moving Targets

I

For an anthropologist pushing 80 and feeling it push back, there seems little else to do on a ceremonial occasion of this sort dedicated as it is to commemorating a marmoreal figure whom most people remember, so far as they remember him at all, as a cloistered Edwardian don who devoted his life to a Causabon-like compilation of the world's exotica, but to reflect upon one's own, rather different, but hardly less transient, career in a related line of work and try to suggest what time and change have done to it. Not that this will avail against what time and change have done, and will continue to do, to it. There is nothing so dead as a dead academic, and any Ozymandian dreams one might entertain will be quickly dissolved by the simple device of looking up the Collected Frazer Lectures, 1922–32 on the Amazon web-site bestseller list and finding them placed at 2,467,068. I want, I hope without undue self-reference or illusions of permanence, simply to put into the record a particular encounter with a particular time.

And a particular subject: the anthropology of religion. Why I have spent so much of my time and energy since wandering into anthropology from the Humanities studying (in heavy quotation marks, here and throughout) "religion"— in Southeast Asia, in North Africa, in the past, in the present, increasingly in the world at large—is not entirely clear to me, particularly as I have myself no particular religious background or—so far anyway, and as I say, it's getting late—commitment. Some of it, this concern, not to say obsession, with faith, worship, belief, sanctity, mystery, world-view, sorcery, propitiation, and the adoration of trees (on which, you will remember, Frazer has no less than five separate chapters) certainly has to do with that Humanities background: literature and philosophy do incline the mind to recherché subjects. But far

Originally published as a Sir James Frazer Memorial Lecture entitled "Shifting Aims, Moving Targets: On the Anthropology of Religion," *Journal of the Royal Anthropological Institue* 11, no. 1 (March 2005).

more, I think, it is due to the continuing centrality of the description and analysis of myth, magic, rite, and spiritual tonality in anthropology from E.B.Tylor [1889], William Robertson Smith [1889], R.R. Marrett [1917], and Frazer [1890] forward through Bronislaw Malinowski [1948], Raymond Firth [1967], E.E. Evans-Pritchard [1956], Godfrey Lienhardt [1961], Victor Turner [1968], and Mary Douglas [1966], to essay only a local—Oxbridge, London, and Manchester—genealogy. (My own, of course, is American: Ruth Benedict [1927], Gladys Reichard [1923], Robert Redfield [1953], Clyde Kluckhohn [1962].)

Along with kinship, with which, via totemic classification and the incest taboo, it was directly linked from the beginning, religion has been so much at the centre of anthropological thought that anyone concerned, as I was and am, with the emblems and insignia of the human way of being in the world would be immediately drawn toward it as a field of research. And so, when the powers at Harvard, having organized a group of graduate students to go to Indonesia on a team project to study kinship, village life, peasant marketing, the Chinese shopkeeper minority, and local government, found themselves in need of someone to "do" religion, I jumped at the chance and wrote my doctoral thesis and my first book on the interplay of Islamic, Hindu-Buddhist, and Malayo-Polynesian currents in the spiritual life of the Javanese, and have been worrying over the complexities and puzzlements encountered—theoretical ones, empirical ones, philosophical ones, sectarian ones, perhaps most important, practical ones—ever since.

Thinking back, not to that particular project, or to my work there as such, both of which are by now more or less archival, but to the whole period—the immediate post-World War II, incipient Cold War 1950s—it seems clear that there was around that time a major shift in both the aims and the objects of the anthropological study of religion: what it was looking at, and what it was looking for. Virtually all of the previous forays had been into tribal or archaic beliefs and ceremonies (Australia, the Ancient Semites, Native America, the Trobriands, the Nilotes, the Chuckchee), with the assumption, implied or open, that rudiments and foreshadowings of Judaism, Christianity, Hinduism, Islam, and the other so-called "High Religions" could be seen there and thus the elementary forms of the religious life, in Émile Durkheim's famous slogan, could be defined, classified, and reduced to rule. Now, however, an effort got under way to address the "High Religions" directly and in their immediate and contemporary, emotionalistic forms, less to ferret out their common features than to place them within the social and historical—dare I say, in this venue, "cultural?"—contexts within which they emerged and upon which they acted. What had been comparative folklore in search of parallels and prefigurations—shamans as priests, cockfights as sacraments, regicide as redemption (what Frazer called "our debt to the savage")—became a comparative ethnography in search of consequence: import, impact, significance, weight. How, precisely, and how much, does "religion" matter in the ongoing course of things? Wherein lies its appeal and force? Its reach? Its persistence? What, as we came soon to put it, is it—the imagery, the discipline, the fervour, the theatrics, the obsessiveness, the storytelling—all about?

This "turn," or "move," or "paradigm shift" was, of course, but part, and a minor part at that, of a general shift in anthropological attention away from deserts, jungles, and arctic wastes, to what came to be known as The New Nations, The Developing Countries, The Third World, The Emerging Powers, or The Non-aligned States [Geertz 1963]. Someone setting out to study India, Iran, Nigeria, Egypt, China, or Brazil, or, as I was, Indonesia, found themselves faced not with an ant-hill assemblage of myths, spirits, and psychical practices to label and sort out, but with massive, deeply historical, and conceptually elaborated social and cultural formations, complete with officials, texts, economies, and ratified names. Complex societies, "civilizations" if you wish, some of them as large as subcontinents, with multicultural populations, bundles of languages, and spiritual connections across half the world, presented those of us who, trained on *benge* and Blessing Way, came to be engaged with them not just with a new object of study, but with a revised conception of how to study it—what it was we wanted to find out.

With regard to Java, that anthology of the world's best imperialisms, poised to become the nucleus of a rambling and precarious, conceptually ill-defined political entity, this meant two things: first, a recognition, forced upon one by the merest contact with local life, of adversative, religiously phrased divisions within a single, many-minded society; and, second, the realization that these divisions and this many-mindedness did not preclude, but in fact produced, a distinct and particular sort of spiritual temper—a bent, a humour, a stamp, a moral climate. If the "function" of religion was, as we were still taught to say in those days, "the tuning up of ultimate value attitudes of the society," the tuning here was various, contrastive, and contrapuntal, and so were the attitudes. What Denys Lombard [1990: vol. III, pp. 89 ff.], the Braudellian historian of "*le cas javanais*," called "*le carrefour des réseaux asiatiques*," precariously balanced between "*le fanatisme*" and "*la tolérance*," between "*les frictions de la concurrence*" and "*la volonté d'harmonie*," turned out to be an excellent site on which, first, to take apart the very idea of "religion" and then to try, somehow, to put it back together again.

The conceptual equipment available for performing this sleight of hand—separating out clashing and discontinuous spiritual currents and then reconnecting them in the muddled, composite flow of everyday life—was sparse and cursory. "Pluralism," "syncretism," "communalism," "denominationalism," "sectarianism," the received terms for describing competing traditions animating common situations, all seemed inadequate to the tumbling intricacy and intensity of things. The suspicions and jealousies, along with the headlong aspirations to national unity, that drove the early Republic, and before long came within inches (or hours) of destroying it, were far wider and more all-embracing than even the metaphorically or analogically "religious." And yet they were, those suspicions and jealousies, and the aspirations as well, coloured and reinforced at almost every point by world-view variations centuries in the making.

It was not so much the ingredient traditions as such—Hinduism (or "Hindu-Buddhism"), which had been there from the ninth century; Islam, which entered in the fourteenth and fifteenth; Christianity, propagated by European missionaries and plantation managers in the eighteenth and nineteenth; and the Austronesian undercurrent, which remained visible in the witchery and spiritism of popular observance—that most challenged description and explication. They were recognizable, familiar, and not all that distinctive: the usual grist for the ethnographical mill. It was the way in which those traditions, and the mentalities they generated, were stretched taut across the deepest and most divisive fissures of social, political, and economic life, and, in fact, defined and constructed those fissures—shaped them, sustained them, drove them on—that demanded a methodological change of plan.

The details of how all this worked out "in reality" are again on the record: the progressive polarization of these closed and hardened casts of mind as the passions of the Cold War intruded upon the local scene and attached themselves, like ideological parasites, to one or the other of them; the foundering of electoral politics and parliamentary government as the polarization advanced to all-out culture-war; the eruption of mass violence—hundreds of thousands dead—when factional killing broke out along these lines across the whole of the island. The causes of all this, and of the forced and artificial reintegration which followed it and kept the country in a state of political and intellectual suspension, a sort of cultural time-warp, for thirty-five years, were, of course, various. But that the crash and clatter of religious dispositions was prominent among them is quite clear.

As I say, this sort of difficult intricacy, the interplay of local traditions and world religions, confronted not just myself and my Java-project colleagues thrown into the middle of a forming country; it confronted the whole generation of anthropologists who turned, in the 1950s and 1960s, to the study of old societies trying to become new (or, anyway, newer) states. India, with the communalist division of its nationalist movement and the agonies of Partition, was perhaps the most spectacular case. But Nigeria, with its Islamico-Christian sectionalism and its ethno-evangelical civil war; Sri Lanka with its Sinhalese-Buddhist vs Tamil-Hindu violence; intra-religion discordances, suspicions, and moral distancings in Landino-Indian Meso-America; Sunni-Shi'i sectarianism of small differences in Iraq and Pakistan, Orthodox-Roman ones in Serbo-Croatia; Muslims, Christians, and Jews tumbled together across the Middle East and North Africa; lowland Buddhism and up-country Christianity glowering at one another in Burma; Spanish Catholicism, American Evangelism, and Islamic Revivalism jammed together and set apart in the island Philippines—all these presented anyone concerned to explore their spiritual constitution with a rather different sort of task than that which had faced Reo Fortune and his sorcerers in Dobu, Max Gluckman and his chiefs in Swaziland, or Claude Lévi-Strauss and his jaguar stories among the Bororo.

The first question it raised, and the one most productive of abstract debate, is one that was, of course, tacitly there from the beginning, but which could, now that such variousness, multiplicity, rivalry, and clamour were involved, no longer be silently and unreflectively answered by the simple device of training our attention on cults and customs that seem at least generally analogous to ones considered in our own society to have something to do with the divine, the supernatural, the holy, the sacred, the numinous, or the transcendent—namely, "What Is Religion?" What is to be included under this rubric? Where are its borders? What are its marks? What, when you get down to it, is "belief," or "worship," or "observance," or "faith"? My dissertation was called 'Religions in Java,' the book that emerged from it, cut, polished, and renamed for public consumption, *The Religion of Java* [Geertz 1960]. It had sections on everything from shadow plays, the *hajj*, yoga, and speech styles to possession, quranic schools, funeral feasts, and political parties. It is still not clear what its subject was.

II

The issue here, how we are to name and classify cultural formations in other societies that are at once broadly similar to ones in our own and oddly *sui generis*, strange and different, is quite general in anthropology: a recurrent crux. Whether it is 'the family,' or "the market," or "the state," or "law," or "art," or "politics," or "status," deciding just what goes into the category, as we say, cross-culturally, and why it does so, is an essentially contested matter, a circular discussion that stirs polemic, never ends, and only marginally, and then rather diagonally, advances. The usual tack is to begin with our own, more or less unexamined, everyday sense of what "the family," "the state," or, in the case at hand, "religion" comes to, what counts for us as kinship, or government, or faith, and what, family-resemblance style, looks . . . well . . . resemblant, amongst those whose life-ways we are trying to portray.

This hardly results in determinate species-and-genera taxa, a Linnaean catalogue of cultural kinds. What it results in is a persistent issue over which endlessly to argue—The Definition Problem: "What Do We Talk About When

We Talk About Religion?" In good part, surely, what we talk about is "meaning." If there is any general, immediate, and (at least until it is looked into more carefully) perspicuous category, direct and intuitive, apparently coherent, under which the cabbages-and-kings material of ethnographic accounts of "religion" in today's potpourri "new state" societies can be comparatively subsumed, it is that. The oblique, family-resemblance connections between the sorts of phenomena—beliefs, practices, attitudes, imaginings—that we group, casually and unreflectively, "ordinary language-wise," under the commonsense designation 'religion' for ourselves, and those that we so group, hardly more deliberatively, in connection with societies we see as at least somewhat distant and unlike to our own—as "Other"—are essentially ones we regard, in either case, as having something critically to do with the overall "purpose," "point," "sense," "significance," or "design" of things: with, broadly and momentously, often enough parabolically, "the meaning of life."

Put that way, it might seem that all we have succeeded in doing is replacing one obscurity with another; the indefinite with the indistinct. But there is, or so it seemed to me as I struggled to determine what it was I had in fact been trying to bring to integral description in the Javanese case, one advantage of re-focusing matters in such a way: namely, that a large and expanding set of precise and powerful speculative instruments—conceptions, theories, perspectives, modes of discourse, frames of analysis—has been emerging in the human sciences which can be mobilized to sort the unsortable, connect the unconnected; to define researchable questions and devise ways to research them. Putting anthropology, and most especially the anthropology of religion, into the conceptually more complex and self-conscious context of contemporary linguistics, literary criticism, semiotics, psychology, sociology, and, most especially, philosophy is not to obscure what it has to say with imported abstractions or pump it up with concocted jargon. It is, in Charles Peirce's famous advisement, to try to make our ideas clear. Not least to ourselves.

In the flood of work that has appeared since—shall we say C. S. Peirce and Ferdinand de Saussure, Gottlob Frege, and Roman Jakobson (who seem to me to have, in their several ways, started most of it off)—with respect to the analysis of what, simply to have a covering term, we can call "meaning systems," or, as I came to prefer, "cultural systems," three lines of thought seem to me of particular value in connection with focusing and ordering our comparative understanding of religion.

The first of these is what has been called 'the autonomy of meaning' thesis. (The phrase is due to the American philosopher Donald Davidson [1984], but the *locus classicus* formulation is Wittgenstein's—no first name needed there— private language argument [Wittgenstein 1953; cf. Colebrook 2002: 70 ff.].) Meaning is not a subjective matter, private, personal, "in the head." It is a public and social one, something constructed in the flow of life. We traffic in signs *en plein air*, out in the world where the action is; and it is in that trafficking that meaning is made. We must, as Stanley Cavell, another American philosopher with Wittgensteinian tendencies, has, with appropriate paradox, put it, "mean what we say," because it is only by "saying" (or otherwise behaving, acting, proceeding, conducting ourselves, in an intelligible manner) that we can "mean" at all [Cavell 1969].

The second thought-line, implicate in the first, is that meaning is materially embodied, that it is (and here one searches for the appropriate term) formed, conveyed, realized, emblematized, expressed, communicated, via ponderable, perceptible, construable signs; symbolical devices, like passage rites or passion plays, differential equations or impossibility proofs, which are its vehicles. (What makes a device 'religious' is not its structure but its use: Pythagoreans, we are told, worshipped right triangles and the square-root of two.) Despite the difficulty of formulating it in a simple, straightforward way, something due to the haunting of our language by the ghosts of departed epistemologies, this is a more or less obvious idea, once those ghosts, Platonic or Cartesian, Comtean or Christian, are properly exorcized. That culture (language, art, science, law, religion, marriage, politics, merriment, common sense—the whole kit and caboodle) consists not of bodiless ideas suspended in impalpable mental states, delicate motions of the soul and spirit, but of what the American action theorist, social critic, and all-round man of letters Kenneth Burke [1941] has called "equipment for living," equipment that is substantial, at hand, usable, and used, ought not by now to be so difficult a notion.

And finally, connecting all this more directly with religion and worship, there has been the development, important in the human sciences since Max Weber's *Religionssoziologie*, but which has a long and serpentine history in apologetical speculation of all shapes and varieties and in certain branches of recent theology, of the conception of "limit," or "ultimate," or "existential" problems of meaning: the notion that it is at the point at which our cultural resources fail, or begin to fail, where our equipment for living creaks and threatens to break down in the face of the radically inexplicable, the radically unbearable, or the radically unjustifiable—irresolvable confusion, ineluctable pain, invincible evil, the primitive surds of finitude—that the sort of concern, often enough itself referred to as "ultimate," that we recognize as religious comes into play [Jaspers 1971; Tillich 1952; Weber 1965]. To cite, as I have done more than once elsewhere, a passage by Suzanne Langer, another unclassifiable, freelance American social theorist:

> Man can adapt himself somehow to anything his imagination can cope with; but he cannot deal with Chaos. [Our] most important assets are

always the symbols of our general orientation in nature, on the earth, in
society, and in what we are doing: the symbols of our *Weltanschauung*
and *Lebenanschauung* . . . [In] a primitive society, a daily ritual is incorporated in common activities, in eating, washing, fire-making . . .
because the need of reasserting the tribal morale and recognizing its
cosmic conditions is constantly felt. In Christian Europe, the Church
brought men daily (in some orders even hourly) to their knees, to enact,
if not to contemplate their assent to the ultimate concepts [1959: 287].

Equipped, then, with these three general notions, that meaning is autonomous, that it is conveyed in signs or symbols, and that religious meanings so
conveyed are directed toward points at which impasse looms, I tried, just
about forty years ago now and, curiously enough, here in Cambridge at a famous hands-across-the-sea ecumenical conference designed to gather younger
British "social" and younger American "cultural" anthropologists into a common discourse community (little hope, apparently, was held out for the elders,
most of whom avoided the event), to set forth a brief, general account of "Religion as a Cultural [or, again, "meaning"] System," by means of which I hoped
I could identify and locate the centre of gravity, so far as there was one, in my
dispersed and ad-hocish, engage it first, interpret it later, approach to things
[Banton 1966: 1-46; Geertz 1973].

This involved, in the first instance, a tentative, rather awkward, rather diffuse, effort to construct a definition, not, as I thought I quite explicitly and
insistently, even repetitiously, stated, to isolate "an ontological," "universalist,"
"transhistorical" "essence of religion for now and for always," but to control,
guide, and render more explicit, an, at that time anyway, still rather angular
and unfamiliar line of argument.[1]

This road-map, *tour d'horizon* "definition" (it was really more of a provocation than anything else, directed toward upending the complacencies at once
of structuralism and functionalism, then the reigning paradigms in ethnologi-
cal research) was mainly concerned with stressing the way in which a people's,
a group's, or an individual's most comprehensive ideas of order, their world-
view, and the pervading tone and temper of their lived life, their ethos, are
made to complete and reinforce one another in religious practice: in ritual, in
myth, in spiritual discipline, in the reflexive pieties of everyday life. "Religion," to quote myself, "tunes human actions to an envisaged cosmic order
and projects images of cosmic order onto the plane of human experience"
[Geertz 1973: 90; for an earlier, less technical, statement, see Geertz 1958]. It
gives, as the epigraph I took from George Santayana's neglected *Reason and
Religion* put it, a particular and idiosyncratic "bias to life," constructs (a be-
liever might say, I suppose, "discovers") "another world to live in." And "an-

other world to live in—whether we expect ever to pass wholly over into it or not—is what we mean by having a religion" [Geertz 1973: 90].

In any case, having thus collected my thoughts as best I could manage for the moment and set them out for the powers to contemplate, I rather quickly tired of position-taking and polemical exchange, the here-we-are and there-we-are of programmatical discourse in scholastical places, and wanted to return to the mine-face, where, once again, the action is after all, to see if all this came to anything useful in understanding, as we say, "the real world"—the one which people live in, but anthropologists only visit. Accordingly, I began yet another long-term, up-close encounter with another historically old, politically new, or anyway renovated, religiously emphatic society (Java at that time was fully in the throes of the pandemic violence I mentioned earlier)—namely, Morocco.

Like Java (or Indonesia—but let us leave that problem aside), Morocco, is, of course, nominally, publicly, and at least semi-officially "Islamic," has been so for the whole of its written history, and seems highly unlikely soon to change. But, unlike Java, it is Arabo-Berber, rather than Malayo-Polynesian, in its ground-bass infra-culture; and, unlike Java, it has been largely—not entirely, but largely—free of direct involvements with and intensive influences from other "high," "world," "organized," "doctrinal," or "scriptural" religions. (There was, for a very long time, an enclave Jewish presence and, for a much shorter period, a supervenient Christian one, but neither had much effect on the overall drift and tenor of things.) As a result, instead of the diffuseness and conglomeration, the sense of eclecticism, dispersion, and continuous position-taking which marks Java, Morocco presents a much severer, much more focused and concentrated spiritual picture: "Islam" *sans phrase*. Against Java's delicate *carrefour* balance between "*les frictions de la concurrence*" and "*la volonté d'harmonie*," Morocco seems (in its temper, at least—its social structure is another matter) direct, uncluttered, spare, and monophonic.

To bring this contrast out, to unpack it, and to demonstrate the usefulness of the meaning system approach in focusing issues, I gave a series of rather brief, schematical, and in some ways reductive lectures after returning from North Africa in the late 1960s, in which, rather than offering an encyclopaedic survey of whatever seemed to have something or other to do locally with "religion," as I had for Java, I attempted to trace how a single, long-established, highly codified, extraordinarily self-conscious, not to say self-absorbed "world religion," Islam, had worked itself out in quite different ways with quite different effects in quite different settings: the farthest Maghreb, the most distant Indies. Published later as *Islam Observed* [Geertz 1968] (which was supposed to be a pun, though I don't know that anyone noticed), my discussion was organized around the construction in each of the two societies of what I called

their "classical styles" of religious expression: in Java, a hierarchical, syncretistic, and rather diffuse, experience-seeking intuitionism; in Morocco, a strenu-
ous, confrontational, and rather puristic, world-correcting moralism. The va-
lidity of these capsule characterizations aside (it is not possible in such matters
to describe without misdescribing; exception and contradiction are so deeply
built-in), my concern was to show how comprehensive, overall ideas of order,
some of them derived from Islamic texts and traditions, some of them not,
and particular, locally developed, locally accented social practices played into
one another, dialectically if you like that sort of language, reciprocally if you
don't, to produce concrete and particular *trains de vie*—distinctive ways-of-
being-in-the-world.

But a funny thing happened on the way to the argument. In both countries
(and, it all too soon became apparent, in the world at large) the closeness of
the tie between large views and local circumstances began to grow drawn and
attenuated, transformed to a plane of abstract defensiveness and identity panic,
even as I watched. What had been a fairly direct and immediate interplay between the everyday experiences of life among others and deep-laid notions of
significance and collective purpose became, at least for large and growing seg-
ments of the two populations, though again in characteristically contrastive
ways, a much more elusive, intricate, unsteady, and uncertain matter.

To name this phenomenon, and in part to characterize it, though its force
and scale, as well as its staying power, remained quite unclear, I coined, for the
nonce, the nonce-phrase "religious mindedness."

> In the course of their separate social histories, the Moroccans and the
> [Javanese] created, partly out of Islamic traditions, partly out of others,
> images of ultimate reality in terms of which they both saw life and
> sought to live it. Like all religious conceptions, these images carried
> within them their own justification; the symbols (rites, doctrines, objects,
> events) through which they were expressed were, for those responsive to
> them, intrinsically coercive, immediately persuasive—they glowed with
> their own authority. It is this quality that they seem gradually to be los-
> ing, at least for a small but growing minority. What is believed to be true
> has not changed for these people, or not changed much. What has
> changed is the way in which it is believed [Geertz 1963: 17].

Whatever you want to call it (and, as I say, "religious mindedness" does not
seem to be quite the right term, for it suggests a certain superficiality and falling away from genuineness which I don't think was the case), there seemed in
both countries to be a change, then still limited but rapidly accelerating, in the
way in which religious convictions were brought together with the workings
of everyday life. The relations between the two were less simple, less immedi-

ate, and less direct—more in need of explicit, conscious, organized support. The forms which this took in both countries—back-to-the-Quran reformist movements, political-party organization of religious interests, the efflorescence of propaganda, apology, and doctrinal argument—brought nothing so much to mind as another line from Santayana, this one about persons (he called them "fanatics," but that too is not quite right) who, having lost sight of their aim, redouble their effort.

III

A great deal has happened, both in Indonesia and Morocco particularly and in the Islamic world generally, since those lectures were delivered in what turned out to be the *après nous le déluge* year: 1967. Indonesia has had five presidents since, two of them strong Muslims, three of them more syncretic in outlook. Morocco has had two kings, one of them emphatic and hard-handed, the other hesitant, elusive, and hard to read. The Cold War, which pumped foreign-born ideological passions into home-grown social tensions to the point where the combination threatened to disintegrate politics and dismantle the state, has ended. There are only a few Jews left of what was once a flourishing, if besieged, community in Morocco. Indonesia's rather nativistic Communist Party, once the largest outside the Sino-Soviet bloc and poised for revolution, has been completely destroyed after a failed coup and a popular massacre, its leaders killed, imprisoned, disgraced, or exiled. And, perhaps most important from the point of view of our subject, the "religious mindedness" vs "religiousness as such"—self-conscious, doctrinarian belief as opposed to everyday reflexive faith—that I saw as just beginning to become prominent in the two countries as "salafism," "scripturalism," "reformism," "purism," and "double-mindedness" has since become pervasive across the whole of the Muslim world under such generalizing rubrics as "Islamism," "Political Islam," "Neo-Fundamentalism," and "Jihadist Islam." Khomeini, Le Front Islamique du Salut, the Taliban, and Osama have occurred since. So have the Al Aksa Intifada, the attack on the World Trade Towers, the American invasions of Afghanistan and Iraq, the bombings in Bali and Casablanca, the de-Sovietization of Central Asia, and the massive migration, increasingly permanent, increasingly contested, of Near Eastern and Asian Muslims to Western Europe and the United States.

Such, indeed, are the perils of trying to write history as it happens, as I was, in part, attempting to do. The world will not stand still till you complete your paragraph, and the most you can do with the future is sense its imminence. What comes, comes: the important thing is whether, when it comes, it makes any sense as an outgrowth of the directive processes you think you have seen. History, it has been said, may not repeat itself but it does rhyme. And from that point of view, looking back from what I see now to what I saw then, though I am both worried and disheartened (I had hoped for better), I don't feel particularly embarrassed, chastened, defensive, or apologetic. Sensing rain, I may have gotten a flood; but it was, at least, a corroborative one. However unformed and gathering the clouds where then, and however uncertain I was about what to make of them, they were real. And so, it now turns out, was the storm they portended.

In the second half of the twentieth century, The Long Postwar, the study of religion in the social sciences was, with a few prominent exceptions, Peter Berger and Thomas Luckmann [1967] and Robert Bellah [1970] in sociology, Victor Turner [1968] and Mary Douglas [1966] in anthropology, still pretty much of a backwater, and the reductive version of the so-called "secularization thesis"—that the rationalization of modern life was pushing religion out of the public square, shrinking it to the dimensions of the private, the inward, the personal, and the hidden—was in full cry. Though spirits and goblins, and even high gods, still had purchase among peripheral peoples and submerged classes, and the churches remained open, the illusion had no future as a broadly consequential social force. It might, indeed probably would, persist for a while, in this place or that, as a primitivist hangover and a drag on progress; but that it would ever again be the directive power, forcible and transformative in social, political, and economic affairs that it had once been, in the Reformation, the Middle Ages, or the Axial Age, was scarcely conceivable. That, of course, may still turn out to be the case, and Weber's nightmare—"specialists without spirit, sensualists without heart"—may yet come to pass [Weber 1958: 284]. But it didn't look like that to me and my out-of-step fellow travellers in 1967. And it certainly does not look like that to anyone now. Hindutva, Neo-Evangelism, Engaged Buddhism, Eretz Israel, Liberation Theology, Universal Sufism, Charismatic Christianity, Wahhabis, Shi'ism, Qtub, and "The Return of Islam": assertive religion, active, expansive, and bent on dominion, is not only back; the notion that it was going away, its significance shrinking, its force dissolving, seems to have been, to put it mildly, at least premature.

Summing up in a handful of sentences what has happened to "religion," here, there, and around the world, in the closing decades of the last century and the opening one of this is, of course, quite impossible, a mug's game (or an ideologue's [Geertz 2003a]); and I have, after what I have been through, better sense than to attempt it. But it is possible to suggest a few characteristics of the contemporary scene, within Morocco and Indonesia as well as without, within Islam as well as the other "world religions," that seem to be at once something rather new under the sun and logical extensions of settled trends.

Of these, I will mention here only two, though they are but part of a much larger social picture and they rather come down to two ways of saying the same thing: (1) the progressive disentanglement, for want of a better word, of the major religions (and some of the minor ones—Soka Gakkai, Mormonism, Cao Dai, Bahai) from the places, peoples, and social formations, the sites and civilizations, within which and in terms of which they were historically formed: Hinduism and Buddhism from the deep particularities of Southern and Eastern Asia, Christianity from those of Europe and the United States, Islam from those of the New East and North Africa; and (2) the emergence of religious persuasion, inherited or self-ascribed, thinned-out or reinforced, as a broadly negotiable, mobile and fungible, instrument of public identity—a portable persona, a movable subject position.

The spread of the named and textualized world religions from their points of origin and most immediate relevance to foreign climes and contexts is, of course, of very long standing; that is why they are called "world religions." The missionary expeditions of Protestantism into Asia and Africa, the migration of Roman Catholicism along with Iberian conquest culture into Latin America, Islam's explosive thrust east and west from its backwater Arabian heartland, even the rather more elusive, harder-to-trace radiation of Buddhism out of India into China, Japan, and Southeast Asia or that of Rabbinic Judaism out of the New East into Spanish, Slavic, and Germanic Europe—all these demonstrate that beliefs, creeds, faiths, *Weltanschauungen*, "religions," travel, change as they travel, and work themselves, with varying degrees of success and permanence, into the finest of fine structure of the most local of local histories.

What is new in the immediate situation, or anyway different enough to represent something of a sea-change, is that whereas the earlier movement of religious conceptions and their attendant commitments, practices, and self-identifications was largely a matter of centrifugal outreach in one form or another—missionization, conquest, calico-trade proselytizing, and colonial intrusion; itinerant clerics, outpost academies, *in situ* conversions—the present movement is both larger and more various, more a general dispersion than a series of directed flows; the migration, temporary, semi-permanent, and permanent, of everyday believers of this variety or that, this intensity or that, across the globe. There are an estimated twenty million Indians living outside of India, five million Muslims living in France. There are Buddhists (Thai, Burman, Sri Lankan, as well as some autopoetical ones) in London and Los Angeles; Christians, Western expatriate ones, in Tokyo, Riad, and Bangkok, Filipino guest-worker ones in the Gulf, Australia, and Hong Kong. There are Muride street peddlers from Senegal in Turin, Turkish and Kurdish grocers in Berlin. Latin-American Indio-Catholics will soon outnumber, if they don't already, Euro-American ones in the United States. "The world," in a phrase I quoted years ago from Alphonse de Lamartine when all this was just getting started and I was just beginning to get interested in the ideologization of religious traditions, "has jumbled its catalogue" [Lamartine 1946: 328].

This scattering, piecemeal, headlong, fitful, and, except for a certain amount of kinship and neighbourhood chaining, unorganized, of individuals (and families) born into locally rooted, culturally particularized setting alters the whole climate of public belief and spiritual self-consciousness, both for those who move, for those into whose midst they move, and for those who are left behind. The formation of diaspora communities, even religiously marked diaspora communities, is also hardly a wholly new phenomenon in world history—Jews in New York, Maronites in West Africa, Hadramautis in Southeast Asia, Gujeratis in the Cape. But the scale on which they now are forming (50,000 Moroccans in Amsterdam, 100,000 Malians in Paris, 150,000 Bangladeshis in London, 250,000 Turks in Berlin, and, most wonderful of all, 10,000 Tamils in Switzerland—virtually all arrived there in the last two or three decades) surely is. It is not just capital that is being globalized, not just doctrine that is spreading.

The transformation of more or less routinely transmitted, compliantly received conceptions of the good, the true, and the actual into explicitly asserted, vigorously promoted, and militantly defended ideologies—the move from "religiousness" to "religious mindedness" of various sorts and degrees of intensity—that was "observed" as getting underway in Moroccan and Indonesian Islam in the mid-1960s as those countries began seriously to reconsider their religious history is now a quite general phenomenon in a world where more and more people and the selves they have inherited are, so to speak, out of context: thrown in among others in ambiguous, irregular, poly-faith settlements. It is not just Muslims, and not just North Africans and Southeast Asians, who are undergoing this sort of spiritual reorientation. Nor is it only happening to migrant populations. The jumbling of the world's catalogue is altering both the form and the content of religious expression, and altering them in characteristic and determinate ways, changing at once the tonalities of conviction, its reach and its public uses. That much, whatever else is or isn't happening, is quite clear.

Being a Muslim abroad (or a Hindu, a Christian, a Jew, a Buddhist . . . but I must return to my sheep), outside the Dar Al-Islam, is, as increasing numbers of Moroccans and Indonesians gone elsewhere to work, study, tour, or marry are finding out, a rather different matter than being one at home. Going among non-Muslims induces in many, probably in nearly all, a certain amount of conscious reflection, more or less anxious, on what being a Muslim in fact comes down to, on how properly to be one in a setting not historically prearranged to facilitate it. There can be and are, of course, a number of outcomes:

an ecumenical "watering down" of belief to render it less offensive to a religiously pluralized or secularized setting; a "double-minded" dividing of the self, and the self's life, into but vaguely communicating inward and outward halves; a turn toward a much more assertive and self-conscious Islamism in response to the perceived faithlessness of the new setting. And just about every possibility in between, including, of course, blind, unfettered, slaughterous rage.

IV

So: one, nervously bounding about over four continents for a half century; the other, calm and settled in his rooms at St John's for a similar period—are we, after all, Frazer and I, in the same business? Is he in my genealogy, am I in his? Does an aim connect us? A history run through us? A field embrace us? It is a very long way, it would seem, from the strange goings-on in the grove at Nemi—the "grim figure," "the drawn sword," "the priest murderer himself to be murdered" [Frazer 1890: preface]—to the political agendas of the salafi madrasahs of central Java or the legitimist ambitions of the sherifian zawias of northern Morocco, to say nothing of the "can we let them wear head-scarves?" comédies of civiste Paris or the "can we let them read Quran?" ones of chapter-and-verse North Carolina [Bowen 2004]. Is "the anthropology of religion" a subject, like "kinship," or "class," or "gender"? An issue, like "the origins of agriculture" or "the evolution of the state"? A discipline, like "palaeontology"? A specialty, like "sociolinguistics"?

It should be clear by now that, at least so far as I am concerned (others may do as others wish), "studying religion" is not, and never has been, a single, bordered, learnable and teachable, sum-up-able thing. It is, and has always been, a matter of sorting through various happenings variously encountered—large, public ones, like national elections or international migrations; small, intimate ones, like household feasts or Quran chants; merely incidental, parenthetical ones, like a broken funeral, a raided cockfight, or a painted-over house façade—all in an effort to determine how overall conceptions of what reality really is and particular ways of going about in it play into one another to sustain the sense that, more or less anyway and on balance, things make sense. "The religion of Java," "observed Islam," and the "jumbled catalogue of The Long Postwar" are but chapters, obliquely related, loosely successive, arbitrarily titled, in a fitful history of meaning-making.

It is that, as I look back over Sukarno's Java, hectic with hope and disappointment, Hasan II's Morocco, half-emergent from 'asabiya, feud, and hommes fétiches, and, now, the tumblings and scatterings of the post-modern post-millennium, which seems to run through the whole and make of it all, after all, a confinable subject—something to regard, steadily and whole.

At each stage, in each place, on each occasion, one is presented with a wild multiplicity of individuals, groups, and groups of groups trying to hold their lives together in the face of change, circumstance, and (Sartre's hell) one another. One doesn't, after all, so much "examine" religion, "investigate" it, or even "research" it, as circumambulate it. Skulking about at the edge of the grove, one watches it happen.

We are, most all of us now, not just anthropologists, folklorists, or connoisseurs of the odd and arcane, thus somewhat employed. The jumbling of the world's catalogue is, by now, general to the point of near universality. Cheek-by-jowl contrast, not only of religious allegiance, but of ethnic background, "race," language-community, place of origin, and God knows what other allegiance or marking people may contrive to distinguish themselves from one another and persuade themselves of their own solidity, is pervasive, not just in Western Europe and North America, towards which migration has recently been perhaps the most marked, but also in Asia, Africa, and Latin America, drawn with increasing force and inevitability into the whirl of the world's variety. It is, of course, possible that all this here-we-are-and-there-we-are will in time sort itself out and large, neat, hermetic blocs of cultural commonality, what we used to imagine 'nations' to be, will either re-emerge or be created anew. But, so far as I can see, there is at the moment precious little sign of it. Jumble is with us late and soon.

References

Asad, T. 1983. Anthropological conceptions of religion: reflections on Geertz. Man (N.S.) 18, 232–59.

Banton, M. (ed.) 1966. *Anthropological approaches to the study of religion* (ASA Monograph 3). London: Tavistock.

Bellah, R. 1970. *Beyond belief*, New York: Harper & Row.

Benedict, R. 1927. *The concept of the guardian spirit in North America*. (American Anthropological Association Memoir 29). Menasha, Wis.: American Anthropological Association.

Berger, P., and T. Luckmann 1967. *The social construction of reality*. Garden City, N.Y.: Doubleday.

Bowen, J. 2004. Muslims and citizens: France's headscarf controversy. Boston Review, Feb./Mar.

Burke, K. 1941. *The rhetoric of literary form*. Baton Rouge: Louisiana State University Press.

Cavell, S. 1969. *Must we mean what we say?* New York: Scribner.

Colebrook, C. 2002. *Irony in the work of philosophy*. Lincoln: University of Nebraska Press.

Davidson, D. 1984. *Inquiries into truth and interpretation*. Oxford: Clarendon Press.

Douglas, M. 1966. *Purity and danger*. London: Routledge & Kegan Paul.

Evans-Pritchard, E.E. 1956. *Nuer religion*. Oxford: Clarendon Press.

Firth, R. 1967. *The work of the gods in Tikopia* (Second edition). London: Athlone Press.

Frazer, J.G. 1890. *The golden bough*. London: Macmillan.

Geertz, C. 1958. Ethos, world view, and the analysis of sacred symbols. Antioch Review, Winter.

———. 1960. *The religion of Java*. Glencoe, Ill.: Free Press.

———. (ed.) 1963. *Old societies and new states*. New York: Free Press.

———. 2003. "Which way to Mecca?" In this volume.

Jaspers, K. 1971. *Philosophy of existence*. Philadelphia: University of Pennsylvania Press.

Kipp, R., and S. Rodgers (eds.) 1987. *Indonesian religions in transition*. Tucson: University of Arizona Press.

Kluckhohn, C. 1962. *Navaho witchcraft*. Boston: Beacon Press.

Lamartine, Alphonse de. 1946. Declaration of principles. In *Introduction to contemporary civilization in the West: a source book*. New York: Columbia University Press.

Langer, S. 1959. *Philosophy in a new key*. New York: New American Library.

Lienhardt, R.G. 1961. *Divinity and experience*. Oxford: Clarendon Press.

Lombard, D. 1990. *Le carrefour javanais*. 3 vols. Paris: Ecole des Hautes Etudes en Sciences Sociales.

Malinowski, B. 1948. *Magic, science, and religion*. Boston: Beacon Press.

Marrett, R.R. 1917. *Primitive ritual and belief*. London: Methuen.

Redfield, R. 1953. *The primitive world and its transformations*. Ithaca, N.Y.: Cornell University Press.

Reichard, G.A. 1923. *Navaho religion: a study of symbolism*. New York: Pantheon.

Smith, W.R. 1889. *Lectures on the religion of the Semites*. Edinburgh: C. Black.

Tillich, P. 1952. *The courage to be*. New Haven: Yale University Press.

Turner, V.W. 1968. *Drums of affliction*. Oxford: Clarendon Press.

Tylor, E.B. 1889. *Primitive culture*. New York: Holt.

Weber, M. 1958. *The Protestant ethic and the spirit of capitalism*. Glencoe, Ill.: Free Press.

———. 1965. *The sociology of religion*. London: Methuen.

Wittgenstein, L. 1953. *Philosophical investigations*. New York: Macmillan.

What Was the Third World Revolution?

I begin with a passage from a 1954 essay of Irving Howe's, reprinted in the recent *Fifty Years of Dissent* volume, called, premonitorily enough, "The Problem of U.S. Power":

> The central fact [he writes] is that we continue to live in a revolutionary age. The revolutionary impulse has been contaminated, corrupted, debased, demoralized; it has been appropriated by the enemies of socialism. All true. But the energy behind that revolutionary impulse remains. Now it bursts out in one part of the world, now in another. It cannot be suppressed entirely. Everywhere except in the United States, millions of human beings, certainly the majority of those with any degree of political articulateness, live for some kind of social change. The workers of Europe are consciously anti-capitalist, the populations of Asia and South America [and he might have added, the Middle East and Africa] anti-imperialist. These are the dominant energies of our time and whoever gains control of them, whether in legitimate or distorted forms, will triumph.

Between 1945 and 1965, about fifty-four, depending on how you count, new, independent states, with borders, capitals, armies, leaders, policies, and names appeared in the world. Between 1965 and the end of the century, depending again a bit on how, and whom, you count, fifty-seven more appeared. All the major colonial empires—British; Dutch; French; Spanish; Portuguese; American; German; Australian; and, via the Pacific war, the Japanese; via the collapse of communism, the Russian—dissolved, most relatively peacefully, a few—India, Algeria, the Belgian Congo, the East Indies, Kenya, Indo—China-amid spastic outbursts of generalized violence. An international system, with sixty or so officially recognized players (forty-two countries were members of the League of Nations at its start; another sixteen joined later, and one has to add the United States and a couple of other recalcitrants) was succeeded by

Originally published as an Irving Howe Memorial Lecture, *Dissent* (Winter 2005).

one with, by the most recent UN membership count, a hundred and ninety-one. The world resegmented, refounded, and reformatted in the space of a few decades. It was, clearly, some sort of revolution. But what sort—what it was that was turned around, and in which directions—was, and still is, imperfectly understood.

Indeed, its thrust and import, what it signifies for our common future, seems less clear today than it did at its outset, when the infinite grandeur of beginnings that attends all mold-breaking political transformations in the modern age clothed it in a dense symbology of selfhood, progress, solidarity, and liberation. In the Bandung Days of the late 1950s and early 1960s, the charismatic hero-leaders—Nehru, Sukarno, Nasser, Nkrumah, Ben Bella, Kenyatta, Ho, Azikwe, Lumumba, Nyerere, Muhammad V, Solomon Bandanaraike, cheered on by two-and-a-half worlders, Chou, Tito, Castro—projected a heady vision of radical nationalism, cold war neutrality, collective opposition to Western imperialism, and great-leap-forward material progress: a vision that was bound to come apart as the diversity of the interests, the variousness of the histories, and the incoherence of the worldviews it was designed to contain became apparent. Within ten or fifteen years, a generation of parochial and hard-fisted leaders appeared—Bukassa, Suharto, Gowon, Marcos, Boumedienne, Mobuto, and Indira Gandhi all came to power in 1965–1966; Hassan II and Ayub Khan a little earlier; Qaddafi, Assad the Elder, and Idi Amin a little later—replacing popular mobilization and national cheerleading with the pressures and calculations of disciplinary rule. That approach, too, in good part a product of the great-power alliance-balancing and aid-brokering that the spread of the cold war beyond Europe and its regional intrusions and intensifications made possible, didn't last. A few relics or throwbacks, like Mugabe or Niyazov, or isolate outliers like Than Shwe or Ben Ali, aside most of the present-day leaders of the now not-so-new states—Mbeki, Bouteflika, Abdullah, Obasanyo, Manmohan Singh, Mkapar, Yudhoyono, Karzai, Muhammad VI, Salih, Macapagal-Arroyo, Kibaki, Assad the Little, even situational equilibrists like Sharon and Musharraf—are suited and circumspect managerial politicians, not mini-leviathans or world-stage superstars.

It would be a mistake, however, to conclude that things have come full circle, that Howe's revolutionary impulse in a revolutionary age, "the dominant energies of our times," left things, in the end, only cosmetically altered. Clearly, something transformative happened to the way the world works, or doesn't work, in the forty-odd years from the partition of India to the fall of the Berlin Wall, and, variously visible, spastically explosive, the process continues. The problem is that, imprisoned in categories of analysis designed for a less multiform, and less dispersive politics, and caught up in large misperceptions of our own situation ("the problem of U.S. power"), we have only the sketchiest of ideas, and most of those dubious, as to what that something might be.

My interest in all this, in what *istiqlal, merdeka, uhuru, swaraj,* and the rest have come to as practical realities, and what they portend for the general direction of things, stems most immediately, of course, from my involvement, up-close and personal, as an anthropologist—an *American* anthropologist, with American commitments and American concerns—working in and on post-colonial Indonesia and Morocco over almost the whole span of my career and their existence. I first went to Indonesia in 1952, a little over a year after the new republic was founded. (I arrived, in fact, on the day of the first anti-Sukarno coup attempt, which, with his usual élan, the Voice of the People—"all tongue and no ears"—talked down on the steps of Parliament.) I first went to Morocco in 1963, shortly after the country's café society Prince Hal, Hassan II, came suddenly and emphatically to power, brandishing tradition and pursuing back-country malcontents. (His hero-father, Muhammad V, had just died—a freakish, premature, politically destabilizing death.) Since then, I have shuttled back and forth between them, both physically and in my research attention, as they attempted to find their way in a fractionated world as volatile and shape-shifting as they were themselves. In Indonesia, populist hyper-nationalism gave way to factional mass murder, which gave way to military *Gleichsaltung,* which gave way to nebulous and dispersive, ethnically inflected factional politics. In Morocco, royal restoration was followed by a couple of spectacular, near-miss outdoor coup attempts by renegade aides and student soldiers, pitiless exercise of sovereign revenge, and imperatorial expansion toward the Sahara, which was followed by hesitant and indefinite moves toward quasi-constitutional, quasi-democratic quasi-monarchy.

This sort of *in media res,* "what next?," education, particularly when combined with a concern to relate what is taking place in front of you with developments elsewhere similar enough to be interestingly different, gives, inevitably, a particular and peculiar cast to one's mind and character, and, especially as one ages, a desperate urge to sum the unsummable and order the unorderable. In all this indirection, finding direction out is, admittedly, a formidable enterprise. But not, I think, a bootless one, and for several reasons.

In the first place, most of the new or newish states, and especially the more consequential ones, have by now a track record, a half-century or so of fitful and multifarious but nonetheless patterned change. Political styles, as opposed to mere regimes and governments, which pass, like their leaders, with the headlines, have begun to take form, with the rudiments, at least, of distinct and recognizable casts and complexions. "Nation-building," the slogan-goal of the fifties and sixties, may still be more notional than real in most places, or a supposititious cover for endemic separatism; imagined communities largely imaginary. But locally specific ways of asserting claims and countering them— "the way things work around here"—have developed virtually everywhere. You don't have to be in Indonesia or Morocco for more than a few months (or, I daresay, in Nigeria, India, Sudan, or the Philippines; the African Great Lakes, the Sahel, the Caucasus, or stanistan Central Asia) to get a definite sense of how the collision of interest and the play of power characteristically proceed, however amorphous or divided the society, the state, or the national body.

Second, the central impulses driving the original thrust toward revolt and independence may have stalled, been diverted, or grown diffuse, but they continue to loom over collective life as a general background, a half-remembered, half-envisaged frame of hope and expectation. Developmentalism, the drive toward technological modernity and sustained growth; integralism, the political solidification of inherited peoples and devolved territories under a capable and responsive government; and particularism, the cultural articulation of an original and singular social personality remain the founding purposes of national existence, if not as realities at least as ambitions. Economic takeoff, effective sovereignty, and bona fide peoplehood are still the third world, postcolonial, new-state mythos: Howe's social change that millions, articulate and inarticulate alike, irrepressively live for.

Third, and in my view most critically, all this—the formation of distinct and persistent political styles, the deceleration of nation-making, and the lingering hold of liberationist ideals—is taking place in the context of the global reformatting that decolonization and the dismemberment of empire brought into being. The capital founding, the border fixing, and the multiplication of consequent actors, the general scrambling of the world's catalogue, form the overall environment in which we all—what Sukarno used to call the "Nefos" and the "Oldefos" (the new emerging forces and the old established forces)— nowadays collectively function.

The irregular and miscellaneous dynamics of this altered landscape—the runaway urbanization (Cairo, two million in the fifties, sixteen million today; Bombay-Mumbai, four and fourteen million; Lagos, three-hundred thousand and ten million—not to speak of Shanghai, Mexico City, Bangkok, or São Paulo); the headlong, multidirectional migration (twenty million Indians live outside of India, a couple hundred thousand of them in northern New Jersey; there are nearly a quarter million Turks in Berlin, forty thousand in Amsterdam; movement from the third world accounts for two-thirds of this country's, and all of California's, annual population rise; 90 percent of United Arab Emirates residents are foreigners; God only knows how many Chinese are now "overseas"); the explosion, one after another, like invisibly connected firecrackers, of ethnic and ethno-religious, primordialized violence (Rwanda, Sri Lanka, Aceh, Darfur) and after-the-border-drawing micro-wars (Timor, Kashmir, Chechnya, Eritrea, Bougainville, Rio De Oro)—not only threaten to overwhelm our machinery for managing them, they escape, or nearly, the established categories of our understanding. It is not just our policies that are inadequate, or our analyses and explanations. It is the conceptual equipment we use to think them with.

A simple thought experiment, concrete and elemental, can, I think, help us see this. Visualize, or try to, what—assuming there to be such a thing—the prototypical new state of the last half-century—just emerged from a disused and distanced colonial past into a world of intense and implacable great-power conflict—had to address—*ab initio*, from a standing start. It had to organize, or reorganize, a weak and disrupted, "underdeveloped" economic system: attract aid, stimulate growth, and set policies on everything from trade and land reform to factory employment and fiscal policy. It had to construct, or reconstruct, a set of popular (at least ostensibly), culturally comprehensible political institutions—a presidency or prime ministership, a parliament, parties, ministries, elections. It had to work out a language policy, mark out the domains and jurisdictions of local administration, elicit a general sense of citizenship—a public identity and a peoplehood—out of a swirl of ethnic, religious, regional, and racial particularisms. It had to define, however delicately, the relations between religion, the state, and secular life; train, equip, and manage professional security forces; consolidate and codify a thoroughly pluralized, custom-bound legal order; develop a broadly accessible system of primary education. It had to attack illiteracy, urban sprawl, and poverty; manage population growth and movement; modernize health care; administer prisons; collect customs; build roads; shepherd a press. And that was just for starters. A foreign policy needed to be established. A voice in the expanding and proliferating system of trans-, super-, and extra-national institutions needed to be secured. Attitudes toward the half-hated, half-loved, politically discarded but very much not forgotten, metropole civilizations—London, Paris, Amsterdam, Madrid—needed to be rethought, their heritage, the only even quasi-modern one the country had, reassimilated; which meant, among other things, turning nationalism around from a restive and reactive, what-we-are-not, separationist ideology to a persuasive image of a natural, organic, what-we-are, historic community, ready for deals, development, and practical alliances: Mazzini modernized. It was a heady time. No wonder it was followed by ambiguous successes, precipitate turnarounds, sobering disappointments, and, often enough, murderous disruptions.

If a standard, prototypical third world state is too great an imaginative stretch—which, given the dishevelment of a category that includes India, Tunisia, Equatorial Guinea, Belarus, Laos, Qatar, South Africa, Suriname, Yemen, Myanmar, and Vanuatu, it well may be—consider, instead, one of my own referent cases: Indonesia. In the fifties, the velocity of public life there had to be experienced to be disbelieved. A long, strung out, irregular archipelago of six thousand large, small, and microscopic islands, its extent fixed by the mercantile reach of Dutch navigators in the seventeenth and eighteenth centuries, it was home to fifteen or so large ethnic groups and hundreds of small ones, their demarcations and definitions uncertain and mobile; to three or four or five hundred languages, depending on how you count; to Muslim, Catholic, Protestant, Hindu, and so-called "animist"—now upgraded to "indigenous"—religious groups; to a Chinese commercial minority, a Papuan racial one, resident Arabs, in-migrant Indians. And, of course, there were intruding Westerners—economists, businessmen, technical experts, diplomats, tourists, journalists, spies, anthropologists, all trying, they said ("here, let me show you") only to help. To set up a going nation, to use a term itself worn and imprecise, in the midst of all this was at once a magnificent aspiration and a mug's game.

Or, again, if the Land Beneath the Winds (as the Portuguese called it) seems extreme, or far too complicated, consider my other, less generally obtrusive, more compact and homogeneous referent case. Where Indonesia had to pull some sort of collective existence out of a potpourri of language, custom, faith, and locality, accidentally assembled, Morocco, ostensibly a kingdom but actually a tilting field of fractious and parochial jousting strongmen, had to define one against the enfolding background of a much more continuous regional civilization—"North Africa," "The Maghreb," "The Arab West"—diplomatically divvied up by France, Spain, Italy, and Britain into more or less arbitrary, sketchily configured, shallowly rooted administrative bailiwicks. Colonized for fifty years rather than two-and-a-half centuries, wall to wall Arabo-Berber, wall-to-wall Muslim (except for a Jewish merchant minority, soon self-exiled when the Israel option became available), and more a collection of oases, piedmont, and mountain-pass micro-polities than island-scattered culture communities, its everyday political life was a bit less hectic, its thrust toward nationhood a little less desperate. But faced, nonetheless, with about the same calendar of clamoring exigencies, things that had to be done and immediately, it responded, or tried to, with a similar mix of received formulas, local contrivances, stop-gap evasions, and borrowed institutions.

It is in this emblematical and iconical sense, not in any standard, average statistical one (something that, with so irregular and discontinuous a distribution, a collection of outliers and singularities, is really not meaningful here), that the two countries can serve, suitably massaged and redescribed, as type examples, diagnostic expressions, point-of-fact instances, of the third world revolution—what frog, worm, and fruit-fly biologists like to call model systems. What makes them so is neither (or anyway not only) their ethno-religio-linguist complexity nor their culturally arbitrary, externally determined frontiers. That they share with virtually all ex-colonies. (Think India, Nigeria, Myanmar, Lebanon, Papua New Guinea.) It is their common subjection to a common phenomenon, characteristic not only of them but, to some extent at least, of just about every inchoate Nefo country, and increasingly, as the masses move, some of the supposedly more crystallized Oldefo ones as well: that is, the dissociation of what in the modern West we have come, since Westphalia, to regard as near synonyms, interchangeable forms of one another, connatural and coincident, internally connected, ingenerately bound collective realities—"State," "Nation," "People," "Land," "Society," and "Culture." These, the master concepts of modern political description and understanding, the terminal frames of loyalty, identity, membership, sovereignty, and support, marked on our maps as colored spaces, and in our vocabulary by gazetteer names, grow not only increasingly awkward of sense and application, they project an evolution toward commonality and consolidation not, on the face of it, in fact evolving.

The unific vision of classical liberalism (John Stuart Mill: "It is generally a necessary condition of free institutions that the boundaries of government should coincide in the main with those of nationality"; and Ernest Barker: "[There is emerging] a worldwide scheme of political organization in which each nation is also a State and each State is also a nation"—quotations I owe to Walker Connor, one of the few contemporary political scientists, virtually all of them closet Wilsonians, not entranced by it) seems in a world of Indonesias and Moroccos—Congos, Iraqs, Sri Lankas, Georgias—an intellectualist dream from before the flood. Divergence and irregularity, plurality and overlap, the derangement of categories and the confoundment of loyalties seem here to stay, as does—think Singapore, Nepal, Cyprus, the United Arab Emirates, Saudi Arabia—the vast variety of political form. Whatever the third world revolution was, it was not, as promised, a homogenizing force.

Of course, the so-called "developed" or "mature" or "modern" nation-states of Europe and North America have not always been quite the "one-country, one language, one people" monads they represented themselves, both to themselves and to each other, to be; and to the degree that they were, they became so fairly recently, and not without incident. Eugen Weber has shown how slow, difficult, and incomplete the process of turning "peasants into Frenchmen" was. Linda Colley has done something similar for the emergence of "Britons" out of English, Scottish, and (rather more uncertainly) Irish Protestants in the religio-cultural alliances and oppositions of the eighteenth century. And even Mazzini is supposed to have remarked that having made Italy he had yet to make Italians. The crystallization of Turks, Serbs, Bulgarians, Romanians, and Hungarians out of the Ottoman-Hapsburg mélange, generating majority-minority problems of fearsome complexity, are more recent examples, almost proverbial. Canada and the United States, both of them settlement areas, variously populated, have never really been more than notionally compact—racial, ethnic, cultural, and geographical assemblages, put together piece by piece, and then represented, not without strain, as fixed and irreducible natural kinds. And so on and so forth, not to speak of "Germany," "Russia," "Spain," or "Brazil."

But, whatever the illusions and strategic suspensions of disbelief involved, not to speak of the internally directed *Blut und Boden* propaganda, the conception of a world composed of consolidated peoples distributed into discrete territories and impartible states—Renan's implicit *plébiscites de tous les jours*—developed with increasing rapidity over the period that we, perhaps prematurely, call modern, materializing most completely, I suppose, and certainly most passionately, in the marching nationalities of the two world wars. And it is this order of things, real or putative, that the third world revolution has made to look less like a developmental endpoint, the convergent attractor toward which all statecraft moves, or ought to, than a rickety and obsolescent, class-invested *ancien régime*. As imagery and representation—an ideological figuration of Barker's "worldwide scheme of political organization"—the colonial-era map of a small set of well-formed nations, mostly West European, projecting their institutions and their identities onto shapeless countries, irregular societies, and exotic peoples, worked more to obscure how notional, how arbitrary, and, what with respect to British India has been called "the illusion of permanence," how temporary, that scheme really was than it did to instantiate it or render it effective. The imperial imaginary, to use for the moment some up-market terminology, was just that: counterfactual make-believe, designed to contain a scramble of odd points and disparate particles within a manageable set of standardized boxes—ordered categories, broad and familiar.

What made the upheavals and separations of 1949 to 1991 so genuinely transformative of how we think, or should, about our political world, and so disruptive of our received procedures for acting in it, defending our interests or advancing our ideals, is not, however, simply the rearrangements of citizenship and government, or even the shifts in legitimacy, they brought about—the map changes. What made them transformative is the curiously double-edged set of ideas, equivocal and counteractive, that drove them and in terms of which they had almost everywhere their indeterminate outcomes: what, to have a name for it, we can call "the nationalist paradox."

Paradox, because the ideological basis on which the would-be new states, or anyway their leaders, sought autonomy and independence—"Freedom!" "*Merdeka!*" "*Istiqlal!*"—was, of course, the same assertion of a broad, intrinsic coincidence of nation, state, country, culture, and people upon which the imperial powers—even, beneath its soviet disguise, Russia—based their own claims to identity and sovereignty, legitimacy and self-rule. The "oil drop" view of the diffusion of third world nationalism from Bolivar's Latin America, via Europe and the United States, and then on again to Asia and Africa on the spreading currents of print literacy, most closely associated perhaps with Benedict Anderson, and the mobilization for modernization view, which sees it as a reflex (or perhaps it is the cause) of the evolution of a village-centered agrarian civilization into an urban-centered industrial one, *à la* Ernest Gellner, may have their historical difficulties and their polemical simplifications. But that the third world vanguard built its arguments and its program out of a reworked version of the same conception of integral nationality that solidified, or tried to, Britain, France, Spain, Belgium, Russia, and the Netherlands, the regimes that half-enfolded them into foreign selves, is clear enough, as is, indeed, the ambiguity that doing so introduced into their struggles and into the volatile outcomes, excursive and unlooked-for, that followed.

Again, my model-system referent countries exemplify the case, especially if I may excerpt, not to say plagiarize, from some of my earlier and more elaborated writings on their short but originative histories.

In Indonesia, the first five decades of self-rule have consisted of one after another impassioned and determined ideological thrusts—Nationalist, Communist, Praetorian, Islamicist—attempting to fasten a unique and definite identity upon the country—each of which has failed, none of which (except perhaps in its original form, and then only literally, the Communist) has gone away, and all of which have brought on an even stronger sense of difference and disunion. Whatever the effort to construct a proper, spiritually pulled-together nation-state may have come to elsewhere, here it has been, to this point anyway, an elusive, spasmodic, disruptive project.

The Indonesian independence movement essentially got going, in general imitation of European models, in the twenties and thirties of the last century. Under the theatrical leadership of Sukarno—a speaking subaltern if ever there was one—it was a radically unitistic movement in a radically pluralistic situation—a characterization (or a fact) that applies, as I say, to the whole course of the republic's political history. During the fifties and early sixties, this attempt to provide a conceptual foundation for integral nationhood (it involved an odd and eclectic hodgepodge combination of nativist Indo-Javanese symbolism, Dutch social-democracy, and a Maoistic sort of peasant populism) increasingly faltered under the combined pressures of factional conflict, the induced hostilities of the cold war, and—not the least important—the uneven impact of economic change across the strung out and discontinuous regions of the archipelago, energizing some, marginalizing others, and inducing a strong sense of distributional injustice between the resource-rich regions—oil, timber, minerals—where exports originated, and people-rich Java, where the imports they paid for were consumed. (Or, at least so it was thought: an otherwise sedate national newspaper was banned in the late fifties for printing on its front page, bare and without comment, a bar graph depicting just that.)

In 1958, after the first general election demonstrated how incorrigibly divided the country really was (Nationalists, Islamists, and Communists—there were more than forty parties in all, versions and counter-versions of one another—split the vote more or less evenly), open rebellion against the government in Jakarta broke out in several of the regions. Sukarno put it down and suspended parliamentary government in favor of his famous, or infamous, "guided democracy." By the late sixties the country was so intensely beset by culturally inflected partisan conflict that, after a palace coup failed in Jakarta, it was caught up in an enormous hand-to-hand bloodbath. Hundreds of thousands died, thousands more were exiled or jailed, and an authoritarian soldier-government, General Suharto's suggestively denominated "New Order," took power in Jakarta. But, though Suharto turned away from Sukarno's hapless populism toward army-enforced disciplinary rigor, he continued to base the country's idea of itself and where it was going on the sort of synthetic and symbolic, culturally eclectic coordination Sukarno had put it place. And when he, in turn, fell after thirty-five years of astringent rule, a good deal of officially backed violence, ethnic, regional, and religious conflict flared up again over a large part of the country.

I need not continue this chronicle through its most recent phases, which you can glean from the newspaper: the riots, bombings, and insurrections, the Timor catastrophe (itself in part, at least, of elaborate nation, state, and culture confusions pressed into the space of a single, small, colonially severed island); the recovery of parliamentary government and popular elections; the rapid and dizzying succession to leadership of a vaguely Muslim, vaguely nationalist, German-trained technocrat, a flamboyant, erratic, blind, and progressive Islamic cleric, Sukarno's elusive and traditionalist, *de haut en bas* eldest daughter, and, just now, a restrained and circumspect Forts Benning and Leavenworth military bureaucrat. And of course—never aloof from any available form of disruptive difference—there have been the jihadist atrocities in

Bali and Jakarta. The country still holds together, so far anyway. But it does so more by managing the clashes and discontinuities in which it consists—blunting, deflecting, and desperately juggling them—than it does by aligning them or spiritually enfolding them into (Renan again) an overriding *grande solidarité*.

Morocco, as I indicated, does not have the jumble of languages, religions, peoples, cultures, and habitats that Indonesia has, nor has it experienced the same succession of differently conceived mega-ideological programs designed to give it identity, direction, and world-position. Its problem has been rather to define such an identity, compact and original, against the background of a diffuse and encompassing, some might say suffocating, world-historical social formation, what Samuel Huntington, raising the people-equals-culture-equals-polity illusion to a higher level, would call, I suppose, a "civilization"—the so-called Arab World. Morocco is defined neither by its edges, which as a matter of fact are both faint and porous and at points contested, the product of exterior negotiations among exterior powers, nor by its cultural specificity, which hardly sets it off from the other new-state countries around it: Mauritania, Algeria, the rest of the Arab West Maghreb, even the stricken and shattered Sahel into which it fades, and which fades into it, to the east and south. It is defined by the presence at its center and apex of a peculiar, and peculiarly ambiguous institution, at once archaic, traditional, perseverant, and thoroughly remodeled: the Alawite monarchy.

Once more, I need not go into the details of the matter here: the long, semi-mythic history of the monarchy ("Alawi" is the name of the present dynasty), stretching back to the days of Arab Spain; its evisceration under the French protectorate; its reinstitution as a consequent force after the confused struggles of the divided and disorganized independence movement, at once less massive and less excited than the Indonesian; its passage from the sainted, hero-king Muhammad V to his son, the implacable Hassan II, to his grandson, the faint and faintly reformist Muhammad VI. The point is that, if it is a sequence of incomplete (and possibly incompletable, though that, admittedly, remains to be seen) thrusts toward national consolidation that defines post-Indies Indonesia, it is the monarchy, or more accurately, persistence of the monarchy, the country's singular and singularizing institution, that defines (again, so far anyway) post-*Protectorat* Morocco.

The peculiarity of the monarchy is not just that it exists, a traditionalist curiosity unique in the Maghreb among a collection of parvenu regimes led by upstart soldiers (Qaddafi, Ben Ali, Bouteflika, al-Bashir, Ould Taya), but that, through the grand upheavals and transformations—modernization, political mobilization, decolonization, collective self-assertion, administrative rationalization, popular government—that have marked, however partially and irregularly, what I have been calling the third world revolution, it persists. There are monarchies elsewhere in the third world, but either they are the products of late-colonial manipulations, as in Jordan, Saudi Arabia, and the Gulf, or ceremonial hangovers of a reclusive past, like Thailand, Bhutan, Cambodia, or Tonga. The Moroccan monarchy, however, is neither a pretense nor a relic. It is both formally sovereign and practically consequential, and just about every scholar, foreign or domestic, who has reflected on the political life of the country has asked essentially the same question: what is it that sustains it and its occupants in a world of elections, parliaments, ideologies, corporations, newspapers, labor unions, and political parties? What is a Medici prince doing in a century like this?

The answers, of course, are complex and very much in the process of appearing. But one thing he, or, more exactly, the position he occupies and the role he plays, surely does, and emphatically, is mark out the population, and, with the population, the space, over which nationality or citizenship or subjecthood—that is, "Moroccan-ness"—extends. At once, as "king" (malik), head of the all-too-secular palace-managed government at Rabat, and "Commander of the Faithful" ('amir l-mu'minin), the sacred, charisma-charged head of the religious community that spreads out around it, the local *ummah*, the king makes the country: not by decree, not even by the force of arms—though both are more than marginally involved—but through the network of loyalties and attachments that surrounds and leads up to him. The country has borders, a capital, a bureaucracy, an international personality, an army, and a name. But it is neither cultural distinctiveness nor collective solidarity, nor even a demarcated territory, but the personal reach of the king, insofar as he in fact has it and displays it, that makes them real.

Not that this way of turning a place into a polity has been smooth, cumulative, uniform, and complete, any more than the irregular thrusts toward symbolic, all-over belief-system unification that are its equivalent have been in Indonesia, though it has been, to date, those flamboyant assassination attempts aside, a bit less crisis-ridden. The throne has had its successes: the more or less peaceful integration of Tangiers and the former Spanish zone into the new state; the forceful turning back of tribalist challenges to central power; the bringing to heel, violently or otherwise, of *rive gauche* republicans and renegade soldiers; and most spectacularly the enormous, royal-decreed and royal-led "green march" incursion—thousands of ordinary Moroccans streaming across the dotted-line border on foot into the Spanish Sahara. But the very conditions of the monarchy's ascendancy are at the same time the source of its difficulties, large and growing, in maintaining its position as the ordering center of a would-be nation.

In particular, as the dispersion of the Moroccan population beyond its indefinite homeland and the impassioned politicization of North African Islam advance—the one feeding off the other as traditionalist Muslims find themselves projected into settings not historically pre-arranged to support their faith and affirm their identity—both the traditionalist-secular and the charismatic-religious foundations of royal rule come under pressure. There are nearly three million Moroccans out of a total of thirty-some (though the figures vary, depending upon who's counting and to what purpose) now living in Europe: six-hundred thousand in France, two-hundred and seventy thousand in Belgium and the Netherlands, a hundred-twenty thousand in Italy, ninety thousand in Germany and, most fatefully in terms of recent events, eighty thousand in Spain. Though increasingly inclined to become resident abroad, rather than temporary sojourners, they remit—again, the figures are shaky, and vary year to year—nearly two billion U.S. dollars home annually (let us not talk of smuggling), and hundreds of thousands of them return periodically across the narrowing Mediterranean, now virtually a ferry-crossing, transforming thus the very shape of the country. (By comparison, ethnically involuted Indonesia has exported less than 1 percent of its citizens, against Morocco's 10 percent or so, and four-fifths of those to immediately neighboring Malaysia and Singapore.)

The degree to which the king's writ still runs with these relocated subjects of his is something of an open question, and the religious anxiety that seems to arise from trying to live as a Muslim in a non-Muslim environment raises even more serious issues along these lines. The recent terrorist attacks in Casablanca and Madrid (the Rabat government has rounded up more than twelve hundred of its citizens in connection with one, the other, or both of them, and the Spaniards have detained dozens more), along with the appearance of serious religiously based dissent in domestic politics—Sufi sheikhs and Salafi mullahs—suggest that maintaining an ascendancy and control over so distended a community, much less turning it into a unific nation, is a delicate enterprise at best, even for a sacralized prince.

The nationalist paradox—that a series of loosely interconnected, similarly inspired movements to liberate one-people, one-country, one-culture political communities supposedly concealed beneath the artificial surfaces of the colonial map should have led to a deconstruction of the very terms in which those movements were cast—is, perhaps, not in itself so entirely surprising. Revolutions, if they are real, have a way of bringing about the inverse of their intentions.

Indonesia and Morocco, are, as I say, but cases-in-point, part-for-whole examples unique in themselves and broadly illustrative of the overall process that has produced the chopped-up and irregular world in which we all now live. Sudan, with its seemingly endless racial, religious, and ethnic clashes arrayed along its line-in-the-sand perimeters, is plagued at once by Indonesian diversity and Moroccan indefiniteness, without the buffering eclecticism of the one or the center-making monarchism of the other; and, unlike Holland in the Indonesian case or France in the Moroccan, it has been more or less totally abandoned by the Britain that, largely for its own purposes, originally invented it. Sri Lanka, with its Sinhala-Tamil frozen civil war, now more than forty years old, is a binary version of Indonesia's pluralism in which nearly half of the population has to contrive, somehow, to live effectively as a permanent minority, something true as well for Indians in Fiji, Chinese in Malaysia, blacks in Guyana, and Sunnis in Iraq. In Rwanda, Burundi, and the northeast Congo, tribalized factions, artificial and arbitrary, tumble backward and forward across territorial borders, also artificial, also arbitrary, in a cacophony of intimate violence, and something similar takes place in the northern Caucasus and the southern Philippines. India and Nigeria are geographical agglomerations, their component peoples—Punjabis, Bengalis, and Tamils, Yorubas, Ibos, and Fulani-Hausas—spilling diffusely over country frontiers. Singapore and Taiwan are cultural fragments, Myanmar and Lebanon administrative relics. And, as for that supposed monopolist of power, legitimacy, and cosmopolitan expression, so absorbing to Weberian political theorists and café radicals, "The State," the enormous variety of its forms and expressions and the multiplicity of the regimes it houses and of the politics it supports render the very idea elusive, awkward, protean, and problematical. There is talk of "failed states," "rogue states," "super-states," "quasi-states," "theatre states," "contest-states," "orphan states," "presumptive states," and "micro-states"; of "tribes with flags," "imagined communities," and "regimes of unreality." China is a civilization trying to be a state, Saudi Arabia is a family business disguised as a state, Israel is a faith inscribed in a state, Iran is—hippogriffically—a populist theocracy. And who knows, aside from a postal address or a tourist destination, what Kyrgyzstan is?

Then there are the so-called "international" organizations, public and private, regulatory and remedial that have emerged in such abundance and variety since the end of the Second World War in the effort to bring these places and populations into some form of effective relationship with one another or to keep their champions from one another's throats, and which, considering the problems they address and the ways in which they address them, are perhaps more accurately to be called "trans-," or "extra-," or even "counter-national."

The United Nations, originally an attempt to restore and extend the lamented League, has proved to be more of a complicated device, occasionally successful, more often frustrated, for setting up ad hoc arrangements to address ad hoc crises than it has the institutionalization of self-determination, collective security, and world-state supergovernment originally envisaged in San Francisco and Lake Success. (As with nationalism itself, its founding language remains: forced, abstract, nostalgic, not a little phantasmal. Roméo Dallaire, the Canadian general in command of UN forces, such as they were, during the Rwanda upheaval in 1994, has noted with well-earned bitterness that the phrases in which the UN assembly framed that crisis and the ones in which it is now framing that in Sudan a decade further on, are essentially identical— "reaffirming its commitment [the resolutions read] to the sovereignty, unity, territorial integrity and independence of [Rwanda/Sudan]" . . . something of a sick joke—even though what it was really trying to do was to put together a nonce coalition of reluctant African states, stand-aside Western governments, some ground-level nongovernmental organizations, and some of its own special agencies as a momentary stay against murder, rape, rampage, and ethnocide.)

So far as the European Common Market to Community to Union—six members become fifteen become twenty-five—is concerned, the arc is similar. From postwar dreams of forming some sort of neo-Carolingian super-state in the Treaty of Rome, through the pragmatic adjustments and distinctions of Maastricht ("pillarization," "subsidiarity"), to the expansion, south, north, and east, beyond any even approximate coincidence of history, culture, polity, and society (Latvia? Malta? Cyprus? *Turkey?*), the move has also been from the fabrication of unities to the navigation of difference. Similarly with the evolution of extra- or counter-national economic institutions that began with Bretton Woods and proceeded on through trade treaties, multinationals, adjustment programs, and various sorts of summits and clubs, to that collection of speeded-up mobilities of capital, labor, organization, and technique we refer to, uncertainly, as globalization. Multiplicity, "the world in pieces," is with us now, late and soon.

So, to wrap all this up for the moment and escape a drawn conclusion: What, slightly more than half a century after Howe's characteristically hope-in-the-face-of-history, resolve-in-the-face-of-evidence essay, does what he would never have consented to call his "problematic"—The Problem of U.S. Power—come to now? His immediate targets then, McCarthy ("[he] may suffer defeats, but the political mood he personified will not disappear"), "Ikeism" ("tideland oil, tax 'relief' for corporate business, plundering of national resources, acceptance of a reserve army of four to five million unemployed . . . fear, cowardice, suspicion, anti-intellectualism, swagger, distrust, denunciation"), and "the men who rule in Washington" ("[they] sincerely believe that material strength, wealth, money, technology, *know-how* will vanquish all obstacles; that the sum of these constitutes a policy") have something about them of the remembered evils of a remembered darkness, and of the uneasy awareness all of us foolish enough to traffic in the present immediate have that today's polemics wrap tomorrow's fish. But they also project, and more profoundly, the unnerving sense that the more things change the more we are trapped in the Eternal

Return. The Problem of American Power is still the same problem in 2004 as it was in 1954. Only more so.

It is hard for me, trying to make sense of my experience as an exterior observer in the third world and a political subject in the first, to take in the fact that not only were Howe and I very near contemporaries (he was six years the older), but that between us we rather frame the reach and catalogue of the America we separately lived through. (We met only once, that I remember—as co-honorary doctorands with—can you believe it?—Dizzy Gillespie and Isaiah Berlin at a New School commencement. He asked me for references to anthropological accounts of "little stories that seem to encapsulate a culture's feelings," because he was working, he said, on the use of anecdote in "pre-urban" writers—Leskov, Sholom Aleichem, Twain, and Silone.) It is not merely that he came out of Great Depression New York amid Trotskyists, Shactman-ites, YPSLs (Young Peoples Socialist Leagues) and other urban accumulations and I out of New Deal San Francisco, amid Okies, war plants, Japanese displacement, and Wobbly rural radicals; that he was headlong, declarative, and confrontational and I tentative, parenthetical, and indirect; or that we both spent the Second World War, he in Alaska, I in the Pacific, waiting for a life-test that, thanks to the A-Bomb, never came. That our central concerns, not to say obsessions, mine with the transformation of the global structure of identity and difference by the coming into public consequence of the dispersed and particulate voices of Asia, Africa, Latin America, and the European near-abroad, his with—quoting him again—"the tragedy of American power [that] becomes more terrible and terrifying every day [as communication] between America and the remainder of the world become[s] increasingly uncertain, sporadic, bitter," should now, at this time, so converge is about as inevitable as it is surprising.

As American power has grown over the past half-century, to the point where it is the only "supergrand" (they say that we now account for nearly a third of the world's GDP and two-fifths of its military spending, and we have a hand in or an option on a lot of the rest), and the country's internal heterogeneity, always very great, has accelerated and grown obvious, hedgehog nationalism, the desire to make everything whole again as it never really was, and managerial imperialism, the hope for a coordinative control beyond our reach and right, spread and flourish. "There has developed in this country," Howe wrote in that same, at once dated and prescient, 1954 article,

> such a concentration of wealth and power, with so many new attendant values, as to make America increasingly isolated from the rest of the world . . . The power potential of the country, its unprecedented emphasis on . . . accumulation and efficiency, its literal incapacity to understand

and irritated refusal to sympathize with the patterns of thought which dominate Europe and the Third World [he actually wrote "Asia," but I think he would be content with the change]—these are the factors . . . which make America into a lonely power colossus . . . sincerely convinced that only by the imposition of its will can the world be saved. But the world resists this will; it cannot, even if it would, surrender its own modes of response.

Howe's response to this, his recipe for countering it and turning it around, from the side of American power, was, of course, in his famous allusion to the story of the man hired to wait for the Messiah, "steady work": the patient and determined effort to make things clear so as to make them tractable. And so is mine, hardly less exhausting, hardly more promising, from the side of the third world revolution, the nationalist paradox, and the explosive dispersion of the post-colonial directions of transformational change. Michel Foucault remarks somewhere in his vast and tangled corpus that we usually know what we are doing, we sometimes know why we are doing it, but we almost never know what our doing does. We had, I should think—and with this I am sure Irving Howe, however he might have regarded the rest of what I have had to say here, would thoroughly agree—damn well better soon find out.

ACKNOWLEDGMENTS AND EDITORIAL DETAILS

Cordial thanks are due to the *New York Review of Books* for allowing me to plunder their pages in such a way as to provide two thirds of this book, and to do so without charging any fee. In this connection I would like particularly to thank their member of staff, Patrick Hederman, who was an unfailing source of help during compilation. In addition, thanks are due to the editors and publishers of the following journals for permission to republish, also without fees, essays from their pages: *International Journal of Middle East Studies* (with gratitude to Adam Hirschberg for his generosity), *Annual Review of Anthropology* (and thanks to Claire Tilman-McTigue), *Current Anthropology* (and thanks to Lisa McKamey and Emily Dendinger), *Journal of the Royal Anthropological Institute* (with particular thanks to the editor, Simon Coleman), *Dissent* (and similar thanks to Maxine Phillips for her promptness and enthusiasm). My gratitude is also due to Amy Jackson, Clifford Geertz's secretary at the Institute in Princeton for very many years, and for her help in retrieving and providing various originals for this collection. Karen Blu, Geertz's widow, supported the venture all the way and I devoutly trust she approves the finished product. Finally and as ever, I am grateful to my old friend, Quentin Skinner, for his loyal support of the idea and actuality of this book. He was for almost forty years a close friend of Clifford Geertz, and shares my judgment that the more we have of Geertz's work and thought to read, the better.

I should point out that I have made a few excisions in the text of the essays and last lectures provided here. In the case of two essays—"Toutes Directions" being the first—I have taken the liberty of removing the very heavy scholarly apparatus of notes which accompanied the original, making the assumption that the reader is more interested in the place of this essay in Geertz's thought and oeuvre than in its significance within the subject of anthropology. So, too, with his autobiographical self-reckoning, "An Inconstant Profession," where the prodigious range of references, obviously important to the special occasion at which the lecture was given, would have seriously impeded the satisfaction and comprehension of a reader in a less specialized context. In both cases, however, I should emphasise how the weight of these deleted references bore striking testimony to the way in which Geertz kept himself confidently abreast of an immense amount of contemporary scholarship in his own and adjacent subject areas, and did so right up to the end of his life.

Notes to Introduction: The Comic Vision of Clifford Geertz

1. *New York Times*, 26 October 1988.
2. "Found in translation: on the social history of the moral imagination" in *Local knowledge: further essays in interpretive anthropology* (New York: Basic Books, 1983), p. 43.
3. Clifford Geertz, *Available light: anthropological reflections on philosophical topics* (Princeton: Princeton University Press, 2000), p. 137–8.
4. Friedrich Nietzsche, *The gay science*, W. Kaufmann trans. and ed. (New York: Random House, 1974).
5. Geertz (as he told me more than once) admired Alasdair MacIntyre's 1979 essay "Social science methodology as ideology," reprinted in *The MacIntyre reader*, K. Knight ed. (Cambridge: Polity Press, 1998).
6. R. G. Collingwood, *The principles of art* (Oxford: Clarendon Press), 1938, p. 111.
7. Ibid., p. 118.
8. Robert Darnton, "On Clifford Geertz: field notes from the classroom," *New York Review of Books*, 11 January 2007.
9. Kenneth Burke, *On symbols and society*, (Chicago: University of Chicago Press, 1989), p. 188, pp. 170–72.
10. Clifford Geertz, *Works and lives: the anthropologist as author* (Stanford: Stanford University Press, 1988), p. vi.
11. Clifford Geertz, *Negara: the theatre-state in 19th century Bali*, (Princeton: Princeton University Press, 1980), p. 136.
12. R. G. Collingwood, *An autobiography* (Oxford: Clarendon Press, 1939), p. 115.
13. In the essay of that name in his *Local Knowledge*, pp. 19–35.
14. These remarks made at an informally welcoming party for the appointment of Joan Scott to the Institute in 1985.

Note to On Malinowski

1. Raymond Firth (ed.), *Man and Culture*, Routledge & Kegan Paul, 1957.

Notes to On Foucault

1. This is about a hundred years too late by his more general schema as set forth in his central work, *Les mots et les choses* (translated in the United States as *The Order*

of Things). But Foucault denies that historical periods are integrated by any sort of over-all Zeitgeist; and he rejects any pervasive "synchrony of breaks." He concentrates instead on actually discovered archaeological connections and disconnections, which can be quite different from subject to subject. This failure of different sequences to correlate is not a contradiction to his approach but rather a problem arising within it that—aside from some vague references to "the dispersion of epistemic domains"—he has yet to face up to. In fact, the "strata" of the various "sites" he has so far "excavated"—insanity, medical perception, linguistics, biology, economics, punishment, and, just recently, sex—are, like those of "real" archaeology (where this issue emerges as the question of establishing "horizons" as opposed to "phases"), only approximately coordinated with one another in time.

2. The quotation is from "Revolutionary Action: 'Until Now,' " one of Foucault's political pieces (an *après*-68 discussion with several far-left *lycée* students) included in a useful collection of his essays, *Language, Counter-memory, Practice*, edited by D.F. Couchard and just published by Cornell University Press, which also contains a number of his more celebrated theoretical articles: "What is an Author?," "Theatrum Philosophicum," "Nietzsche, Genealogy, and History," etc.

3. "Theatrum Philosophicum," ibid.

Notes to Ethnography in China

1. For the supposed impossibility of purely "consanguineous" (here, purely matrilineal) kinship systems, see G.P. Murdock, *Social Structure* (Free Press, 1996), pp. 41ff.; cf. D.M. Schneider and K. Gough, *Matrilineal Kinship* (University of California Press, 1961). Of course, "consanguineous" ties are not always phrased in terms of "blood," as they are with us. Among the Na, the idiom is "bone": matrilineally connected individuals are said to be "of one bone."

2. Hua includes the Na vernacular for these various phrases in his text; I have removed them and repunctuated accordingly.

3. David M. Schneider, *A Critique of the Study of Kinship* (University of Michigan Press, 1984), p. 196. Italics original.

4. The Communists of course came to power in 1949, but the Na area remained essentially Kuomintang country until 1956, when the Party installed its own local government, placing Han commissars in the region and effectively ending the traditional chiefship system.

Note to The Last Arab Jews

1. L. C. Briggs and H. L. Guede, *No More Forever—A Saharan Jewish Town*, (Cambridge: Peabody Museum of Archaeology and Ethnology, Harvard University, 1964).

Notes to On Feminism

1. The first quotation is from Elizabeth Fee, "A Feminist Critique of Scientific Objectivity," in *Science for the People*, Vol. 14 No. 4, p. 8, cited by Sue V. Rosser, in Tuana, p. 10; the second from Virginia Woolf's *Three Guineas*, cited in Sue Curry

Jansen, "Is Science a Man? New Feminist Epistemologies and Reconstructions of Knowledge," *Theory and Society*, Vol. 19 (1990), p. 235.

2. "Panel Discussion: Construction and Constraint," in Ernan McMullin, ed., *Construction and Constraint: The Shaping of Scientific Rationality* (University of Notre Dame Press, 1988), p. 242. The whole volume is an excellent survey of the range of positions in the debate.

3. For a review of the intense, unstable debate over the meaning and value of the concept of gender in feminist writing generally, see Joan Wallach Scott, "Gender: A Useful Category of Historical Analysis," in her *Gender and the Politics of History* (Columbia University Press, 1988), pp. 28–50.

4. The quotation is from W.V.O. Quine, cited, negatively, as "dogmatic metaphysics," in Richard Rorty, "Is Natural Science a Natural Kind?" McMullin, p. 50.

5. Evelyn Fox Keller, *A Feeling for the Organism: The Life and Work of Barbara McClintock* (W.H. Freeman, 1983); reviewed in *The New York Review*, March 29, 1984.

Notes to Indonesia: Starting Over

1. Hal Hill, *Indonesia—Industrial Transformation* (Singapore: Institute of Southeast Asian Studies, 1997), p. 1, references removed; Steven Radelet, *Indonesia's Implosion* (Harvard Institute for International Development, 1998), p. 1.

2. For the closest thing to a blow-by-blow account of what happened, see Jeremy Wagstaff, "Dark Before Dawn: How Elite Made a Deal Before Indonesia Woke Up," *The Wall Street Journal*, November 2, 1999 (the event itself took place on October 20). For a brief description of the presidential election and its postscript outcome, see R. William Liddle, "Indonesia 1999: Democracy Restored," *Asian Survey*, XL2, forthcoming (2000).

3. Volcker, the former head of the Federal Reserve, is quoted from a video conference on "international financial architecture," in *The Calendar and Chronicle*, Council on Foreign Relations, March 2000, p. 4:

> I [have] spent my life worrying about [supervision, bank capital standards, disclosure, and risk management] and . . . none of it is going to prevent an international financial crisis. . . . Large and volatile capital flows are coming up against small, undeveloped . . . financial systems, which is a recipe for a train wreck under the current international structure.

As an investment banker, Volcker may be suspected of having a bias toward pessimism; but, in the same conference, the former head of Clinton's upbeat Council of Economic Advisors, Laura D'Andrea Tyson, is only marginally more sanguine:

> The goal is not to eliminate financial crises. The question is, can we reduce their intensity and number? . . . I think you can reduce vulnerability by having better regulatory environments, better accounting environments, and greater transparency.

Since there is no sign on the horizon of "better regulatory environments," or indeed of any serious change in "the current international structure," except perhaps to render it even more unstable by crippling the few institutions that seek to manage it, this is rather cold comfort.

Notes to On the Devastation of the Amazon

1. *In Trouble Again: A Journey Between the Orinoco and the Amazon* (Atlantic Monthly Press, 1988), pp. 17–18. Italics in original.
2. *Darkness in El Dorado*, p. 14.
3. In Claudia Andujar, *Yanomami* (Curitiba, Brazil, 2000), p. 100. This is a fine book of art photographs of the Yanomami, with a brief ethnographic description of them by the French anthropologist Bruce Albert and personal reflections by Andujar, the photographer, and Davi Kopenawa Yanomami, a leading spokesman for the Yanomami people.
4. October 15, 2000.
5. Turner headed an earlier American Anthropological Association Special Commission to Investigate the Situation of the Brazilian Yanomami, in 1990–1991; Sponsel was chair of the Association's Committee for Human Rights from 1992 to 1996. There are, as yet, no accepted conventions for the citation of Internet communications, which often have long and roundabout, not always recoverable, transmission routes, hyperlink upon hyperlink, before they arrive on one's screen. (Precise source-referencing may be another elderly tradition on the way out.) I have not attempted to provide the relevant addresses for my on-line quotations: they tend to be long and cryptic, as well as, often enough, fugitive, disappearing like electronic wraiths when you look back for them. I have kept a list of them, which I can post on the Net (!) if there turns out to be a demand. An extensive, but given the volume of traffic necessarily incomplete, index of "over 300 links" (the true number is probably closer to a thousand or two by now) relevant to the debate can be found at www.anth. uconn.edu/gradstudents/dhume/index4.htm.
6. See Patrick Tierney, "The Fierce Anthropologist," *The New Yorker*, October 9, 2000, pp. 50–61; John Tooby, "Jungle Fever," *Slate*, October 24, 2000, 4:00 PM PT; "The New Yorker Replies," *Slate*, October 27, 2000, 4:45 PM PT. In a separate release, "The Muddied Waters of Amazon Anthropology," the *New Yorker* editors say that Chagnon originally agreed to be interviewed in connection with Tierney's piece, and then backed out, threatening suit. For all this, see *Inside Media*, another on-line magazine, October 3, 2000, 6:54 PM.
7. And the beat goes on: Tierney, having perhaps caught his breath as well, has recently (December 3, 2000) issued, via his publishers, W.W. Norton, a response to the critiques of John Tooby and Bruce Alberts. Tooby, he says "is not a neutral observer," but president of the Human Behavior and Evolution Society, of which Chagnon was president before him, and "co-director of the University of California at Santa Barbara's Anthropology Department," which has funded some of the Yanomami work. Tierney says that Tooby ("who has been trying to block the publication and fair reviewing of [my] book") conflates his work with the Sponsel-Turner e-mail, where the accusations against Neel and Chagnon are dif-

ferent, and less careful, than his own, and he lists ten examples of "errors" and "misrepresentations" in Tooby's piece for *Slate*.

Against Alberts (whose press release seems, in fact, to have been more a personal response than an officially deliberated Academy statement), he admits a few minor errors, but again denies that he accused Neel of purposefully starting the measles epidemic; he merely criticized his activities once the outbreak occurred. He also charges Alberts with distorting a number of his arguments, and remarks, "The prepublication assault [on *Darkness in El Dorado*] has been nothing short of extraordinary, but not surprising given the stakes in the controversy . . . [which] has been spun to make [the book] seem a book only about a measles vaccine and . . . epidemic in the Amazon . . . [when it is actually] a work with a broad and encompassing theme."

The text of the American Anthropological Association's Executive Board decision following the November meetings, which promises some sort of a decision in February, can now be found on the Association's Web site, www. ameranthassn .org/press/eldorado.htm.

8. James V. Neel, *Physician to the Gene Pool: Genetic Lessons and Other Stories* (John Wiley, 1994), p. 302. This is a combination autobiography and homiletical treatise in "genetic medicine." Neel goes on to say, "One of the major disappointments of our fieldwork was that, despite much brainstorming, we could never devise a field test of Yanomama 'smarts'—and if we had devised one, the Yanomama would have no motivation to take it seriously." To Tierney, he confessed, in a 1997 phone interview, that his failure to isolate the alleles for his "Index of Innate Ability," and thus pin down his big man/big smarts/big reproducer theory directly, "was the greatest disappointment of my life."

9. Neel, *Physician to the Gene Pool*, p. 134.

10. John J. Miller, "The Fierce People," *National Review Online*, November 20, 2000.

11. Napoleon A. Chagnon, *Yanamamö: The Last Days of Eden* (Harcourt Brace Jovanovich, 1992), p. xiii. Italics in original.

12. Chagnon, Yanamamö: The Last Days of Eden, p. xi.

Notes to Which Way to Mecca? PART I

1. *Approaching the Qur'an: The Early Revelations*, translated by Michael Sells (White Cloud Press, 1999); Oriana Fallaci, *The Rage and the Pride* (Rizzoli, 2002).

2. Stephen Schwartz, *The Two Faces of Islam* (Doubleday, 2002); Daniel Pipes, *Militant Islam Reaches America* (Norton, 2002); *What the Koran Really Says*, edited by Ibn Warraq (Prometheus Books, 2002); Noah Feldman, *After Jihad: America and the Struggle for Islamic Democracy* (Farrar, Straus and Giroux, 2003); Graham E. Fuller, *The Future of Political Islam* (Palgrave MacMillan, 2003).

3. Vartan Gregorian, *Islam: A Mosaic, Not a Monolith* (Brookings Institution Press, 2003); Paul Berman, *Terror and Liberalism* (Norton, 2003). And this is but the tip of a very large iceberg: I have read more than fifty recent works in preparing this commentary.

4. See Samuel P. Huntington, *The Clash of Civilizations and the Remaking of the World Order* (Simon and Schuster, 1996). The use of "Islam" to mean both the

"religion" and the "civilization" it animates—the lack of a Christianity/Christendom-like distinction—has hampered the discussion here somewhat. The late Marshall Hodgson, whose *The Venture of Islam* (University of Chicago Press, 1974) is the (usually unacknowledged) founder of this world-historical approach to Islam—see my review in *The New York Review*, December 11, 1975—suggested "Islamicate" for the latter meaning, but it has not, unfortunately, much caught on.

5. *Buddha* (Viking, 2001), *In the Beginning* (Knopf, 1996), *The English Mystics of the Fourteenth Century* (London: Kyle Cathie, 1991), *A History of God* (London: Heinemann, 1993), *The Battle for God* (Knopf, 2000), *Tongues of Fire* (London: Viking, 1985), *The Gospel According to Woman* (London: Elm Tree Books, 1986), *Through the Narrow Gate* (St. Martin's, 1995), *Beginning the World* (St. Martin's, 1983).

Notes to Which Way to Mecca? PART II

1. See the discussions of the books by Bernard Lewis, Thomas W. Simons Jr., M.J. Akbar, and Karen Armstrong in the first part of this commentary, "Which Way to Mecca?" *The New York Review*, June 12, 2003. For other examples of this synoptic approach to things, see John L. Esposito, *What Everyone Needs to Know About Islam* (Oxford University Press, 2002); Charles Lindholm, *The Islamic Middle East: Tradition and Change* (Blackwell, 2002); Seyyed Hossein Nasr, *Islam: Religion, History, and Civilization* (Harper, San Francisco, 2003); Bassam Tibi, *Islam between Culture and Politics* (Palgrave, 2001); F.E. Peters, *Islam: A Guide for Jews and Christians* (Princeton University Press, 2003).

2. Originally published as *Jihad: Expansion et décline de l'islamisme* (Paris: Gallimard, 2000). I have slightly reordered the wording and altered the punctuation of the following paragraph, without benefit of indication, in an effort to restore at least some of the readability an unusually leaden translation has, here as throughout, destroyed.

3. See "Which Way to Mecca? Part I" As Kepel himself notes, his own work follows upon that of his mentor, Olivier Roy, whose *The Failure of Political Islam* (Harvard University Press, 1998; first published in Paris in 1992), "a book full of ideas that went against current opinion and forged the way for a new approach to the problem of Islamism," first advanced the view that political Islam had entered into a period of more or less final decline. In his most recent work, *L'Islam Mondialisé* (Paris: Seuil, 2002), not yet translated into English, Roy reasserts and extends this notion, which rests, in the first instance, on a sharp distinction between "Islam as a Religion" and "the concrete practices of Muslims," considered as an assemblage of social, not cultural, facts. The first may be left, along with the Koran, "to the theologians"; the second is "a world-wide phenomenon, which supports [*subit*] and accompanies globalization." As "all explanations [of social and political matters] by religion are tautological . . . the Huntingtonian notion of a civilization founded on religion explains nothing." The present tensions "associated today with Islam are symptoms of its distorted [*mal vécu*] Westernization and the cascading crises this has provoked," not of some intrinsic "clash of cultures." "It was not St. Peter's in Rome that bin Laden attacked. It was not even the Wailing Wall. It was Wall Street."

4. After completing his book (but before publishing it), Schwartz, by then Washington bureau chief of the Jewish *Forward*, went to work for the Voice of America, but was soon fired by its news director for attacking the Voice for airing interviews with Muslim militants in the interest of balance. A public controversy, initiated by a William Safire column in *The New York Times* and continued by a good part of the neoconservative press, then broke out, in which the firing was attributed to pressure from Colin Powell's "dovish" State Department in its struggle against Vice President Richard Cheney and the Pentagon "hawks." See William Safire, "State Out of Step," *The New York Times*, July 1, 2002; Ronald Radosh, "State Department Outrage: The Firing of Stephen Schwartz," *Front Page Magazine*, July 2, 2002; Timothy Noah, "The Weekly Standard's House Muslim," *Slate*, July 3, 2002; Justin Raimondo, "The VOA Follies—'Voice of America' Loses a Writer—and the War Party Gains a Martyr," Antiwar.com, February 18, 2003.

5. For a clearer, shorter, more scholarly, and more nuanced (though hardly less hostile) account of Wahhab and Wahhabism, see Hamid Algar, *Wahabbism: A Critical Essay* (Islamic Publications International, 2002). Algar, who is a translator and admirer of both Qutb and Khomeini, is mainly concerned to question the conflation of Wahhabism with Islamism generally, a conflation upon which Schwartz's book (which Algar doesn't, at least directly, discuss) is founded.

6. *Terror and Liberalism*, which has pretensions to broad philosophical significance, has already been reviewed—and tellingly, in my view—by Ian Buruma in *The New York Review*, May 1, 2003. Here, I am concerned, and very much *en passant*, with its place in the "constructing Islam" literature.

Notes to On the State of the World

1. Jared Diamond, *Guns, Germs, and Steel: The Fates of Human Societies* (Norton, 1997). Richard Posner, *Aging and Old Age* (University of Chicago Press, 1995); *Public Intellectuals: A Study of Decline* (Harvard University Press, 2001); *Sex and Reason* (Harvard University Press, 1992), *The Economics of Justice* (Harvard University Press, 1981).

2. Under the general rubric of "the anthropology and sociology of science," such a monographic literature about particular disasters has begun to appear. See, on the Ukraine case, Adriana Petryna, *Life Exposed: Biological Citizens After Chernobyl* (Princeton University Press, 2002); on the Union Carbide tragedy in India, Kim Fortun, *Advocacy After Bhopal: Environmentalism, Disaster, New Global Orders* (University of Chicago Press, 2001); on the commercial exploitation of Indonesia's forests, Anna Lowenhaupt Tsing, *Friction: An Ethnography of Global Connection* (Princeton University Press, 2005).

Notes to The Near East in the Far East

1. Geertz, C., The Religion of Java (Glencoe, IL: The Free Press, 1960).

2. See, inter alia, Geertz, C., *Islam Observed: Religious Development in Morocco and Indonesia* (New Haven: Yale University Press, 1968).

3. On the history of the Asian trade in the Indonesian archipelago, see van Leur, J.C., *Indonesian Trade and Society: Essays in Asian Social and Economic History* (The Hague and Bandung: W. Van Hoeve, 1955).

4. On such states, see Schrieke, B.J.O., "Ruler and Realm in Early Java," in *Indonesian Sociological Studies,* vol. 2 (The Hague and Bandung: W. Van Hoeve, 1957); for a (late) example, see Geertz, C., *Negara: The Theatre State in Nineteenth Century Bali* (Princeton: Princeton University Press, 1980). See also Pigeaud, Th., *Java in the Fourteenth Century: A Study in Cultural History* (The Hague and Bandung: M. Nijhoff, 1960–62).

5. On the bazaar states, see Schrieke, B.J.O., "The Shifts in Political and Economic Power in the Indonesian Archipelago in the Sixteenth and Seventeenth Century" (sic), in *Indonesian Sociological Studies*, vol. 1 (The Hague and Bandung: W. Van Hoeve, 1955).

6. For a general history of East Indies formation and development, see Vlekke, B., *Nusantara: A History of the East Indian Archipelago* (Cambridge, MA: Harvard University Press, 1943).

7. Bali was, and still, being "Hindu," is the exception to all this. The reason for its relative isolation from this development are complex, but the absence of good harbors on the Java Sea side of the island was surely of importance.

8. On the *pesantren* complex in Indonesia generally, see Abaza, M., "Madrasah," in *The Oxford Encyclopedia of the Modern Islamic World* (New York and Oxford: Oxford University Press, 1995). For some concrete examples, see Geertz, C., *The Religion of Java. Pesantren* teaching, though mainly oral, was not entirely so: a written tradition of Malay and Javanese language commentaries in Arabic script, which at least some of the students could read, grew up. See van Bruinessen, M., *Kitab Kuning: Pesantren dan Tarekat* (Bandung, 1995).

9. Hurgronje, C. Snouck, *Mekka in the Latter Part of the Nineteenth Century* (Leiden: Brill, 1931). The estimate of the present number of *pesantren* is from Abaza, "Madrasah."

10. Geertz, C., *Religion of Java*. See also Geertz, C., *The Social History of an Indonesian Town* (Cambridge, MA: Harvard University Press, 1965).

11. On the history of nationalism in Indonesia, see Kahin, G., *Nationalism and Revolution in Indonesia* (Ithaca: Cornell University Press, 1952).

12. Lapidus, I., *A History of Islamic Societies* (Cambridge: Cambridge University Press, 1988), p.568.

13. Geertz, C., *Islam Observed*.

14. On Muhammadiyah, see Peacock, J., *Muslim Puritans: Reformist Psychology in Southeast Asian Islam* (Berkeley: University of California Press, 1978); Noer, D., *The Modernist Muslim Movement in Indonesia, 1900–1942* (Singapore and New York: Oxford University Press, 1973).

15. On Nahadatul Ulama, see Hefner, R., *Civil Islam: Muslims and Democratization in Indonesia* (Princeton: Princeton University Press, 2000).

16. Geertz, C., "The World in Pieces," in *Available Light: Anthropological Reflections on Philosophical Topics* (Princeton: Princeton University Press, 2000).

17. For a brief account of his ascent to the Presidency, see Geertz, C., "Indonesia: Starting Over," *New York Review of Books*, May 11, 2000.

Note on What Is a State If It Is Not a Sovereign?

1. Headlines respectively from the Sydney *Morning Herald*, March 23, 1999; *Agence France Presse*, February 28, 1999; the *Toronto Star*, March 14, 1999; the *Singapore Straits Times*, March 13, 1999; and the *Far Eastern Economic Review*, March 18, 1999.

Note on Shifting Aims, Moving Targets

1. The epithets are all taken from a particularly obtuse and *interéssé* critique, Asad (1983). For an excellent critique of the critique, see Canton (forthcoming); cf., along the same lines, but more briefly, Kipp & Rogers (1987: 29). For another general statement of my own which addresses some of these issues more directly, in connection with the work of William James, see Geertz (2000: 167–202).